Additional praise for *The Colony*

"Every once in a while, there comes a shocking event that briefly makes international headlines and then vanishes, only to be picked up by a dogged sleuth who finds and tells the *real* story—a much more bizarre and fascinating one—buried beneath. In *The Colony*, Sally Denton burrows into a big, complicated tragedy that crosses borders and cultural divides, and she does so with imagination, resourcefulness, and investigative zeal."

—**Hampton Sides,** *New York Times* best-selling author of
Blood and Thunder: An Epic of the American West

"Sally Denton brings all her skills as an investigative journalist and American historian to this tale of murder, religion, guns, water rights, drugs, and deviant cults. A great read and an important piece of U.S.-Mexico border literature."

—**Nina Burleigh,** author of *The Trump Women: Part of the Deal*

"In a story as American as it is Mexican, as riveting as it is horrifying, intrepid investigator Sally Denton explores the deeper history of a spectacular and terrible moment. Opening with the shocking murders of three Fundamentalist Mormon housewives and their children on a dirt road in Sonora, Denton reveals a tangled web of cult murder, sex trafficking, water wars, and blood feuds bound by political corruption and calculation on both sides of the border. Spellbinding and bone-chilling."

—**Virginia Scharff,** Emeritus Distinguished Professor, University of
New Mexico, and chair of Western history,
Autry Museum of the American West

THE COLONY

The SUV in which Rhonita LeBaron Miller and four of her children were killed in an ambush near La Mora, Mexico, on November 4, 2019. *(Meghan Dhaliwal/New York Times)*

THE
COLONY

FAITH AND BLOOD
IN A PROMISED LAND

SALLY DENTON

Liveright Publishing Corporation

A Division of W. W. Norton & Company
Celebrating a Century of Independent Publishing

For information about permission to reproduce selections from this book, write to
Permissions, Liveright Publishing Corporation, a division of W. W. Norton & Company, Inc.,
500 Fifth Avenue, New York, NY 10110

For information about special discounts for bulk purchases, please contact
W. W. Norton Special Sales at specialsales@wwnorton.com or 800-233-4830

Manufacturing by Lakeside Book Company
Book design by Patrice Sheridan
Production manager: Julia Druskin

ISBN 978-1-324-09408-1 pbk.

Liveright Publishing Corporation, 500 Fifth Avenue, New York, N.Y. 10110
www.wwnorton.com

W. W. Norton & Company Ltd., 15 Carlisle Street, London W1D 3BS

1 2 3 4 5 6 7 8 9 0

FOR JOHN L. SMITH,

AND

FOR MY MOTHER, SARA DENTON,

WITH LOVE

Contents

THE COLONY

PROLOGUE

She Was the Whitest

❋

ON THE MORNING of their murders, the three young mothers felt uncommonly apprehensive as they prepared to leave the village of La Mora in northern Mexico. Their sport utility vehicles were packed for the six-hour journey, which would include a desolate twelve-mile stretch on a dirt road dividing the states of Sonora and Chihuahua. Each woman had made the trek dozens of times between the sister communities of La Mora and Colonia LeBaron. They were well aware that the isolated and unpatrolled road was also the regular route for Mexico's criminal cartels to transport drugs into the US. But because their interrelated families, who had dual American and Mexican citizenship, had lived in the area for more than a century, and were well known by the cartels, they believed that they were protected from the violence of the drug trade.

The lonely road was rarely used by local farmers and ranchers; outside of the cartels, it was almost exclusively traveled by La Mora and LeBaron family members, for whom it was a shortcut through the mountains. "Sometimes they get the warning that it is better not to use it: bullets are predicted," a family member said, referring to communications between the cartels and La Mora and LeBaron. In the weeks prior to the attacks, the victims had been alerted repeatedly not to travel the road, but for some reason they had neglected to take the threats seriously.

Each of the three women had an intuition that something was wrong, but they forged ahead, perhaps even knowing they were tempting fate. On

November 4, 2019, they departed in their three-SUV caravan, figuring there would be safety in numbers. Each of the women was married, and they were taking with them a total of fourteen children between the ages of seven months and fourteen years old. By all accounts, the caravan was unarmed.

Thirty-year-old Rhonita LeBaron Miller was traveling with four of her seven children. She placed Titus and Tiana, her eight-month-old twins, in their car seats. Howie and Krystal, twelve and ten, respectively, were strapped in with their seat belts, excited about going on a road trip with their mom and helping her with the babies. Rhonita, or "Nita," as her family called her, planned to drive partway with the other two women and then veer off northwest toward Phoenix. Her husband, Howard Miller, was flying in that afternoon to Sky Harbor Airport from North Dakota, where the couple had been living for most of their thirteen-year marriage. Ever since Howard's brother had died several months earlier in an ultralight-aircraft crash, Howard and Rhonita had begun spending more time in La Mora to help in his parents' pecan orchards. Described by one account as "a typical American mom," the blue-eyed blonde had a Pinterest page and frequently posted family photographs on Facebook and Instagram. Known for her sense of style, Rhonita wore diamond stud earrings, willowy sundresses, and fashionable hats to protect her fair skin. A "spunky lass," as one of her aunts described her, she had an infectious smile and relentless energy and "could charm everyone."

Just six weeks earlier, she and her husband had decided to leave the US permanently—Howard had been working with some of his brothers in a fracking business in North Dakota—and resettle in their native Mexico. Howard had been reared on his father's large farm at La Mora, in the municipality of Bavispe in the state of Sonora. Rhonita had grown up across the Sierra Madre mountain range in the village of LeBaron, in the municipality of Galeana in the state of Chihuahua. At sixteen, she married Howard, her handsome seventeen-year-old second cousin, and now they were building their dream home on a hill overlooking LeBaron, where they would raise their growing family. Rhonita and Howard expected to spend a few days in Phoenix, enjoying the city and shopping for a wedding gift for Howard's sister, before returning to Mexico to begin the new phase in their lives.

Thirty-one-year-old Christina Langford Johnson was traveling from La

Mora to LeBaron with her seven-month-old infant, Faith. Born in La Mora, Christina was the common-law wife of a native of LeBaron—a cousin of Rhonita's named Tyler Johnson—and had been raising their six kids in La Mora while Tyler, like Howard Miller, lived and worked in North Dakota. She had recently decided to join Tyler and the large community of La Mora and LeBaron relatives living in and around Williston, North Dakota. "Though she loved raising their children in La Mora—in the country, surrounded by high-definition views of uninterrupted landscape," as one journalist put it, "they missed living together." That weekend, her family had held a going-away party for her in the home where she had grown up. The next day, she was heading to LeBaron, where she and Tyler would begin the process of moving their family to the US.

A lively brunette with warm chocolate eyes, Christina was a gifted pianist and composer. Her late father, Dan Langford, had been the founder of La Mora, and Christina was a "fireball" who had "her dad's temper," according to her mother. "She reacted instantly to everything. She could fight with somebody . . . but then a minute later, she was completely repentant and fixing it." Determined and focused, Christina was "very disciplined, and yet she was sunshine," said her mother. "Every time you see her, she had a smile."

Forty-three-year-old Dawna Ray Langford would drive the third SUV in the convoy. The oldest of forty-nine children, Dawna was like a second mother to her younger siblings and was beloved by the many sisters and mothers she supported as they reared their own large broods. Fun-loving and mischievous, she was known as "Aunt Dawna" to dozens in the La Mora community who frequently sought her open smile and sage advice. "Dawna could take mundane happenings and turn them into stories with a moral," according to one relative, "even if it might mean exaggerating or bending the facts of that story a tad." The plural wife of David Langford, Dawna was looking forward to celebrating their twenty-fifth anniversary a week later. She was taking nine of her thirteen children—ranging in age from nine months to fourteen years—to LeBaron to attend a wedding and have playtime with their many cousins.

Rhonita, Christina, and Dawna were all raised in polygamous families, "model people," a close relative said—"God-fearing women" committed to rearing good children. They were related by blood and marriage and had just celebrated together in La Mora to wish Christina Godspeed in her new life in North Dakota.

On the morning of November 4, a Monday, the three assembled at the home of Christina's mother, Amelia Langford, to load their Chevrolet Suburbans. They packed snacks and toys and puzzles for the children, milk bottles for the babies, and, in Rhonita's case, infant seats for the twins, as well as strollers and overnight bags for her visit to Phoenix with Howard. "We were at my house, and everyone left at the farm gathered to say good-bye," Amelia would later tell a BBC reporter. "We talked about it. About how stupid we are as women, traveling these roads alone, and with our kids." Christina had laughed, her mother remembered, and said, "I'm not afraid of anything." Though she then added, "I am a little bit, but why should I be? There's a bunch of us going together. I won't be alone."

The women traded tales about the *sicarios*—the cartels' hired killers who manned the checkpoints between the two Mexican states. "We'd been a lit-tle more nervous the last couple of months," Rhonita's sister-in-law would remember. "But we still felt like we were OK."

Rhonita was as knowledgeable as anyone about the intensifying violence in the region, but she was naïvely optimistic about her trip and her immunity from it. She had been born and raised in LeBaron. Her mother, Bathsheba Shalom, known as Shalom, was one of her father's four plural wives. The sixth of Shalom's twelve children, Rhonita had bounced back and forth across the Sierra Madre range her entire life.

"She thought her innocence would protect her," said her sister Adriana. "Who's going to mess with a woman and her kids? Nobody is that evil."

Still, Rhonita paused before leaving La Mora that morning. "I have a bad feeling about this," she told her mother-in-law, Loretta Miller, who later said they had all talked about security concerns the previous night. "Maybe I shouldn't go." Then she slid into the front seat of her SUV.

* * *

Under a clear sky, the seventeen women and children struck out across the high desert. But just five miles outside of La Mora, a ball bearing on the front

Rhonita Miller.

passenger wheel failed on Rhonita's black SUV. They couldn't call for help because cell service was out, for some unknown reason, so Rhonita and her four children crowded into the other two vehicles and headed back to her in-laws' house for a replacement vehicle. "Do you think it's a sign?" Rhonita asked Loretta when they arrived back in La Mora. "Well, you decide," Loretta said, "but if you want to borrow my car, you're welcome to."

It was already after 9 a.m., and Christina and Dawna, eager to get back on the road after the delay, headed out again while Rhonita put her kids in Loretta's Chevy Tahoe and followed behind them. When Rhonita arrived back at the broken-down Suburban, she transferred the car seats and luggage into the Tahoe, while the other two women continued on. Rhonita then rushed to catch up. Not far behind her was her eighteen-year-old brother-in-law, Andre Miller, who was bringing a trailer to tow the disabled Suburban back to La Mora. It was 10:20 a.m. when Andre reached the Suburban and saw a column of black smoke about a mile up the road, and then a fireball exploding upward. Fearing that Rhonita had been in an accident, Andre raced to the scene. He found the Tahoe engulfed in flames, the inferno so intense that he couldn't get closer than thirty feet to see whether anyone was inside. He was only able to identify the SUV by its license plate. He saw half a dozen men dressed in black and carrying automatic weapons, and they sped away in what looked like brand-new SUVs. Andre then spotted another three black-clad men wearing military helmets walking away from him on the road toward Chihuahua. "I couldn't tell if they were inside the car or not," Andre recalled, referring to Rhonita and her children; he wondered at first whether they had been kidnapped.

He hurried back to his parents' house in La Mora, yelling that there had been an attack on Rhonita's car, and that he didn't know what had happened to her and the children. A family member sent up a drone to check the area, and, once they saw that it was clear, several of the men in the Mormon community gathered, forming a posse. Uncertain about what they would find, and fearful that the armed gunmen Andre had seen were still in the area, they joined members of the nearby Sonora Cartel who were also assembling to investigate the attack.

The La Mora community had long coexisted with the cartel that controlled Sonora—an offshoot of Joaquín "El Chapo" Guzmán's powerful Sinaloa Cartel—purchasing gasoline from them while giving them a wide berth. In "an arrangement more forced than agreed upon, the two sides maintained a largely peaceful, if uncomfortable, arrangement." The previous year, one of the violent cells of the Sinaloa/Sonora Cartel had ordered the Mormons not to purchase gasoline from anyone but them, even though it was cheaper in the neighboring state of Chihuahua. In return, they promised to warn the community when there might be violence.

The cartel members had heard the explosion and immediately suspected that their rival, La Línea—the enforcement wing of the Juárez Cartel in Chihuahua—had encroached into their territory. Sonora footsoldiers—"50 or 60 of them, armed to the teeth"—loaded into a convoy of six "hard trucks, Tritons, with blacked-out windows," and raced off toward the site of the ambush with the Mormon men following. The family stopped at the still-smoldering Tahoe while the cartel men continued up the road to confront the attackers.

Kenneth Miller, Rhonita's father-in-law, was the first to look inside the incinerated car. He recorded a cell-phone video, choking up in anguish. "This is for the record. Nita and four of my grandchildren are burnt and shot up!"

he cried. The video would go viral as family members posted it to Facebook, WhatsApp, and Twitter in urgent pleas for help; they were still unable to get cell service, so they used portable Wi-Fi devices and satellite phones. "Howie's wife and four kids have been killed," read a WhatsApp message that appeared on the family thread just after noon. "Christina and Donna [*sic*] are not accounted for. Were traveling with them." Kenny LeBaron, then thirty-two, who owns a trucking company in Williston, recalled that the messages "are hard to listen to but you get the whole story from them."

"They shot the shit out of my grandchildren, my daughters, daughter-in-law—just burned them to a crisp," said a family member in a voice message shared among relatives in Mexico and the US. "There's nothing left. Just a few bones." Rhonita's sister-in-law would later describe the horror to NBC News. "It was awful seeing the babies' little skulls just sitting there on the floor of the car, burnt and broken." Another relative recounted the grisly attack on the Chevy Tahoe: "They just unleashed hell on this vehicle. Fired shots, raided them, and burned the passengers alive." The front passenger door was open, and the ashen remains of twelve-year-old Howie were falling half out of the vehicle, as though he had been trying to escape. The twins' car seats were belted in the second row, and Krystal's burned body was in a fetal position in the SUV's third row, tightly holding onto a tiny pink leather purse.

Relatives of Christina and Dawna began to panic, as neither woman had been heard from since they left La Mora two hours earlier. Family members frantically called the US Embassy, the Mexican federal police, the attorneys general of both Sonora and Chihuahua, and the Mexican military, begging for help to rescue the other two women and ten children—thought to be a short distance farther along the road from where Rhonita was attacked. It turned out that they were eleven miles away—a confusing fact that defeated the security purpose of traveling as a caravan, though it probably had little effect on the tragic results.

Christina had been in the lead as the road narrowed and began its steep incline, with a sheer mountain face to the left and a vertical drop-off to the right. "The location seemed chosen for its vulnerability," observed one of the first reporters to arrive at the scene days later. "An attack could not easily be defended—or escaped. As the women barreled up the road, their vehicles

Cell-phone photo of Christina Langford Johnson with her infant, Faith Marie Johnson. Christina was shot to death during the November 4, 2019, assault on the seventeen-member group of women and children, and "Baby Faith" was found alive in her car seat. *(Adriana Zehrbrauskas/New York Times)*

Cell-phone photo of Dawna Ray Langford, 43, and her son Trevor Langford, 11. The two were among nine women and children killed in an ambush on November 4, 2019, in Bavispe, Sonora, Mexico. *(Adriana Zehrbrauskas/New York Times)*

were easy targets." Sometime after 11 a.m., more than forty minutes after the attack on Rhonita, gunmen opened fire on Christina's Suburban. She quickly placed Faith, who was in a car seat, on the floor behind her, threw a blanket over the baby, and jumped out, waving her hands in the air, begging for mercy and showing she was alone and unarmed. "We're women!" she shouted. But the assailants kept shooting, and she was fatally wounded in the heart.

A few minutes later, when Dawna came upon Christina's body in the road, she started yelling at her nine children to drop to the floor and hide the babies. "Get down right now!" she screamed, while also "praying to the Lord" and "trying to start the car up to get out of there," her thirteen-year-old son Devin later recalled. Bullets rained from a nearby hilltop, killing Dawna, along with her eleven-year-old and two-year-old sons. A late-model red pickup truck drove up to Dawna's Suburban, and the driver told the surviving seven kids to run. Nearly all of them, including a toddler and an infant, were bleeding from gunshot wounds. Although the driver of the truck spoke Spanish, Devin, who was uninjured, understood what they were being told to do. "They got us out of the car and then they drove off." One of Devin's sisters later said that the driver was checking to make sure the women were dead and was surprised to find the vehicle full of children.

Devin gathered his six siblings and began the trek back toward La Mora. But they had walked less than a thousand feet before he realized they were too injured to make it. Fourteen-year-old Kylie could barely walk with her foot wound. A bullet had grazed nine-year-old McKenzie's arm, and eight-year-old Cody had been shot in the jaw. Six-year-old Jake was uninjured but not able to walk a long distance. Xander, four, had been shot in the back, and nine-month-old Brixon, who had an open flesh wound in the chest and a bullet graze on his wrist, was carried by one of his siblings. "Going through my mind was to get help because [my siblings were] bleeding really bad, so I was in a rush to get there," Devin would recall. He knew he had to hide them and continue alone on the long—fourteen-mile—journey home. In a ravine off the side of the road, he found a tree with low-hanging limbs and secreted the children under it, covering them with branches and begging them to be silent while he went for help. For hours, the children heard gunfire in the distance.

By midafternoon, word had reached Shalom and Adrian LeBaron Soto,

Rhonita's mother and father, who were running errands together in Galeana, that Rhonita's car had been ambushed. La Mora and LeBaron are approximately a hundred miles apart as the crow flies, but because of the rugged terrain and the single-lane road, the drive between the two can take as long as seven hours. Departing from La Mora, the route first goes north and then doubles back south toward LeBaron, following the spine of the mountain range. Joel LeBaron Soto, Rhonita's uncle and the family patriarch, along with his adult son, Julian, organized a group on the Chihuahua side of the Sierra Madre to intercept and rescue anyone who might still be alive from the other two vehicles. Julian notified the Mexican National Guard in Chihuahua and asked them to protect the LeBaron family property from attack while they headed to the neighboring state of Sonora. Shalom and Adrian joined the caravan of about a dozen people. But when they left Highway 10 at the small town of Janos to travel the forty miles of dirt road to the Sonoran border, soldiers stopped them, warning that rival cartels were battling in the nearby foothills and the situation was too dangerous for them to proceed.

Dawna's six terrified children huddled together as the hours passed and the temperature dropped. McKenzie finally decided that Devin had been gone too long and that she needed to go find him. She left her five siblings under the tree and took off walking toward La Mora, in spite of the bullet wound in her arm. But she became lost in the labyrinth of dirt roads and took off one of her shoes to fight back a snake, leaving her with a bare foot that was soon scratched and bloody from the rugged terrain.

Devin had traveled as fast as he could, hiding when he thought he was being followed and praying every step of the way. At 5:30 p.m., six hours after the ambush of his mother's car, the exhausted boy came across the search party—the armed posse of men who had set off from La Mora earlier in the day—and he gave them the first report of the deaths of Christina, Dawna, and two of his brothers. He said the shooters carried long guns and wore masks. He related that Christina had gotten out of the car and waved her arms, but the gunmen shot her anyway. "We have to go back! We have to rescue them!" Devin shouted, referring to his brothers and sisters. His armed uncles immediately headed out to find the hidden children, now knowing that most of them were seriously injured. At about the same time, the LeBaron caravan that had been stopped by the military in the small village of Pancho Villa southwest of Janos in Chihuahua was moving down the dirt road toward the Sonoran border, accompanied by federal police.

As family members approached the two massacre sites from both La Mora and LeBaron, a military garrison from Agua Prieta, seventy miles north of La Mora on the Arizona border, joined them. For eleven hours, frightened people from both communities scoured the rough landscape in search of the children, whether dead or alive.

Shortly after 7 p.m., the caravan from LeBaron descended the Sonora side of the mountain range, beating local authorities to Christina's and Dawna's bullet-riddled Suburbans. They found Christina's body on her back fifty feet from her vehicle, wearing a T-shirt and jeans. "The first [person] that came across the bodies, the crime scene, was me!" Julian later told a reporter, incredulous and outraged that no Mexican authorities had arrived to investigate by that point. "She was shot with her hands in the air!" Shalom LeBaron echoed Julian's anger: "We never dreamed that we'd see Christina's body still lying in the road."

The group's despair turned to unfathomable joy when they opened the car door and found baby Faith, blood-spattered but unscathed except for a scrape from shrapnel on her head. Still strapped into her car seat—a bullet hole in its base—the baby was soaked in urine and was in shock. "She opened her eyes, like, 'What's up?'" Julian recalled. It was a miracle, they all agreed. "When we found out the baby was alive, it was just a whole new level of rejoicing," said her grandmother, Amelia. "It was a relief." The starving and dehydrated infant cried through the entire evening, as Shalom gave her capfuls of Pedialyte she found in Christina's car, while others in the party continued toward Dawna's nearby Suburban.

Dawna's body was slumped over the steering wheel, "so full of bullets they stopped counting," said one family member. The bodies of two of her young sons were also in the car. Around the same time, the group from La Mora arrived at the nearby spot where Dawna's surviving and severely injured children, except for McKenzie, were hiding. Devin had guided the group.

Cold, hungry, hurting, and scared, the children were desperate for medical attention and nourishment. The emotional scene then became hysterical when the rescuers realized McKenzie was missing. As darkness fell, a desperate search ensued. Finally, almost two hours later, Kenneth Miller and some soldiers who had escorted the La Mora group found her by tracking her footprints, which alternated between a bare left foot and a right running shoe. The nine-year-old had walked on rocky ground and through brambles for nearly ten miles, often in the wrong direction, bloodied by her gunshot wound and shoeless foot. When they found her alive, on the side of the road, the men wept with gratitude. Another miracle.

Back at the site of the attack on Christina's SUV, Shalom had gotten Faith hydrated enough to make tears, and the men took charge of transporting the baby to La Mora, where Amelia would find a nursing mother in the community to feed her. "When they brought her to us, she was very weak," Amelia told a reporter. "They tried to give her a bottle, but she wouldn't really drink it." But after nursing, "she greeted everyone with a smile and was happy to be with people again."

With the rescued children being taken by ambulance to the medical clinic in Bavispe, Shalom and Adrian planned to drive the eleven miles to Rhonita's car, but it was now dark, so the couple continued on to La Mora, returning before dawn the next morning to the site of their daughter's murder. They were stunned that, more than eighteen hours after their daughter and four grandchildren had been shot at close range and set on fire, Mexican law enforcement still had not begun to investigate the crime scene.

Pulling on rubber gloves in order to preserve evidence, Adrian—a solid, deep-voiced man who had an authoritative demeanor—began searching the scorched Chevy Tahoe. Crying and praying, Shalom could not make sense of the heinousness—her daughter's beautiful life spirit reduced to bones and ash. Rhonita's seat was reclined, her upper body completely immolated. It would later be confirmed by medical examiners that she and her children had been burned alive. The window glass and much of the car's chassis were melted. Next to the car, Adrian and Shalom gathered shell casings from AR-15, AK-47, and M16 assault rifles. Adrian seized on the casings as proof that his community "had clearly been targeted"—that the attack was neither a case of mistaken identity nor accidental crossfire, as the Mexican Government would later contend. "They knew it was the women and children. They don't give a shit," one family member said.

Also shocking to Rhonita's parents was the evidence that she had been robbed and the vehicle looted before it was burned. They found her checkbook, postage stamps, loose change, and other items from her purse scattered on the ground nearby. Shalom kept a vigil with her daughter's body until forensic investigators from law enforcement finally arrived—thirty hours after the ambush. In the freezing morning air, she spoke to her deceased daughter. "She would cry and talk to her and then get overwhelmed and go sit on a rock and dry her eyes out for thirty minutes," said one of Rhonita's sisters.

Not trusting anyone in the Mexican Government, Adrian and Shalom got into their SUV and drove five hours north, crossing the border into Arizona to hand over the evidence they had collected to the FBI, imploring the US agency to help investigate the murders. It was an unusual entreaty, and American involvement initially would be blocked by Mexican authorities. "All the conclusions that we've reached is [sic] that it was something that was almost premeditated against [our] community. They knew that they were killing women and children," Adrian told the *Mexico News Daily*. "We know that if we want justice, we just have to do it ourselves," he said to the *New York Post*. "And I won't stop until I get it."

Some thirty hours after the attacks, Mexican national police arrested a man in Agua Prieta attempting to cross the US border near Douglas, Arizona. In his vehicle were two bound and gagged hostages, four assault-style weapons, high-caliber ammunition, and spent magazines. The police seized a cell phone and on it found a video taken by one of the assailants on November 4, showing twelve to fifteen gunmen—dressed in black, wearing masks and bulletproof jackets and carrying assault rifles—circling Rhonita's vehicle just moments after the barrage. "Burn it! Burn it! *Quemalo!*" yelled one of the gunmen from the top of a nearby hill. When twelve-year-old Howie tried to escape from the burning car, someone yelled, "Shoot him! Don't trust!" Details about the unnamed suspect, and the video evidence, confirmed the family's suspicions that Rhonita's SUV had been intentionally destroyed, contradicting official reports that the bullets had sparked the blaze. "It was a massacre, 100 percent a massacre," said a family member. At first, the Mexican authorities claimed the arrested man wasn't tied to the killings, but they later admitted that he had become a confidential informant in the investigation and that his video was firsthand evidence.

Hundreds of .223- and 7.7mm shell casings were found at the two scenes. "They shot us up, burned our vehicles to send a smoke signal into the sky," a relative told the international media that eventually swarmed to the sites. "This was deliberate and intentional," said Loretta Miller. "We were the targets. We just don't know why."

* * *

Of the three murdered women, none had deeper bloodlines in the immense LeBaron family than Rhonita LeBaron Miller. Rhonita's great grandfather, Alma Dayer LeBaron, had founded Colonia LeBaron, which the family calls "the colony"; he was the patriarch of a powerful polygamous empire. LeBaron remains one of the largest, if not the largest, fundamentalist Mormon community in Mexico today, dwarfing La Mora. Adrian LeBaron Soto, fifty-eight at the time, told reporters he had four wives, and, up to the day of the massacre, thirty-nine children and seventy-nine grandchildren.

"She was the coolest, the whitest and the most Mexican," is how Adrian described Rhonita. "The beautiful LeBaron girl," as she was known, was born on September 15, 1989—the day before Mexican Independence Day, which Rhonita treated as a celebration of her own life as well. "She was sweet and a bit naïve," said her sister Adriana. "You couldn't tell a dirty joke around her because she wouldn't get it." A "flower-power girl," she gave birth to her babies at home. "Going over that mountain range was no big deal," Adriana said of Rhonita's fearlessness and sense of invulnerability in her native land.

Even though Rhonita's seven children were born across the mountains in La Mora, where her husband Howard's extensive family had been since the 1960s, she aspired to raise them in LeBaron. She wanted to give them the best of both worlds, according to her father. On her birthday, just six weeks before her death, one of her relatives had given Rhonita and Howard a choice piece of property for their planned dream home. "She just wanted a fairly large, not luxurious, house," where her Miller in-laws could visit LeBaron and "feel at home," said Adrian.

Two days after the attacks, Jorge Castañeda, one of Mexico's former foreign ministers and a noted scholar, told the press that Rhonita was the primary target of the massacre. Castañeda contended the LeBaron family was marked for violence because of its ongoing clashes with its neighbors. "They had stood up to the drug cartels, and they did have certain frictions either with the cartels or with neighboring communities over water rights," Castañeda said to CNN. "There are long-standing tensions, and apparently the woman who was driving in the first car that was attacked was an activist."

For years, the family had been confronted by escalating threats of cartel violence. The LeBarons had received recent threats, and family members regularly traveled with armed bodyguards, which makes it all the more difficult to understand why three women and fourteen children were traveling unescorted. In the aftermath, both communities were seized with panic. "We're living in a war zone," said Julian LeBaron. "But it's a war zone with little kids running around in the yard."

Family spokesmen dismissed claims made by current Mexican officials that the attack was the result of cartel hit men mistaking the travelers for a rival cartel, or that they were caught in the crossfire among cartels. "We've been here for more than fifty years," another of Rhonita's cousins, Alex LeBaron, who had served as both a US Navy officer and a member of the Mexican congress, told Reuters. "There's no one who doesn't know [us]. Whoever did this was aware. That's the most terrifying." If Rhonita had indeed been the intended target, because her vehicle was the only one that had been torched—possibly by a military-style grenade launcher—many wondered whether the attacks on the vehicles driven by Christina and Dawna were merely, and tragically, collateral damage.

"There is one ominous signal to all this and it is that someone has a bone to pick with the LeBaron family," wrote a Mexican reporter. "The first thing these criminals aim for is not the target himself, but his or her family."

Months after the massacres, when it seemed unlikely that the Mexican Government was going to hold anyone accountable, Adrian LeBaron Soto claimed that his clan was being "persecuted"—a word thick with religious meaning for millions of Mormon faithful. The murders spawned numerous rumors and conspiracy theories about the motives of the attackers, their identity, and the targets themselves. As the months went by without justice for the victims, and only hazy information emerging about suspects and arrests, each theory was more outlandish than the last.

* * *

The attack on the LeBaron clan was shocking, even against the backdrop of the gratuitous violence of the Mexican drug wars. But in the long history of the LeBaron clan, it was not a wholly exceptional event. Any attempt to investigate or comprehend the murders requires first an understanding of that history, which goes back nearly two centuries. The LeBarons' story is not only an epic of pioneer America but also a tale of secrecy, polygamy, blood feuds, conquest, and exploitation, wrapped in a radical interpretation of Mormon doctrine and steeped in a myth of persecution.

Those feelings of persecution exist among members of the LeBaron clan itself. Rhonita's grandfather, Joel LeBaron, was the beloved and martyred Prophet of a Mormon fundamentalist religion called the Church of the Firstborn of the Fulness [sic] of Times. Joel LeBaron was killed in Mexico by his brother, Ervil, in 1972, in a ritualized form of murder called "blood atonement." The most controversial and fanatical doctrine in the Mormon faith, blood atonement is a killing of higher purpose intended to provide the victim with eternal salvation when his or her blood was spilled into the earth. Contemporary church leaders have insisted that blood atonement was "a rhetorical device" meant to keep church members faithful, and that it was never actually put into practice. But numerous scholars over a century and a half have concluded otherwise. The LeBarons did not need to turn to scholarly accounts, however. The family had intimate knowledge of the existence of the practice. From the 1970s into the 1990s, the LeBaron family had been fractured by dozens of these so-called divinely inspired murders among its own.

The modern-day Cain-and-Abel story that began when Ervil murdered Joel set off what US law enforcement described as the longest crime spree in the modern American West. It led to at least thirty-three—and some say as many as fifty—murders on both sides of the border and earned Ervil the moniker of "the Mormon Manson." It was with neither hyperbole nor paranoia that some family members, in the immediate aftermath of the attack on the three women and fourteen children, broached the possibility of the old blood feud erupting. Many observers within the mainstream Mormon church, the fundamentalist Mormon offshoots, as well as members of the LeBaron family, believed that the historic rivalries and tensions remained very much alive and may have played a role in the November 4, 2019, ambush and murders.

"It was the first thing that came to my mind when I learned of the massacre of my cousins," said a relative of all three women.

* * *

This book is an attempt to answer a seemingly straightforward question: Who are the LeBarons, and what drove them first to settle in Utah in the 1840s, and then to colonize a region in Mexico in the 1880s as members of an embittered offshoot of a uniquely American sect? Put another way, why were Rhonita, Dawna, Christina, and their children on that road in the first place? But behind this question looms a more fundamental one.

Although I am not Mormon, I am descended from a long line of Mormon pioneer women, beginning with my great-great-grandmother, who was converted in London in 1849 by a future Mormon Prophet and brought her seven children with her to Zion by sailboat, steamer, and wagon train. Her daughter-in-law, my great-grandmother, made a solo trek from Denmark to Utah in 1851 as a nine-year-old girl. She walked from St. Louis to Salt Lake City, pushing her few belongings in a handcart. In the summer of 1887, my grandmother was born in the mountains of Utah Territory, the twenty-third and final child of my great-grandfather, a church leader and prominent polygamist. When the United States granted statehood to Utah in 1896, requiring the church to abandon the doctrine of polygamy, my grandmother became illegitimate in the eyes of state and federal law—"an outlaw by birth," as one writer described what happened to children born of polygamy.

Today, Colonia LeBaron is a portal into the past, a place where one can glimpse what it must have been like to live within a polygamous community on an arid and dangerous frontier. This book is an exploration of LeBaron—the place and the family—in an effort to explain the impulses that drove thousands of women over generations, including ancestors of mine as well as Dawna, Christina, and Rhonita, to join or remain within a novel American

Members of the LeBaron family mourn on November 5, 2019, while they observe the car in which some of their relatives were killed and burned during an ambush in the Sonora mountains. *(AFP Photo/Hérika Martinez)*

religion based on male supremacy and female servitude. Many did not have a choice in the matter, of course, but many others did, and many embraced their patriarchical world. These women of Zion found themselves in an isolated desert, navigating the often-mysterious complications of plural marriage. What was the attraction? Why did they submit then—and why do they submit even now?

CHAPTER ONE

"We're Not Radical Cultists"

THE APPROXIMATELY FORTY families of La Mora make up a diverse community. Among them are breakaway Mormon fundamentalists, polygamists, Mormon-born worshipers who identify as independents, mainstream Mormons, and "even some agnostics and hippies," as one resident described the conglomeration of believers and nonbelievers. Mexico is home to 1.5 million mainstream Mormons, the largest LDS population outside the US, but La Mora is not affiliated with the official Church of Jesus Christ of Latter-day Saints, whose leaders in Salt Lake City, Utah, were quick to distance themselves from both La Mora and LeBaron after the ambushes. "We are heartbroken to hear of the tragedy that has touched these families in Mexico," said LDS church spokesman Eric Hawkins. "Though it is our understanding that they are not members of [the church] . . . our love, prayers and sympathies are with them as they mourn and remember their loved ones."

Another church spokesman called the attack "terrible and tragic" but pointed out that the church had no information about the event, telling CNN, "as from what I can tell, these were members of a polygamist sect." The victims' family members were deeply insulted by the statements, described by one as "super cold, unfeeling." Dawna's sister-in-law bristled at the portrayals of the La Mora residents by the church and the news media. "I was kind of ashamed of them for that. We're not radical cultists." In contrast, the local LDS church in Williston, North Dakota, where the Millers worshipped, held a candlelight vigil attended by one hundred fifty mourners. "We can never forget what these three mothers did. We can always remember their valiant acts of motherhood," said Bishop Pete Isom.

Colonia LeBaron, located eight miles south of the county seat of Galeana in the state of Chihuahua, is home to approximately three thousand souls, whereas La Mora has only a few hundred. It is the power center of Mexico's fundamentalist Mormons. While many surnames are associated with the LeBaron and La Mora settlements, the LeBaron family was the first to colonize Galeana, carving out a sanctuary for polygamy, and it remains the most prominent Mormon name in the region. LeBarons have lived on both sides of the US/Mexico border since the 1880s, enjoying economic—and, in many cases, political—clout in both countries. In stark contrast to the crushing poverty of their Mexican neighbors, the wealthy Mormon landowners, with vast cattle ranches, farms, and pecan and walnut orchards, are direct descendants of one of the church's pioneer leaders.

In the 1950s, another splinter group of American fundamentalist Mormons emigrated to the neighboring Mexican state of Sonora. Fleeing the infamous "Short Creek" raids against polygamists by the Arizona National Guard in 1953, the Langford family crossed the border to settle a section of land in a river valley they christened Rancho La Mora. It was a hardscrabble place, and the impoverished émigrés eked out a living from the high desert landscape, enduring freezing winters and blistering summers. They went without electricity or running water, cut off from the US and the rest of Mexico. Then the Miller family moved from the US to La Mora in order to practice polygamy. In the 1960s, Kenneth Miller, Howard's father, came with his parents to join the fundamentalist compound they referred to as "the ranch." They were penniless, along with the rest of the community, "living by the river in a tent with no running water," as Kenneth remembered it, and growing potatoes, beans, and corn long before the nut orchards of the twenty-first century. There was little interaction between the Sonoran and Chihuahuan Mormons until the late twentieth century, when a "smattering of marriages would draw together La Mora and the larger, more prosperous Colonia LeBaron." Kenneth married Loretta LeBaron, and the couple raised their fourteen children in La Mora, home-schooling them all.

Residing in luxury Santa Fe–style homes with manicured lawns and gated entries, tree-lined streets, basketball courts, parks, bronze statues, and a nearby private golf course and gun club, the LeBarons have sparred repeatedly with their poorer Indigenous and native Mexican neighbors as well as the notorious drug cartels that surround them. *Welcome to Colonia LeBaron*, on a huge billboard, greets visitors today. *A place where the sun always shines with the light of hope and love*. A large letter "L," formed by white-painted stones on a nearby hilltop, announces the community, and another welcome sign says, *Respect for the Rights of Others Is Peace*.

The road where the ambushes occurred links a string of Mexican villages, but it serves mainly as a smuggling route—for drugs and people—into the US from Mexico, across the remote southern borders of Arizona and New Mexico. The territory has long been controlled by the Sinaloa Cartel, presided over by El Chapo until he began serving his life sentence in July 2019 in the federal SuperMax prison in Florence, Colorado. Three of his more than fifteen sons—Joaquín, Ovidio, and Ivan, who call themselves *Los Chapitos*—succeeded him as drug lords in the largest and most powerful drug cartel in the world. Not only were they at the center of a power struggle with former Chapo lieutenant Ismael "El Mayo" Zambada, but rival groups had also been challenging them, including the Juárez Cartel and the Jalisco New Generation Cartel (CJNG). Known for its savagery, CJNG was making significant inroads into Sinaloa's territory.

The botched capture of twenty-eight-year-old Ovidio by Mexican security forces at his home in the Sinaloa state capital of Culiacán, just two weeks before the Mormon attacks, threw the region into crisis. Instead of immediately taking Ovidio into custody for extradition to the US, the soldiers allowed him to make a phone call. During that delay, Ovidio's four hundred gunmen seized control of the city and repelled the Mexican National Guard, Federal Police, and Army. The battle took place in broad daylight, resulting in the deaths of at least eight soldiers, and Ovidio was freed in a stunning rebuke and humiliation of the Mexican Government. His heavily armed security forces remained at large near the Mormon colonies.

La Mora had forged a time-honored, if unofficial, pact with the Sinaloa Cartel and its offshoots. It was not an alliance as much as a "cordial relationship" with those controlling the roadblocks along the numerous smuggling routes in northern Sonora on Mexico's border with Arizona, according to Loretta Miller, grandmother of Rhonita LeBaron Miller's four children who died in the ambush. But despite the Sinaloa Cartel's reputation for violence, it had never extorted the Mormon community for "protection payments" and had never stolen from them, Adam Langford, a patriarch and two-time La Mora mayor told a reporter. At the same time, the LeBaron community had also forged a decades-long agreement with the Sinaloa Cartel—an implicit understanding of "Don't interfere in our business and we won't interfere in yours." The Sinaloa Cartel was using smuggling routes along Chihuahua's border with New Mexico and Texas. In recent years, though, Colonia LeBaron was increasingly surrounded by the enforcement unit of the Juárez Cartel, a wing of assassins known as *La Línea* ("The Line"). This "line" of former and active-duty police officers was assembled to protect Juárez Cartel traffickers by having sophisticated training in urban warfare and a weapons arsenal to rival government forces. "They marked out the line, that's to say, they enforced order" for the Juárez Cartel, said Mexican security analyst Carlos Rodriguez Ulloa.

The relationships between the two fundamentalist Mormon communities had become more complicated in the months before the murders, as the Mormons in Sonora began to view the cartel *sicarios* in their own area as "the good guys" and those in Chihuahua as "the bad guys," and vice versa—setting up a dangerous and conflicting set of allegiances dividing La Mora and LeBaron. The cartels had also started fighting for control of gasoline distribution in the region—a resource directly affecting the communities' farming operations.

The relatives of the murder victims firmly believed that the brazen massacre was no accident. Perhaps the most damning and poignant evidence came from the surviving children, who gave firsthand accounts of watching their mothers die. Relatives also spoke vaguely of information from other sources. Rhonita's sister-in-law Kendra Miller said that they had received "confirmation that this was orchestrated as a provocation for the cartel over here in Sonora where we are, and our family was picked to be the ones to stir up trouble and to start a war." Miller claimed that the cartel *sicarios* from Chihuahua were "stopping our families." Other family members were also quick to blame the Juárez Cartel for the premeditated murders, arguing that the cell-phone video obtained by Mexican police clearly identified the men involved as theirs.

The LeBaron clan's patriarch, Joel LeBaron Soto, claimed that the massacre was rooted in the political situation in the region, stating that the motive originated in an event that occurred earlier in the state of Sonora, although he declined to pinpoint the event. "I don't want to say more," he told a Mexican television station, before going on to criticize Javier Corral, the governor of Chihuahua, for running a corrupt justice system, which Corral strongly disputed. LeBaron Soto dismissed the local and national governments for presenting the attacks as a confrontation between cartels. Calling that narrative "pure show," LeBaron Soto pointed out that, after the assassins "shot one of the women, they stole her wallet and then set her on fire"—hardly a case of mistaken identity. Not only did they shoot from the top of a hill, they also fired from point-blank range, as evidenced by the hundreds of shell casings near the cars. "The government of Javier Corral has been an accomplice to all kinds of crimes that have been committed against our family," said LeBaron Soto's son Julian, lamenting that the rule of law did not exist in Chihuahua. He stopped short of blaming Corral for the killings.

The massacre sparked outrage on both sides of the border, with Mexican President Andrés Manuel López Obrador ("AMLO," for short) vowing to find the assassins, while American President Donald Trump tweeted an offer to send US troops to "clean out the monsters." López Obrador rejected it. After Trump tweeted, "You sometimes need an army to defeat an army," another of Rhonita's cousins, Alex LeBaron, responded to a reporter: "Want to help? Focus on lowering Drug Consumption in [the] United States. Want to help some more? Stop . . . systematically injecting high-powered assault weapons into Mexico." Alex then joined other family members in presenting a petition to the Trump administration to designate the cartels as terrorist organizations. But the negative response from the Mexican public was swift, and, in a matter of hours, Trump and the LeBarons were attacked on social media under hashtags calling the LeBaron family traitors. The family swiftly backpedaled, insisting that the Trump administration tricked them into signing the petition asking for the terrorist designation in order to justify a military intervention by the US. The petition, they said, marked the family as the cartels' number-one enemy, further endangering them. "What worries me more than anything is how some politicians and some media outlets are using the event as a political weapon to criticize the federal [Mexican] government," Julian told a Mexican newspaper.

The nine murder victims were dual Mexican-American citizens, killed by American-made bullets and assault weapons. Most of the theories posited—on social media blogs and chat rooms—were variations on schemes involving US and Mexican policies for fighting the drug cartels. According to one theory, the massacre was "bait" that would allow the US to invade Mexico and seize the resource-rich northern states of Sonora and Chihuahua under the auspices of a new war on drugs. Another said the Central Intelligence Agency carried out the attack to pressure López Obrador to start a new war against the dominant Sinaloa Cartel so that the US could sell more weapons to Mexico.

In the aftermath of the massacre, the LeBarons' decades-long clash with their neighbors over water rights has also attracted scrutiny. A powerful civil-society organization of local farmers and ranchers calling itself *El Barzón*—for the strap with which oxen are yoked to the plow—has accused the family of siphoning excessive water from the rivers and aquifers for their massive commercial farms. The *Barzonistas* claim the LeBarons have illegally dug hundreds of wells, bulldozed reservoirs meant for Indigenous communities downstream, and cleared common land to grow twenty thousand highly profitable nut trees, which require far more water than regular crops.

As climate change has intensified in the arid land of Chihuahua, many observers view the Mormons' agricultural empire as a potential battleground for the coming water wars in the area. The coalition believes the comparatively wealthy LeBarons are part of a network of power and violence along the US–Mexico border. For their part, the LeBarons have accused *El Barzón* of being a criminal gang that receives protection from Chihuahua's governor.

Notoriously secretive about their weapons, Colonia LeBaron operates like a mini-state and has negotiated special terms with various leaders of the governments of both abutting states. Often referred to by detractors as "the Polygamist Mafia," for more than a century the members of the community have been seen by Mexicans as land-hungry foreign invaders who dishonestly acquired mineral-rich acreage and precious water rights.

Predictably, the aftermath of the massacre saw hackneyed antipolygamy screeds emerge, spawning claims that the killings were "an inside job" in which the mothers and children were murdered because they were trying to publicly expose abuses. Less predictable were reports that the murdered women had ties to the infamous alleged sex-cult NXIVM (pronounced NEHK-see-uhm), and that Colonia LeBaron "is where underlings of NXIVM leader Keith Raniere recruited young women to work as nannies in an upstate New York compound run by the accused cult," according to the *Mazatlan Post*.

Still, while the family had a history of violence with its neighbors and the cartels, many members of the fundamentalist Mormon communities in both the US and Mexico wondered whether the attack was a continuation of the fifty-year-old vendetta among the descendants of Joel and Ervil LeBaron. The threat from their "brand of fringe delusion" had gone "dormant," as Ben Bradlee Jr. and Dale Van Atta reported in their 1981 book *Prophet of Blood*. But law enforcement officials in the US and Mexico had long memories of that feud and remained wary of its revival, fearing it "could again rise up and begin playing itself out as a biblical Western written in fear and in blood," wrote Bradlee and Van Atta.

* * *

The LeBarons' original forebear, Benjamin Franklin Johnson, was an early disciple of the church founded in 1830 by Joseph Smith Jr. Johnson would go on to become an apostle and leader in Smith's church for the rest of the nineteenth century, and, shortly before his death in 1905, he would claim to have inherited Smith's mantle as the church's spiritual leader.

An imaginative farm boy, Joseph Smith was born in Sharon, Vermont, on December 23, 1805, to formerly well-to-do parents whose wealth had been squandered in dubious real estate deals, so he was raised in poverty. His parents, with their eight children, began a pattern of moving westward "to escape irate creditors," ultimately settling in Palmyra, New York, in a "well-chinked four-room cabin," as one historian put it.

As a teen, Smith practiced fortune-telling and magic, dug for buried treasure in graveyards, and dabbled in the occult before receiving what he claimed was an order from an illuminated angel of God named Moroni. Appearing as

a spirit draped in white robes, the angel addressed him by name, telling the
tall, athletic seventeen-year-old that he had been chosen by God to write a
book about one of the mythical ten lost tribes of Israel. Moroni quoted numerous biblical prophecies regarding the Second Coming of Christ, according to
Smith, and said God had chosen Smith as His instrument to reveal to the
world that all religions were false and corrupt, and that he should set the
world straight.

In a white heat, the illiterate Smith dictated the 275,000-word manu-
script, and, in just over two months, his tale of heroes and villains, bloodshed and miracles, warriors and intrigue took upstate New York by storm.
Emulating the King James Bible, the book was a thousand-year chronicle that
Smith averred was a secret and sacred enhancement of the New Testament.
"He began the book with a first-class murder, added assassinations, and piled
up battles by the score," wrote Fawn Brodie, his most famous biographer.
Intricate and thrilling, *The Book of Mormon* included an ancient military figure
named Mormon, the prophet for whom the book was named and the father
of Moroni.

Smith published his book on March 26, 1830, amid the fevered atmosphere of the Second Great Awakening. Reflective of the mystical leanings of
the day, it was an unsophisticated view of the battle between good and evil,
with a Cain-and-Abel story at its center. The *Rochester* (NY) *Daily Advertiser*
published the tome's first review with the headline BLASPHEMY! BOOK OF MOR-
MON, ALIAS THE GOLDEN BIBLE. Stung by the scorn, Smith claimed he was being
persecuted like the Apostle Paul, the first of hundreds of alleged persecutions
that would define Smith's life, death, and legacy. Just two weeks after publication, Smith formally established his church and announced to his followers, who then numbered six, that his official title was "Prophet, Seer, and
Revelator." A month later, their ranks would swell to forty, and more than a
thousand would be converted within a year.

It was a new and exciting religion. At its core was a belief that all churches
had deviated from the true religion of Christianity—in what Smith called
"The Great Apostasy"—and that his divine task was to gather the remnants of
Israel to a latter-day Zion and await the Rapture. Central to Smith's theology
was the doctrine that all male devotees were on the road to godhood, that all

men could create their own kingdoms, and that women, if they were pure and obedient to men, could be "pulled through the veil" to this kingdom to join their "righteous" men as eternal companions in the hereafter. As part of this doctrine of male supremacy, Smith created an autocratic cadre of "worthy males" to rule his Church of Jesus Christ of Latter-day Saints.

"In no other period in American history were 'the last days' felt to be so imminent," as Brodie put it, describing the era as a time when the country was "seized by swiftly spreading fear that the Republic was in danger." In 1830, the United States was only half a century old and populated by fewer than thirteen million people. President Andrew Jackson had assumed office after a bitter election battle that divided the country along partisan lines and fomented theological and political schisms. Into this mix came Smith's millennialist movement, a seductive male-dominated collectivism with an apocalyptic vision that included the fall of the US Government, with his revolutionary theocracy filling the void.

Perceived from the start as a radical faith by most Americans, the religion was neither Judaic nor Christian. Still, *The Book of Mormon* propelled Smith to fame and cemented his status as the sect's leader. He ruled his flock with a holy warrior's passion guided by divine revelation, which gave him an aura of infallibility and repelled any challenges to his rule. Boasting of more than a hundred personal conversations with God, he claimed that he was a higher spiritual being than both Martin Luther and the Pope, with whom God, he said, had never spoken directly. Though widely mocked, *The Book of Mormon* would soon attract hundreds of thousands of immigrants to the United States from Great Britain and Scandinavia, in addition to its many American converts.

"The stupendous claim that this fourteen-year-old boy had seen God and Jesus Christ was soon followed by detailed reports of visits of other heavenly messengers," wrote Verlan LeBaron, great-grandson of Benjamin Johnson. From the start, Johnson and the other ancestors of the LeBarons were avid followers, believing Joseph Smith and the witnesses, accepting him as a Prophet, and "adhering to his teachings."

Mainstream Christians ridiculed the theology of early Mormonism and its claims about the divine power of crystals, along with its secret rituals,

proxy baptisms, blood oaths, celestial marriage, anointings, healings, and
other strange practices. Smith's gospel and its road to godhood was a religious
version of the American dream—not only were little boys told they could
grow up to be president, but they also could become gods. He depicted the
afterlife as a paradise where his male disciples would "progress" to the same
divinity as the God of the Old Testament, who lived on a planet called Kolob,
where he was sexually active with the Heavenly Mother and other wives—
heady stuff for Smith's zealous male disciples.

From the beginning, Smith preached about the virtues of material
wealth, resulting in a clannish prosperity that distinguished Mormons from
their neighbors. "Holy worth" was measured by church members' industri-
ousness and affluence, their private property consecrated to the church, which
then returned to the male members as much as was "needful for the support
and comfort" of their families—a concept that Smith called the United Order
of Enoch, which swelled church coffers. Smith bestowed such biblical titles as
apostle, *elder*, and *patriarch* on his male converts, and, thanks to the evangelical
ferment of the day, his energetic proselytizing was historically fruitful.

Setting themselves apart as God's modern chosen people, and calling all
non-Mormons "Gentiles," reinforced a tribal mentality that would alien-
ate neighbors and help define the religion. In 1830, when Smith's converts
numbered only forty, an angry mob destroyed a dam built across a Palmyra
stream to create a deep pool for the immersion baptisms he was performing.
Yelling "False Prophet!" and foul epithets, they spit on him, which he took as
validation that he was Jesus incarnate. "And thus did they imitate those who
crucified the Savior of mankind, not knowing what they did," he wrote of
his ill treatment and its parallels to Jesus's experience. The nascent Prophet
brilliantly grasped how to manipulate the myth and reality of persecution as
a means to his ends.

His church was not yet five months old when, fearing for his life and the
lives of his followers, Smith turned his attention to finding a location to build
his Zion. He moved the growing flock from Palmyra to an existing communal colony in Kirtland, Ohio, a site that the twenty-five-year-old Smith
pronounced as the easternmost boundary of the Promised Land. His devotees
converted and baptized nearly everyone in their new community.

Benjamin Johnson was born in 1818 in Pomfret, New York. "In the year 1829, in our village paper, was published an account of some young man professing to have seen an angel, who had shown and delivered to him golden plates, engraved in a strange language and hid up in the earth, from which he had translated a new Bible," Johnson wrote later in life. By the following year, "We began to hear more about the 'Golden Bible' that had been found by Joe Smith, the money digger." Johnson and some family members traveled on foot to join Smith in Kirtland, where Johnson was baptized.

A devoted convert, Johnson, thirteen years younger than Smith, would rise quickly in the church, gaining the Prophet's trust and friendship. "It was with a joy almost unspeakable that I realized that I was living in a day when God had a prophet upon the earth." By the summer of 1831, Smith's gathering of "Saints" from New York, Pennsylvania, and Ohio brought together in Kirtland the two thousand members of the church, sending the region into the throes of a speculative craze. Founding a church bank and growing personally rich in Ohio's real estate boom, Smith prospered until it all collapsed during the Panic of 1837, leading to a warrant issued for his arrest on bank-fraud charges.

In the middle of the night, Smith and a trusted apostle fled on horseback, riding eight hundred miles to Far West, Missouri, where he continued his colony building. Smith believed the locale was the true cradle of biblical civilization, the site of the original Garden of Eden, where Adam had been born. Six years earlier, one of Smith's elders had already led several hundred followers to Far West to establish Zion. Part of the area's appeal was its proximity to Indian country, and the Mormons planned to "convert the Lamanites," as *The Book of Mormon* called Native Americans. Restoring "these heathens to the gospel" was considered integral to fulfilling the prophecies of the Angel Moroni. Greeted by fifteen hundred church members, including recent converts, Smith was initially buoyed by the successful gathering of Saints. But it was a short-lived honeymoon. Missourians did not welcome the influx of the insular group, which pooled its resources, voted in blocs, and eschewed "Gentile" businesses. Clashes between the Mormons and their neighbors escalated, culminating in 1838 with riots and the Missouri governor calling for the Mormons to be "treated as enemies" and "exterminated." Once again,

Smith mounted a "fine chestnut stallion" and "pounded up the road" toward yet another new Zion—this time, a wooded hilltop in Illinois on the banks of the Mississippi River. He named the site Nauvoo, meaning "a beautiful plantation" in Hebrew.

When Smith arrived in Nauvoo in 1839, it was a sleepy burg at the edge of the United States. By the summer of 1840, though, Nauvoo was a thriving town of 2,900, its population increasing as eager converts poured in from the proselytizing missions Smith had sent abroad. Smith's charismatic missionaries—including the brash and dynamic Brigham Young—had converted hundreds and then thousands in England, Scotland, and Wales and then established a massive emigration system to bring them to America. The apostles found the English and Welsh manufacturing and mining towns a fertile field in which to plant the seeds of Mormonism, populated as they were with impoverished laborers keen to improve their lot.

Less than a decade after founding his church, Smith had lured his European converts into making perilous ocean crossings and onerous overland passages across half the North American continent to Illinois. By that point, too, many of his fellow Americans had also fallen under his sway and made their way to his Promised Land. By 1844, the religion numbered thirty thousand adherents, with ten thousand of those located in Nauvoo.

Smith envisioned Nauvoo as a wealthy and powerful separatist city-state ordained by God that would rival the young nation's capital. He even petitioned Congress for it to become a completely independent federal territory—with him as Governor of Nauvoo—and he began to organize an administration to rule over his "sovereign Mormon state." Instead, Nauvoo would be Smith's "last stopover on the road to his Celestial Kingdom," as one writer put it. But even though it became Smith's grand finale, the Nauvoo episode was only the beginning for his followers.

Smith controlled all real estate deals in his model city and oversaw every business and personal transaction. He was not only the spiritual leader but also the mayor, judge, architect, hotelier, and banker. He masterminded the design and construction of a spired marble temple, wide streets, lush surrounding farms, and stately private homes and public buildings. He also directed the establishment of a newspaper, a post office, seven brickyards, and steam-driven sawmills. Jonathan Browning, a devout follower as well as a gun manufacturer, provided weapons to Smith's expanding "Army of God," which quickly became the largest militia in the state and nearly one-quarter the size of the US Army.

Benjamin Johnson served as one of Smith's confidants, as well as his private secretary, bodyguard, personal lawyer, legal representative for the church, and trustee for church property, and he held Smith's power of attorney. He would be ordained a high priest and become a member of the church's powerful Council of Fifty, what Johnson described as the "embryo kingdom of God upon earth." This elite and highly secretive body of "princes" in Smith's government, considered "the highest court on earth," would "crown Joseph Smith King of the Kingdom of God."

In 1842, after returning to Nauvoo from a proselytizing mission in England, Johnson met Melissa B. LeBaron, an orphan who, "in appearance, education and ease of manner, had no equal in the vicinity," and it was said there was a money legacy due and waiting her claim in a Rochester (New York) bank. He fell in love with "the heiress," as she was called, and they were quickly married. "Here was one the Lord had placed right before me, a young lady of culture and refinement . . . beloved by all who knew her." It would be the issue from that marriage who would carry Melissa LeBaron's bloodline down through several generations to populate Colonia LeBaron in Chihuahua, Mexico. In turn, those descendants would claim the mantle of the Mormon priesthood as it was bestowed upon their great-grandfather Benjamin Johnson by none other than the Prophet himself.

In Nauvoo, the Mormons first began the widespread practice of polygamy, a practice that had come to Smith through divine revelation years earlier, and one that he and his chosen intimates had already been secretly following before it became official church doctrine in 1843. "Although the prophet's well-known zest for temporal delights surely came into play with polygamy," wrote a twentieth-century chronicler of the church, "indications are strong that the major reason for instituting the Principle was to shore up Joseph's power with his own men. In Mormondom the prophet alone could decide which comely virgin went to which man." Careful at first to keep polygamy concealed so as not to inflame the reviled "Gentiles," or even male and female skeptics in his own congregation, he dispensed the blessing of "the Principle" one by one to his inner circle of loyal male followers. Celestial marriage—with its patriarchal order and promise that any worthy male could rule his own world, accompanied by a select group of wives not just in this life, but throughout eternity—excited many of them.

Many other church members, however, were aghast as Smith expanded his harem, marrying very young girls and even propositioning sisters and wives of friends. Church officials split into two distinct camps—advocates of polygamy and those ardently opposed.

Among the first women Smith took as a plural wife was Almira, one of Benjamin Johnson's sisters. "It was a Sunday morning . . . that the Prophet proceeded to open to me the subject of plural marriage and eternal marriage," as Benjamin described the encounter decades later to a church official. "After breakfast he proposed a stroll together, and taking his arm, our walk led toward a swail [sic], surrounded by trees and tall brush and near the forest line not far from my house." The two men sat on a fallen tree, and Smith told Johnson that "the Lord revealed to him the ancient order . . . and the necessity for its practice and did command that he take another wife." As Benjamin listened, he was stunned. "He came now to ask me for my sister Almira. His words astonished me and almost took my breath. I sat for a time amazed, and finally, almost ready to burst with emotion, I looked him straight in the face and said: 'Brother Joseph, this is something I did not expect, and I do not understand it. You know whether it is right, I do not. I want to do just as you tell me, and I will try to, but if I ever should know that you do this to dishonor and debauch my sister, I will kill you as sure as the Lord lives.' "

Three weeks later, Smith asked Johnson for another of his sisters, a young woman who was already engaged. Johnson instead offered Smith an attractive orphan girl named Mary Ann, whom his parents had taken in as a child and raised as his sister. "No, but she is for you," Smith responded. "You keep her and take her for your wife and you will be blessed." Smith then conferred on the twenty-three-year-old Johnson a patriarchal blessing, first sealing him for eternity to his own young wife Melissa, and then sanctioning his second marriage to Mary Ann. Smith "gave me my first plural wife," Johnson later wrote of his new bride Mary Ann. From that point forward, Johnson was able to overcome his "Puritanical Ideas of Monogamic Marriage."

Throughout his life, Benjamin Johnson claimed to be closer to the Prophet than most others. "Even so close as to give him enemas when needed and to receive such from him," recorded Hyrum L. and Helen Mae Andrus in their famous book *They Knew the Prophet*. A highly respected Mormon scholar, authoritative source, and lifelong student of Joseph Smith's life and teachings, Hyrum Andrus taught church history and doctrine at Brigham Young University. After giving Johnson a second wife, according to Andrus's account, Smith then sealed Johnson to himself as his adopted "son," making him a member of the Royal Family.

The LeBaron forefather was now a High Priest bound for eternity to the Prophet as both his putative son and his brother-in-law.

* * *

Once polygamy became official, the Mormons were irrevocably estranged from their Protestant neighbors, and there were rampant defections from within Smith's own ranks. While some male adherents were appalled by the concept, others were intrigued. "To men who loved their wives, it was pleasant to hear that death was no separation," as historian Fawn Brodie put it, "and to men who did not, it was gratifying to hear that there could be no sin in taking another."

As rumors swirled about Smith's secret marriages to nearly fifty women, a groundswell of anger and derision rose against him from within and without. He became increasingly reckless, lashing out against his enemies and triggering more hostility against him and his sect. Clashes between the Saints and their neighbors increased as polygamy became more conspicuous and as many Missourians recoiled at what they saw as an invasion of foreign converts. The heightened tension prompted Smith to reinforce his 2,500-man militia, the Nauvoo Legion. As angry anti-Mormon mobs from Missouri, Iowa, and Illinois gathered near Nauvoo, which by this time had a population of twelve thousand, Smith mustered the Legion.

In 1844, Joseph Smith announced his candidacy for the US presidency, pledging to create a Mormon-ruled theodemocracy. He viewed capturing

the presidency as part of the prophecies and mandate of his church. He fore-
told the emergence of "the One Mighty and Strong"—a leader who would
"set in order the house of God"—and claimed that mantle for himself. That
summer, he declared martial law in Nauvoo, and the thirty-eight-year-old
Prophet—now calling himself "General Smith"—led his Legion in a parade
up Main Street, sitting atop his stallion Charlie, who pranced to the cadence
of a brass band. Smith took his place on the reviewing platform, resplendent
in a blue uniform with epaulets and gilded buttons. Giving a boisterous and
sermonizing final address to his followers, he raised his sword skyward: "Will
you stand by me to the death?" he shouted. He was answered with a "thun-
derous 'Aye!' "

Just days later, the mutual fear and hatred between the Mormons and
the people in surrounding communities reached a fevered pitch, and Smith
was criminally charged for inciting a riot. He rode twenty-five miles southeast to Carthage, the county seat, to stand trial. Once in custody, Smith was
charged with treason and denied bail. There, on June 27, 1844, an armed mob
stormed the Carthage Jail and shot Smith to death. The town of Warsaw, a
center of opposition to Mormon settlement in Illinois, had raised an armed
militia of 250 men to attack Smith. The first American religious leader ever
to be assassinated, Smith's self-inflicted martyrdom was equivalent to that of
Jesus Christ in the eyes of his Saints.

"To attempt to delineate the feelings of woe and unutterable sorrow that
swelled every heart too full for tears I need not attempt," Benjamin Johnson
wrote years later. "I stood up dazed with grief, could groan but could not
weep. The fountain of tears was dry. Oh God, what will thy orphan church
and people now do?"

A succession struggle began immediately, as more than a dozen distinct
cabals grasped for control over Smith's religious and financial empire. But
before the internal chaos could topple the church, Brigham Young, a Smith
loyalist, appeared. Young had been in the eastern United States, working to
elect Smith to the presidency. Now, back in Nauvoo, at the meeting of the
Council of Fifty, the forty-six-year-old New England carpenter "arose and
roared like a young lion," recalled a church leader who witnessed him jumping onto a platform and imitating the style, voice, and aura of Smith.

This "American Moses," as George Bernard Shaw later dubbed him, would lead the Saints' exodus from Nauvoo and rule them for decades in their Kingdom of God on Earth—or KOG, as they called it. Born in 1801, the son of impoverished farmers, Young was among Smith's earliest converts and rose quickly in the Prophet's shifting hierarchy. "One of the most remarkable Americans of any age," as one historian called him, Young received "only eleven days of formal schooling." In 1832, after Young was baptized in his "own little mill stream," he preached and proselytized for Smith's new church. He served ten missions, including wildly successful stints in Great Britain; he reported seeing angels; and he was acknowledged by Smith to be a "Prophet and Seer" as early as 1836. Upon ascending as the new leader of the church, he announced that he had received a divine revelation directing him to move his flock out of America, where they were being tirelessly persecuted. He was now, like Smith had been, in the role of "Revelator." Knowing he could not compete with Smith in receiving direct orders from God, he assured his fellow Mormons that the Prophet had left behind enough revelations to guide them over the next decades.

Searching for Zion, Young settled on a remote, sparsely populated Rocky Mountain region then belonging to Mexico, and he started planning to build a colony there. After Smith's murder, the Saints' increasing paranoia had become intense agitation. As a result, the Saints would adopt a siege mentality during the exodus to their new homeland on the ancient bed of Lake Bonneville, which had been covered with twenty thousand square miles of fresh water in prehistoric times but now was a vast expanse of salt flats. The land Young intended to claim for his people put the Mormons outside the dominion of what one of his apostles called "the bloodthirsty Christians of these United States."

Many Mormons saw Young as a usurper who ruled with an iron fist and displayed a dangerous desire to avenge the blood of the Prophet, "thus making the entire Mormon people sworn and avowed enemies of the American nation," according to one of the Danites—a consecrated, clandestine band of Mormon assassins (also called the Avenging Angels) trained to silence internal apostates and outside enemies. But most grew to admire, if not worship, their new leader. "There is a tinge of Cromwell and Napoleon about Brigham that is really charming to the very humble Mormons," the nineteenth-century journalist T. B. H. Stenhouse would observe.

Between the time of his return to Nauvoo after Smith's murder and the Mormon trek to the West, Young managed to marry forty women. While still in Nauvoo after Smith's killing, he turned the city into a police state to protect himself from law enforcement in Illinois and began studying the reports and maps of such explorers as John C. Frémont, who had charted the West. He "vowed he would kill any man" from Illinois law enforcement who would attempt to arrest him on polygamy charges. As violence against the Mormons increased, Young accelerated his plans. In February 1846, he told his people it was time to "Flee Babylon by land or by sea" for their latter-day Israel.

Young was called the "Lion of God" for moving his fourteen thousand Saints more than a thousand miles across the Great Plains to an isolated desert valley, and his hegira was hailed as the emigration feat of the age. His forceful personality and determination inspired confidence and devotion, as thousands of Mormon men, women, and children marched across a vast, mostly unmapped territory to an unknown homeland.

First glimpsing the valley on the morning of July 24, 1847, Young reportedly said, "This is the Place!" though that declaration is widely considered apocryphal. That very day, the Saints set to work in the place Young called *Deseret*—meaning "Land of the Honeybee" in the Jaredite language from *The Book of Mormon*—to carve out a homeland and establish their own nation-state. They unhitched their horses and plowed the soil; by the next day, they had already planted the potatoes, corn, beans, and peas they had brought with them and had begun digging ditches to divert the runoff from the snow-capped mountains of the Wasatch Range.

Brilliant and resourceful, Young turned the Mormons into disciplined and ingenious pioneers who would build what one writer described as "the Holy City by the Dead Sea." Creating a sophisticated irrigation system unparalleled in the history of the American West, they were "laying the foundation of the most ambitious desert civilization the world has seen," as eminent environmental historian Marc Reisner has described the Mormon effort. Under Young's direction, the Saints diverted the precious water into canals that steered the liquid into the newly planted fields on the dry and barren desert floor. Young envisioned his City of Saints surrounded by orchards, vineyards, acres of vegetables and alfalfa, and green fields full of Texas longhorn cattle and hot-blooded Kentucky thoroughbreds. The expertise gained in establishing Deseret would serve Benjamin Johnson's descendants well when they left for northern Mexico, where similar challenges awaited.

Also on the first day in their new Zion, Young set out the laws of the new Mormon empire, including the principle of blood atonement, which he derived from Joseph Smith. Young would usher in the "Dispensation of the Fulness of Times," signaling Christ's return, and there would be no tolerance for those whose faith was weak.

Over the next half-century in Deseret, Young waged a constant, often violent, struggle with the US Government over sovereignty. Along the way, the Mormons procreated and colonized, preached and converted around the globe. (In 2020, the church became the richest in the world, surpassing even the Catholic Vatican and the Church of England.) From the start, nothing inflamed Young's adversaries in the US Government—and stirred outrage in the American people—more than polygamy. Still, as long as Young's Deseret kingdom was a thousand miles beyond the frontier, little could be done. That changed in February 1848, with the signing of the Treaty of Guadalupe Hidalgo, ending the war between the United States and Mexico.

In the second largest land acquisition in American history, Mexico transferred fifty-five percent of its territory to the United States, including the entire Pacific Southwest. Members of Congress and other federal officials were flabbergasted when Brigham Young immediately claimed this new land for his Mormon empire—a landmass encompassing the later states of Utah and Nevada, two-thirds of California, a third of Colorado, and thousands of square miles of Idaho, Wyoming, and New Mexico. While the treaty ended the war with Mexico, it sparked a new conflict and challenge for the US Government, introducing what historian David L. Bigler described as "nearly fifty years of cold war between the Kingdom of God and an American republic that never quite figured out how to handle the challenge." From the start, Young wanted independence from both the US and Mexico, and he sought the creation of a new nation twice the size of Texas to be called Deseret, inhabited by ten thousand settlers and "with a seaport at San Diego." He cited his tiny far-flung colonies in Southern California and the Sierra foothills of northern Nevada as justification for his colossal domain. To fill his empire, Young planned to rely primarily on the population increase fostered by polygamy. He also turned his attention to Great Britain and Scandinavia, dispatching his ablest men in search of fresh converts with the talents and skills needed to continue building his Zion. But Young's grandiose scheme would not go unchallenged by Washington. The US Government "deliberately snubbed" this proposed free and independent sovereignty, wrote Mark Twain of Young's "accumulation of mountains, sage-brush, alkali and general desolation." Instead, in 1850, Congress decreased Deseret's land area and created Utah Territory—named not for the Mormon Zion but for the region's Native American inhabitants, the Ute tribe—which would be administered by the federal government. Even with the reduction in size, the territory covered at least 220,000 square miles, more than twice the size of the state of Utah today. It also included parts of Nevada, Colorado, and Wyoming.

* * *

In 1847, twenty-nine-year-old Benjamin Johnson and his wife Melissa LeBaron were members of the first pioneer Mormon contingent arriving with Brigham Young in the Salt Lake Valley. Johnson was a loyal follower of the new Prophet, though without the same bond of love, friendship, and intermarriage he had long shared with Joseph Smith. One of Johnson's last testimonies to his descendants conveyed his unwavering firsthand certainty that Smith was "a prophet of God faithful and true to the end of his days." As he wrote, "I know. I traveled with him, slept with him, lived with him. I was his bodyguard, private secretary and business manager for years. I have always loved and revered him and all his successors."

Johnson struck an imposing, almost legendary figure during his half century in Utah. He would serve fourteen terms in the territorial and state legislatures. He took a total of seven wives, including a pair of sisters, and had forty-five children and 374 grandchildren (though none of these figures were particularly extreme among the Mormons). His older brother Joel was considered one of the most significant Mormon poets, revered for his famous 1853 hymn "High on the Mountain Top."

In Deseret, Brigham Young and his flock unabashedly and conspicuously lived "the Principle," as they called the practice of polygamy. The Principle, known as the Law of Abraham, was based on the Old Testament polygamist Abraham and his plural wife Sarah. "God never introduced the patriarchal order of marriage with a view to please man in his carnal desires, but He introduced it for the express purpose of raising up to His name a royal priesthood," Young wrote. Polygamy posed a direct challenge to the laws of the United States, and the Mormons' conflict with the federal government would last even into the twenty-first century.

The national debate surrounding the Mormons evolved with the changing political winds. In 1848, newly elected President Zachary Taylor, a hero of the Mexican-American War, was openly hostile to the Mormons. He viewed them as religious fanatics with aberrant sexual practices. He also saw them as a rival power center in the West at a crucial moment of American imperialism, when the Gold Rush in California was underway. When Taylor died suddenly in 1850 of apparent food poisoning, some believed he had been deliberately fed arsenic. "Taylor is dead and in hell, and I am glad of it," Young shouted at a public celebration, vowing that "any President of the United States who lifts his finger against this people shall die an untimely death and go to hell." (Rumors about Taylor's death continued into the twenty-first century, fanned by conspiracy theorists claiming pro-slavery Southern politicians had killed him. It was not until 2011 that Taylor's body was exhumed for an autopsy, "laying to rest speculation that he was the first president assassinated.") Taylor's successor, Millard Fillmore, no less appalled by polygamy but reluctant to antagonize the Mormons in the run-up to the 1852 election, appointed Brigham Young as governor of the newly drawn Utah Territory.

That uneasy alliance would be cut short after numerous exposés written about polygamy, including the 1852 publication of a book about the Mormons that included surprising details of plural marriage. Written by a revered American military officer and explorer named John Williams Gunnison, who was leading a government survey of the Utah Territory, the highly readable and authoritative book became an immediate bestseller. One of several influential and popular books written about polygamy, it was more even-handed about the Mormons and their Western expansion than many others. Nonetheless, Gunnison's book contained shocking revelations and salacious details that fueled antipolygamy sentiment across America.

A devout Unitarian, Gunnison went to great lengths to avoid passing moral judgment on Mormonism. Even though "spiritual marriage" went against his personal religious convictions, he was most affronted by the lowly status and abuse of women in the polygamous authoritarian male regime. In the Mormons' patriarchal system, a woman could enter heaven only as an appendage to a man, yet a man could take as many women to the eternal kingdom as he pleased. Gunnison wrote that polygamy introduced a "great cause of disruption and jealousies" in families, and that the practice was "highly distasteful to the young ladies of any independence of feeling."

Gunnison wrote critically of Brigham Young's immense power over the domestic and conjugal relationships in his colony, for Young (like Smith before him) alone had the authority to grant a man the privilege to take another wife. Some women, however, did not trust their spouses' credentials for entering heaven and sought new couplings with priests with higher standing in the church, leading to intense competition among "worthy men" as well as among striving women.

In national political circles, Gunnison became an in-demand expert on the so-called Mormon question, and his book's disclosures would have far-reaching negative consequences for the church. Gunnison identified many virtues of the Mormon experiment under Brigham Young's leadership, including his belief that they were loyal Americans whose quest for autonomy was naturally fueled by a "tempest" of persecution against them. Gunnison advocated for their self-rule, believing that they would reject authoritative theocracy and pagan rituals in favor of modern Christianity and separation of church and state once they became more educated, and as Young's apocalyptic prophecies failed to materialize. Gunnison eloquently praised the Mormon virtues of generosity and communal spirit, resourcefulness and diligence. In the end, though, for all of Gunnison's fairmindedness, he condemned polygamy, the practice Mormons held most sacred. Young had handed his enemies a sword, allowing critics, including Northern congressmen, to compare it to slavery. In August 1852, Young called an emergency conference of his apostles. He defended the inviolability of polygamy, which he saw as a cornerstone of his advanced civilization, believing that many of society's ills were rooted in the subjugation of the male's sexual needs. Still, he had no choice but to acknowledge the rising apostasy in his ranks and the sharply stunted proselytizing abroad caused by the exposure of the practice of polygamy.

Refusing, however, to abandon the Principle, Young "snubbed his nose at federal officials and the general public alike," according to Mormon scholar Benjamin E. Park, and he and his apostles, including Benjamin Johnson, continued to "go forth and multiply" with numerous wives.

A prosperous farmer, merchant, brickmaker, tavernkeeper, nurseryman, and beekeeper—"a living monument" in the church—Benjamin Johnson waited until after Young died in 1877 to claim that he, not Young, had been the rightful heir to Smith's realm. As Smith's adopted son and early confidant, Johnson revealed (though naturally it could not be verified, and few outside the LeBaron family believed it) that shortly before Smith's death in 1844, the Prophet had passed on to him what the Mormons refer to as the mantle of "the One Mighty and Strong." That mantle, also known as the "White Horse Prophecy," meant that Johnson was God's anointed leader on Earth, comparable to Moses, and that he would oversee the latter days when, according to Mormon scripture, God will send signals that the Second Coming of Christ is imminent. That prophecy was ingrained in Mormon culture and passed down through generations who were taught that the day would come when the divinely inspired US Constitution would "hang like a thread as fine as a silk fiber," and LDS church elders would save the nation.

In 1903, at the age of eighty-five and two years before his death, Johnson, at the request of the First Presidency of the Mormon church in Salt Lake City, penned a sixty-four-page handwritten document for the church archives. In it, he recalled the prophecies that Smith had revealed to him and related how he had been "sealed" to Smith as a sacred son, more binding than blood. Although Johnson remained a faithful member of the church, the church never acknowledged his claim. When Johnson's favorite child—a daughter of his seventh wife—married a nephew named Benjamin LeBaron, Johnson designated the firstborn grandson from that union as the one who would carry the patriarch's proud bloodline into posterity. On March 15, 1904, the day that grandson Alma Dayer LeBaron turned eighteen years old, Johnson placed his hand on Dayer's head and pronounced: "When I die, my mantle will fall upon you, as the mantle of Elijah fell upon Elisha when he ascended to Heaven on a chariot of fire." He then told Dayer that the future of Mormonism on Earth was in Mexico, where Benjamin had been sent by Brigham Young in the 1880s to colonize, spread the gospel among the Catholics and Lamanites, and establish a safe haven for polygamists. The Lord had a special mission for Dayer, his grandfather told him: He was to raise his family in Mexico and carry this blessing down to one of his sons. Believing that his grandfather had indeed conveyed the authority of the priesthood mantle upon him—even if his peers were skeptical—the teenager packed his belongings and left the United States for Colonia Juárez, a prosperous colony of 3,500 Mormons who had settled on a 50,000-acre tract in northern Mexico in 1885.

As Dayer's wife Maud recalled years later, Benjamin Johnson told Dayer that "the great things to transpire in the last days, pertaining to the Kingdom of God, would transpire in the land to the South." In 1911, at the age of twenty-five, Dayer had what he called his "100-year vision" about the future of Mexico. In that vision, he "was walking alone in the desert near the border," recalled his son Alma Dayer LeBaron Jr. "He came upon a house, and a voice told him to go upstairs, from which point he could see Mexico from coast to coast. He saw dark clouds overhead representing ignorance, then the sunshine came and progress was made. He turned to look at America and saw rampant destruction."

CHAPTER TWO

The Englishman and the Danish Girl

※

Come girls come, and listen to my noise,
Don't you marry the Mormon boys,
For if you do your fortune it will be
Johnnycake 'n' babies is all you'll see.
Build a little house and put it on a hill,
Make you work against your will,
Buy a little cow and milk it in a gourd
Put it in a corner 'n' cover it with a board.

—MORMON FOLK SONG

OVER THE LAST TWO DECADES, a handful of LeBaron wives and daughters have abandoned their faith, "escaped" the polygamist Mexican colonies, and written popular yet controversial memoirs. "Where was the excitement I had anticipated as the wife of a leader?" wrote Susan, the sixth—and self-proclaimed "favorite"—wife of one of Benjamin Johnson's great-grandsons who was a Colonia LeBaron patriarch. "Babies, hard work, and poverty were the lot of a polygamist's wife. Our colonies consisted of run-down homes filled with lonely women and children, waiting for the scattered moments when our husbands could find time for a hurried visit home."

From childhood, polygamy shaped and governed her life, wrote Irene

Spencer, another LeBaron plural wife—an essential sacrifice by the women so the men could attain godhood and avoid Hell. Over twenty-eight years of marriage, she bore fourteen children and embraced the "miserable prescription for life and marriage," before mustering the pluck to flee. "Irene was a precious and entertaining scallywag who had the courage to take on the brethren," said a sister-in-law.

In 2007, Spencer published *Shattered Dreams: My Life as a Polygamist's Wife*, which became a *New York Times* bestseller, and followed it two years later with *Cult Insanity: A Memoir of Polygamy, Prophets, and Blood Atonement*. In the second book, she wrote that she had "decided it was finally time for someone to tell it like it is." While Mormonism had adopted polygamy as a commandment from Prophet Joseph Smith, by the twenty-first century it had become a means of turning believers into "submissive pawns," she argued. "Through it, prophets controlled believers and men controlled women, all allegedly in accordance with God's will. No one seemed to acknowledge how terrible it was for everyone to live it—women, children, and men as well." One polygamist impressed upon his daughter that "queenhood" was her "birthright and destiny," but she sensed, even at a young age, that it could be a "hollow title, the booby prize in the great and passionate tableau of life."

The powerlessness of women, and what one described as the "heavy duty brainwashing," was inescapable. "I argued my heart out," said one teenage plural wife who was desperate for an education. "I pointed to John 1:4 from the Bible, that everyone has a right to seek his own answers. But my husband said he prayed on it and said 'the Lord looks on that like a pile of shit.' It was all so tawdry and hypocritical."

Some young women broke free even before they could become plural wives and mothers. "At age nine, I had forty-nine siblings," wrote Anna LeBaron in her 2017 memoir, *The Polygamist's Daughter*, which describes how her parents, who were always evading American authorities, abandoned her in Mexico. "My sisters and I were pawns to be auctioned off to the highest bidder," she wrote. "I understood from watching my mom, along with her twelve sister-wives and my countless siblings, that no one was allowed to question my father's authority. So, like the others, I obeyed."

Ruth LeBaron Wariner, Anna's cousin, wrote in her 2015 book *The Sound of Gravel: A Memoir* that her father, another of Benjamin Johnson's great-grandsons, "believed that polygamy was one of the most holy and important principles God ever gave His people," and that if a man lived the Principle, he "would become a god himself and inherit an earth of his own." The thirty-ninth of her father's forty-two children, Ruth was raised in Colonia LeBaron, suffering poverty and sexual abuse, until she managed a traumatic escape to the US with four of her young siblings. They were rescued in the middle of the night by two brothers who had earlier bolted across the border.

The dramatic accounts of contemporary LeBaron women who fled the community are representative of the experiences of a portion of Mormon women during the era when polygamy was still practiced by members of the mainstream church. But Mormonism also holds an allure for many women in LeBaron and La Mora today, just as it held a fascination for women during the LDS church's polygamy era. For some women, it offered the promise of a new beginning, of adventure and empowerment. Many women converts from Europe and Scandinavia anticipated an exciting wilderness experience amid the majesty of the Rocky Mountain West. Pioneering women from the eastern United States who traveled by wagon train to Utah were drawn to the awe-inspiring landscape, which some saw as enhancing their spirituality.

"It brought out the poetesses and hymnists among them, and a belief that they were being called to be goddesses," said the daughter of a twentieth-century plural wife from Colonia LeBaron. "My mother thought *The Giant Joshua* was our own *Gone with the Wind*, and its author Maureen Whipple our own Margaret Mitchell," she added, recalling how the "modern" Mormon women of the 1950s compared the Utah author's 1941 Mormon epic with Mitchell's classic Southern historical romance. Both books were set in Civil War America—one in Utah's Dixie Cotton Mission in the desert near St. George and the other on a cotton plantation in Georgia. "The writers each had their own 'Dixies' and my mother wooed my father's new wives in Colonia LeBaron with the idea that their romantic new lifestyle was as exciting as *Gone with the Wind*."

Plural wife Marilyn Tucker also remembered the quixotic experiment of Colonia LeBaron. "We all lived in this euphoria," she said. "We felt all this suffering, sackcloth-and-ashes and humility was part of a big plan. We were all going to be greatly rewarded for it. Every day we were imbued with the feeling that what we were doing was spiritually important. We were the chosen people of God having our mettle tested." Sacrifice was necessary, they believed, as part of God's will, and the true believers thought they were doing their part in populating the new Zion. "We felt we were making an important contribution to a community founded upon and rooted in beliefs we all shared," wrote the thirteenth wife of a Colonia LeBaron polygamist. "We were part of an organization, a 'celestial family,' that was going to bring about the restoration of all things good and positive. This, in turn, would usher in the millennial reign of Jesus Christ." Jenny Langford, the first plural wife of the founder of La Mora, agreed: "When God said 'multiply the earth,' we took him literally." Jenny and her sister-wife, Amelia Langford—the mother of Christina Langford Johnson—would live together and raise their twenty-three children.

To other women, especially the young daughters of earlier converts, polygamy was seen as a life-changing decision over which they had no say. For many who joined the church in its early years, the experience brought suffering and ruin. From the start, the isolation and the suppression of women's agency have been part of the story within Mormonism. Yet if modern accounts emphasize the repressive and restrictive effects of polygamy, the daily lives of nineteenth-century Mormon women reveal a similar but overall more complex portrait, in which the dream of a new life is central.

* * *

John Taylor, an Englishman who was an ordained apostle of Joseph Smith, returned frequently to his native Great Britain between 1839 and 1847 to proselytize among aristocrats. An upper-class intellectual who rejected the Anglican doctrine of "sin and unworthiness," Taylor became one of the earliest British converts to Mormonism. He had emigrated to Far West, Missouri, shortly after his 1836 baptism, and he was so close to the Prophet that he was shot several times during the Carthage Jail attack that left Smith dead.

Among the people Taylor converted in England were Jean Rio Baker and her husband, Henry Baker. Taylor had twelve wives back in the United States, but he publicly denied the existence of polygamy, dismissing rumors about the practice as evilly inspired gossip, lest it be off-putting to potential converts. Born in 1810, a daughter of Scottish nobility, Jean Rio was raised in the shadow of London's Guildhall, the only child of prosperous parents. She was educated as though she was a boy and learned to play the harp and the piano from music professors who journeyed to her home for lessons. An avid reader of English literature from the Elizabethan through the Renaissance era, she studied at a conservatory and appeared as a singer and pianist in Paris, Madrid, and Milan music halls.

She married Baker in 1832 and gave birth to nine children—seven sons and two daughters—over the next sixteen years. Child rearing was left to governesses, while a cook and butler handled domestic matters. The family was among the elite of mid-nineteenth-century London society, and often in close proximity to Queen Victoria and the royal family. Tutors instilled in the children "the pure Queen's English," as one of them recalled, and the couple routinely read Shakespeare aloud from a three-inch-thick leather-bound volume of the complete works—a tome that Jean Rio would eventually carry with her by wagon train to Utah.

The children were "taught personal cleanliness, morals, manners, and religion in no uncertain terms," and they dined separately from their parents until the age of fourteen, when, having received training in etiquette, they were invited to the family table. By that time, the children were also expected to have mastered the conversational elements of history and literature. At sixteen, each boy received a gold watch—a symbolic ritual marking him as a proper gentleman from that point forward. Both boys and girls learned horsemanship on the bridle path in nearby Hyde Park, though they could not have known this skill would serve them well in their future lives on the American frontier, where horses were necessary for farming and hunting rather than just for recreation.

Henry was a prominent engineer, but it was Jean Rio who was extremely wealthy, having inherited a fortune in property and cash from her great-uncle, who was the surgeon to the royal family and lived at No. 10 Downing Street in London, the official residence of the prime minister. At first glance, the Baker family would seem to have been the unlikeliest of converts, as the overwhelming majority of Mormons were factory workers, miners, and general laborers; a small percentage were middle class, and a relatively negligible number were upper class.

But Brigham Young had just begun his Utopia-building project in the Great Salt Lake Valley, and he was superb at matching his missionaries to specific missions. Dispatching the cerebral Taylor to London, Young was seeking followers from Taylor's rarefied social stratum who were already steeped in religious questing, and who could bring a refined and enlightened sensibility to the rough-edged Zion. The Bakers were one such family.

Mormon missionaries were "preaching the glory of America along with the glory of the new religion," wrote Fawn Brodie, and Jean Rio was as seduced by the calling of a new land as by the promises of a purer and more authentic Christianity. Tales of Smith's assassination and the persecution of the Saints fortified her zeal. She saw Smith's claim that Mormonism would restore Christianity to the individual as a return to the revolutionary idea that Jesus preached—that God was accessible to every human being rather than only through the dominant male hierarchy of mainstream churches. The missionaries assured her that she could embark on a deeply spiritual relationship with God without a censoring male intermediary. She was drawn to the promised guarantee that women could be members of the priesthood, and that Smith had ordained nineteen "high priestesses." She would aspire to re-create her class standing in both her new religion and her new country.

That Taylor and the British missionaries had lied blatantly about polygamy and its centrality to the new religion would eventually, and predictably, infuriate her. It would not be until she arrived in Zion, however, that she saw that the church under the leadership of Brigham Young had evolved into a steadfast patriarchy and oligarchy, with polygamy at its core. But, like much else, and like many others, she would learn that only after a great deal of hardship and sacrifice.

The Millennial Star was an official church newspaper based in Liverpool that carried a regular column about the urgency of the "Latter Days" and the impending Second Coming. These "signs of the times," as they were called, registered the world's wars, volcanoes, earthquakes, plagues, fires, and floods that signaled the nearing apocalypse. The time was nigh, the missionaries told Jean Rio and Henry, and they agreed to an immersion baptism on the night of

June 18, 1849, in preparation for their emigration to America. Soon thereafter, a missionary baptized the Baker children. Many decades later, two of the missionaries to Great Britain—John Taylor and then an American Mormon named Wilford Woodruff—would succeed Brigham Young as presidents and prophets of the church in Utah. (Benjamin Johnson had lost out to Taylor in the scramble after Young's death.)

Just weeks after the Baker family baptisms, a cholera epidemic struck London, taking Henry and their infant child, who was also Jean Rio's namesake. The loss of her husband and baby propelled her forward, as though it was further evidence of the fast-approaching prophesied Armageddon. She added her husband's property to her already sizable assets and began preparations for the family's trek to the distant, mysterious land.

While the church chartered vessels for poorer converts to sail to America, Jean Rio Baker had the financial means and independence to pay for her family, now numbering eight, as well as for nine other friends and relatives. She booked passage for the group on the 152-foot *George W. Bourne*, an elegant square-rigger built two years earlier in Kennebunk, Maine. She also took her beloved piano, which was dismantled and crated, the crate dipped in tar to weatherproof it for the numerous ocean, river, and stream crossings to come. She packed enough couture dresses made for her by Regent Street seamstresses that she envisioned would suffice for the rest of her life—a wardrobe that would require its own ox-driven wagon across twelve hundred miles of plains. At forty years old, Jean Rio believed she had sufficient resources to live out her years comfortably in Zion. It was with confidence and optimism that she packed her personal library, English Blue Willow china, sterling tableware, damask linens, Queen Anne furniture, and her gold, diamond, and sapphire jewelry.

On January 4, 1851, she wrote: "I this day took leave of every acquaintance I could collect together, in all probability never to see them again on earth. I am now, with my children, about to leave forever my Native Land, in order to gather with the Saints of the Church of Christ, in the Valley of the Great Salt Lake in North America." It was the first of dozens of diary entries, which were begun initially as a letter to a friend. Over the next two years, she would keep a written record of her journey from a stately London mansion to a remote valley in the magnificent Rocky Mountains.

Although missionaries downplayed the dangers, even under the best
of circumstances, the migration of Mormon converts in the 1850s required
immense courage in the face of unfathomable risks. At sea, the perils included
smallpox, measles, typhoid, spoiled food, and seasickness. Then there were
the shipwrecks and hurricanes—"I could only compare it with the boiling of
an immense cauldron covered with white foam, and the roaring of the waves
like the bellowing of a thousand wild bulls," Jean Rio wrote of the latter.

Their arrival in New Orleans would be followed by a thousand-mile riv-
erboat excursion up the Mississippi River to St. Louis, offering new opportunities for calamity. Sandbars, fires, and floods threatened the steamboats, and
American diseases to which British immigrants had no immunity were a further concern. The wagon-train expedition from what is now Council Bluffs,
Iowa, to Salt Lake presented its own array of terrifying hazards, including
buffalo stampedes, lightning strikes, poisonous snakes and insects, sunstroke,
Indian attacks, and wagon accidents.

Families rarely arrived in Zion intact, and Jean Rio's was no exception.
While crossing the ocean, four-year-old Josiah became grievously ill from the
consumption that had killed his father and infant sister. Jean Rio prayed that
the sea air would bring a curative miracle for the child, so one morning, after
they had been traveling for a month, she carried him to the deck to show him
a school of porpoises playing near the ship.

But on February 22, 1851, "my very dear little Josiah breathed his last,"
she wrote. Her brother-in-law prepared the boy for burial, attaching to his
feet a mass of coal heavy enough to bear him to the bottom of the ocean and
enveloping the small body in a canvas shroud. The captain tolled the ship's
bell, announcing that the time had come for her last-born son to be "committed to the deep." She noted the precise longitude and latitude in her diary.
"This is my first severe trial after leaving my native land. But the Lord has
answered my prayer in this one thing: that if it was not His will to spare my
boy to reach his destined home with us, that He would take him while we
were on the sea. For I would much rather leave his body in the ocean than
bury him in a strange land and leave him there." It was but the beginning of
her "severe trials" to come, even though the rest of her journey itself would
be relatively uneventful.

On September 29, 1851, her wagons arrived at the majestic overlook view of Deseret that greeted all arriving Saints.

* * *

Eight-year-old Nicolena Bertelsen stood on a busy wharf in Jutland, Denmark, clutching her favorite doll and crying. Yellow curls tumbled out of the peasant kerchief tied over her head. Swathed in layers of bulky clothing, arm in arm with her beloved sister and playmate, Ottomina, Nicolena begged tearfully as her stern mother, Maren, grabbed the doll from her and stuffed a little Bible into the girl's bundle. "Read it every day, wait on yourself, and never never cry," she said in her native Danish. "Be a good girl and keep clean." There would be no room on her journey for anything but necessities, her mother explained.

Nicolena appealed to her father Niels, who was the more tenderhearted parent and had opposed his wife's decision to send their ten children, variously alone and in pairs, to Utah. Two of Nicolena's siblings had already been sent. But the quiet, God-fearing farmer did not intervene to help her, and Nicolena would be burdened by the heartaches of her childhood for the rest of her life. She would later tell her own children that the trials she endured once in Zion paled in comparison to those feelings of abandonment, fear of the unknown, seasickness crossing the Atlantic, confusion caused by a foreign language, and sheer loneliness.

Even as Brigham Young had shrewdly mined the patrician class of Great Britain, he turned his attention to Denmark, where most men labored under titled landowners, with no hope of personal ownership of their own plots. The Scandinavian country would prove a bountiful recruiting ground for his most avid missionaries—with many Danes flocking toward the promise of becoming lords of the soil in Zion. Young knew that nearly all Danish adults were literate, thanks to the most advanced compulsory education program in the world. They were exceptionally healthy and skilled, and the men, having served a mandatory six years in the Royal Danish Army, were disciplined and proficient soldiers. The Danish women were equally resourceful, making feather beds and pillows from swans' down and clothing from handspun wool. Young saw them as the kind of converts who would help him build—literally, in their case, unlike in Jean Rio's—the industrious and civilized empire he envisioned.

The missionaries' guarantee that he could become a landowner for the price of a survey was irresistible to Niels Bertelsen. His family of twelve lived in a small white cottage in the tiny village of Staarup, in the shadow of the massive manor house. Niels had spent his entire adult life tilling the acreage of the wealthy landlord and foresaw no change in his future. Maren and Niels, like 97 percent of the Danish population, were Lutheran. While Maren was a faithful churchgoer, Niels preferred the almanac to the Bible. So when Mormon missionaries reached their village in 1852, the Bertelsens were eager converts. And when their landlord of twenty-one years evicted them for consorting with the Mormons, they had no choice but to emigrate quickly. Unable to afford travel as a family, they arranged for the children to leave with missionaries returning to the United States. The parents would soon follow, and all would meet again in Utah.

It was Nicolena's fate to go without any of her family. Her parents paid two Mormon elders to take her, and she had no say in the matter. Mystified by the talk of salvation and the Promised Land, she wept uncontrollably as she was ushered off to this so-called Zion with two male strangers. The young girl would board a sailing vessel, and, like Jean Rio—with whom her destiny would entwine in a far-off land—Nicolena would spend three stormy months on the Atlantic Ocean, seasick and homesick. Her destination was New York City; after arriving, she and the missionaries traveled by rail to St. Louis, arriving in March 1854.

Nicolena was consumed with fear and despair when the Mormon elders calmly announced they could take her no farther, but they had found her a position as a nursemaid with a wealthy family. They promised to let her parents know where she was. She found that prayers didn't help much, and she didn't have the language proficiency to read the Bible in English. More than a year went by, with no word from either Denmark or Utah. While she became a beloved member of the St. Louis family—they taught her English and offered her a permanent home with them—Nicolena was a headstrong girl, determined to continue the journey to Utah to join her sisters and brothers. "In her steadfast little mind, she remembers that she had been sent to

Utah, her parents desired it, God was waiting there for her, and she must get there somehow," a descendant would later write.

After two years in St. Louis, she had saved enough of her earnings to pay for transportation up the Mississippi from St. Louis to Council Bluffs, Iowa, which she had been told was the starting point for covered wagons heading to Utah. At Council Bluffs, however, she learned that she had to go to Florence, Nebraska. So she walked five miles, crossing the state line, and found a company of Mormon converts assembling not a wagon train but a handcart company. This new, church-sponsored system consisted of emigrants piling their meager rations of food and clothing onto two-wheeled carts, modeled after the small wagons Brigham Young had once seen used by porters in a New York railroad station. The carts' open beds measured three to four feet long, with eight-inch-high sides. Four or five adult family members were assigned to a cart, with each allowed to carry only seventeen pounds of baggage that had to include clothing and bedding. All of them walking abreast could push one cart, while an ox team pulled a wagon full of supplies for every hundred emigrants.

The carts were meant to be pushed by adults, with their children walking alongside. By the time Nicolena arrived, she found that every handcart had already been distributed and loaded, and no one seemed to have room for a stray nine-year-old. But one emigrant took pity on her and invited her to join his family in exchange for helping his pregnant wife and their young children. She eagerly agreed.

Nicolena would be one of thousands of men, women, and children converts—many of whom spoke little or no English and who were too poor to purchase wagons and oxen—who walked partway across a continent. "Going Home to Zion" was the hopeful message scrawled on the sides of their handcarts. While Nicolena's crossing was treacherous—as were many of the Mormon handcart expeditions—she embraced it as new and exciting. "She was, after all, a child with a child's natural happy outlook," her daughter later wrote. "During the long trek west, the great outdoors, the lure of unaccustomed scenes and activities, and the knowledge that at last she was on her way to Zion made it almost entirely a glorious adventure."

Three months later, Nicolena arrived in Utah, and she considered it nothing less than a miracle when she reunited with her oldest brother and sister, Lars and Letty, who were settled in the small community of Richfield, 150 miles south of Salt Lake City. Her parents and other siblings were still en route, by sea and land, so Letty oversaw the young girl's adolescence. Letty had received a common school education in Denmark, and she tutored Nicolena, who became a fluent reader and learned the skills necessary for all pioneer women: cleaning, sewing, spinning, weaving, dyeing, and nursing.

In 1867, at the age of twenty-two, Nicolena took a job as a maid at the Richfield House Hotel, which was owned by a well-to-do Englishman named William George Baker and run by his wife, Hannah. Since emigrating with his mother, Jean Rio, a decade earlier, the handsome Baker had risen to prominence in Brigham Young's empire. In 1862, Young had sent him to colonize the town of Richfield in the Sevier River Valley and had rewarded him with choice positions commensurate with his status, education, and loyalty to the Prophet and the church. Baker was one of thirty-nine men chosen by Young to locate areas in Deseret that could sustain a growing Mormon population. The businessman and hotelier was the justice of the peace in Richfield, held the lucrative and coveted US Postal Service contracts to deliver mail by Pony Express, and operated a stagecoach line between two other flourishing Mormon colonies. As the first settler in Richfield, he was the founding architect of its municipal government.

One day when he stopped by his hotel, Baker noticed the new Danish girl tripping up the stairs under the burden of clean linen for the bedrooms. "A lovely blonde with luxuriant honey-colored hair of the texture of spun silk," as one account described her, Nicolena was preoccupied with the recent death of her fiancé, a fellow Danish convert named Christian Christensen, who had been mortally wounded in the Black Hawk War the previous year. Chief of the Timpanogos tribe, Black Hawk had led Paiute and Navajo forces in a series of attacks against Mormon settlers encroaching in the tribes' territory. "Her sweetheart lingered for three weeks," one of her granddaughters wrote many years later, and Nicolena had cared for him, while insisting that their marriage ceremony be performed, "though she feared it would never be consummated." Sealed together for eternity, their love story was so romantic and tragic that it became the subject of a ballad sung throughout Utah over the next century. "His death left her all but overwhelmed," and the last thing on her mind that day at the Richfield House was a new romance.

Baker asked one of the hotel employees about the girl, instantly smitten by her "unusual fresh beauty," her pink complexion, slight figure, "shapely ankles," and "alluring shyness." The thirty-year-old father of five observed her cleanliness and efficiency, admired her cheerfulness and modesty, and decided that he would ask his wife Hannah to give her consent for him to woo Nicolena as his second wife. When Hannah agreed, Baker then sought permission from Brigham Young, who eagerly concurred, "setting aside" her deathbed marriage to Christensen. And just like that, Nicolena was to become William's plural wife.

Her bride's nest was a primitive adobe dugout—a small earthen structure carved into a hillside—a few blocks from Hannah's comparatively extravagant two-story log home. Nine months later, Nicolena gave birth to her first child. She would spend the next twenty years pregnant, recovering from childbirth, and rearing ten children who were not legitimate according to American law.

While she did not love William—and for years continued to pine for her beloved Christian—Nicolena was committed to her faith. Once the Prophet had abolished her marriage to Christian in the afterlife, her only avenue to eternal salvation now rested with William, who would "pull her through the veil" to the celestial kingdom. All the while, she groped for an understanding of her role in plural marriage, even as being the wife of such a distinguished man offered her new opportunities. She was a young woman "who hungered and thirsted for knowledge, culture, and beauty," and the highly educated and polished William filled that need. "Even though Lena may not have been in love with him at the time," according to one account, "she realized it was the natural and dutiful thing for a girl to marry a good man and do her part toward the common good," to raise a family in the "new and everlasting covenant."

She vowed that she would make every effort to cultivate love for her older husband. A tall man with wavy black hair and blue eyes, the genteel William was "ever kind, considerate, and gallant—a real lover to his little bride—despite the difficulties of celestial marriage." During his scheduled visits with her, he would sip tea and read aloud from the volume of Shakespeare's plays his mother had brought from England. He told her about his teenage years in London, about the beauty of Queen Victoria, and about how, at public celebrations, she arrived bedecked in fabulous silk and velvet dresses, a jeweled crown, and Parliament robes trimmed with ermine. Such stories carried Nicolena away from her crude shanty in the isolated mountains of Utah. William, musically gifted like his mother, would sing to her in a mild baritone and imparted a love of music to their children. Every Sunday morning, without fail, he would awaken early before church services and shine the shoes of all twenty-three of his children at both homes—placing them in a row smallest to largest, "in a precise line like little black soldiers," as one of them recalled.

With time and maturity, Nicolena's appreciation of William expanded to genuine love, making it ever more painful to share him with Hannah, whose status as the first wife set her apart in the community. "If she ever felt dissatisfaction over sharing her husband with another woman, or over the small injustices which inevitably arose in her situation, she never by word or deed let it be known to her children. Only the occasional stifled weeping, overheard in the dark of night," indicated to them that her life was less than perfect. Her family's abject poverty was underscored by its close proximity to the nearby "first family," her own children pitted for survival against William's thirteen children by Hannah. All the while, Richfield's Mormon bishop pressured Nicolena to tithe ten percent of her paltry assets to the church. "She had been gentle and kind, sparkling and pretty, and somewhere along the line had gotten the short end of things," recalled one of her sons.

As her sons grew older, though, they hauled firewood for her, took care of the horses and cows, cut and baled alfalfa, and eventually supported her with their earnings from driving their father's stagecoach, which brought mail from the mining camps in nearby Nevada. Her younger children oversaw the chickens, garden, and orchards. "The little happinesses, the large griefs, the moves from town to town, the uncertainties of life as a second wife, the sorrows and ecstasies of mothering and rearing ten children, poverty, sickness, and death"—all were typical for a woman of her time and place. What carried her through was a deep tranquillity found in her religious beliefs and an unwavering faith in the Church of Jesus Christ of Latter-day Saints.

* * *

For her part, Jean Rio Baker had been shocked upon her arrival in Zion years earlier. She found that it was far from the Garden of Eden the missionaries had promised, but instead a barren desert starkly different from her native England. And that was only the beginning of her disillusionment. She purchased a large and comfortable adobe-and-brick house on a one-acre plot in Salt Lake City, and though it was numerous steps down from her opulent London residence, she was reconciled to a life of what she regarded as simplicity and humility. In fact, her home, with its English furniture, Persian rugs, bone china, and sterling flatware, was among the best appointed in the city, her cherished piano the centerpiece of her parlor. Only a few months after her arrival, though, as part of his directive that the Saints go forth and create outlying communities, Young would order her to relocate from the relatively urbane city to a remote and uncivilized area thirty-six miles to the north.

She then bought twenty acres in the village of Ogden in Utah Territory, built a small house, and gamely took up farming, relying for help solely on sixteen-year-old William, who was already deeply devout, and another son, fifteen-year-old Charles. The other children were under the age of ten and could not contribute much in the way of labor. The family of Londoners struggled to raise a crop in the harsh, rocky soil on "a little patch of worthless land" and eked out a meager existence.

When Jean Rio arrived in Utah, it had become immediately apparent to her that the rumors of polygamy, long denied by church officials, were indeed true. "Spiritual wifery," as it was called, was a crucial component of one's progression to the celestial kingdom. During the 1856 presidential election, as the outside world turned its eye toward the unruly Utah Territory, polygamy had brought the Mormons unwanted national attention. Labeled the "twin relics of barbarism," polygamy and slavery were linked and appeared alongside one another on the new Republican Party's political platform. *The New York Times* carried lurid reports of prominent Mormon men purchasing girls for polygamous marriages.

That year, disasters struck Deseret on multiple fronts. A swarm of locusts, or "Mormon crickets," decimated the crops in the valley, causing a famine.

Defections hit new highs, as the disappointing realities of daily life led to widespread "escapes" into what was then western Utah (which would become Nevada in 1864). Young began to declaim more strenuously against the US Government, insisting that he would decide which laws would be enforced in Utah Territory. President James Buchanan considered Young's actions to be treasonous, so he prioritized armed intervention in the territory. Then he announced to Congress that, in order to restore the supremacy of the Constitution and the law of the land, he was sending three new federal judges, a US marshal, and a Superintendent of Indian Affairs to the insurrectionist theocracy—accompanied by twenty-five-hundred American soldiers.

When he learned that US troops were marching toward Utah in the spring of 1857, a defiant Young responded with his "Mormon Reformation," a massive spiritual inquest designed to cleanse his flock of sin and disobedience, and he declared that all backsliders would be "hewn down." Church historians would later refer to this terrifying period as the "Reign of Terror." Loyalist enforcers interrogated other Saints, and Young preached incendiary sermons about blood atonement. "There are sins that the blood of a lamb, or a calf, or of turtle doves, cannot remit, but they must be atoned for by the blood of the man," he thundered. As the US military force drew close, Young imposed martial law and ordered all non-Mormons to leave the Utah Territory.

Amid the famine and the new wave of fanaticism in Zion, many Saints began abandoning their unproductive farms and turning toward newly settled California. A move to California, however, became synonymous with apostasy, and those who fled did so in darkness and secrecy. Jean Rio encouraged her son, Charles Edward, now twenty-one years old, to take his younger brother, John, and make a getaway. She helped them with their plans while keeping everything secret from family members and neighbors—especially their polygamist brother, William. "The brothers sneaked away from Utah in the middle of the night on two horses," according to one of their descendants. They knew that if they were caught, they would be put to death. "Brigham Young didn't like people leaving, especially if they took horses."

After a harrowing journey over the Sierra Nevada, Charles Edward and John arrived safely in San Francisco, and both young men went on to have illustrious careers in California. "They could not stand poverty any longer so ran away from it," Jean Rio wrote. Nine years earlier, she had brought her five sons to what she had excitedly described as "the city in the tops of the mountains." Now, two sons were dead (Josiah had died on the passage from England, and another, nine-year-old Charles West, had died in Utah after being kicked by a horse), two sons had apostatized and struck out on their own to the edge of America, and another, the polygamist William, lived too far away to be of any help to her.

Jean Rio would be hit hard by Brigham Young's "Law of Consecration," requiring Saints to give all of their property to the church, which claimed it would distribute the combined possessions of the Mormons among followers according to need. It did not work out exactly that way. How much money Jean Rio carried with her to Utah is unknown, but she was forced to surrender it, was reduced to poverty, and watched with disdain and dismay as Young used the collective wealth of his followers to support the construction and maintenance of his mansions—the Beehive House and the Lion House—and other homes, and to pay for servants for his many plural wives. "My

Brigham Young dining with some of his many wives in Salt Lake City. This October 1857 *Harper's Weekly* illustration accompanied an article entitled "Scenes in an American Harem."

20-acre farm turned out to be a mere salaratus [*sic*] patch, killing the seed which was sown instead of producing a crop," Jean Rio recalled years later when, shortly before her death, she wrote an addendum to her diary, which she had stopped in 1852. "I came here in obedience to what I believed to be a revelation of the most high God, trusting in the assurance of the Missionaries whom I believed to have the spirit of truth. I left my home, sacrificed my property, broke up every dear association, and what was and is yet clearer than all, left my beloved native land. And for what? A bubble that has burst in my grasp. It has been a severe lesson, but I can say it has led me to lean more on my Heavenly Father and less on the words of men."

Among her conveyances to Young, the "Trustee in Trust" of the church, was her treasured piano. Some accounts indicated she had traded it to Young earlier for wheat to feed her starving family. Whether traded or appropriated, the ornate inlaid Collard & Collard grand piano wound up in the Gardo House, dubbed the "Amelia Palace," which was the home of Young's twenty-fifth and favorite wife, Harriet "Amelia" Folsom. "Tall and symmetrical of form, dignified and graceful of manner," as one account described her, the beautiful Amelia was called the "Queen of Mormon society." Young was "lovesick" for Amelia, who could not only play the piano but also sing his favorite song, "Fair Bingen on the Rhine." The piano has been on display for years in the Mormon Temple Museum in Salt Lake City. It remains a symbol not only of the power of the faith to attract those hungry for an intense religious experience, but also of how Mormonism failed some of its most devoted early converts, women above all.

CHAPTER THREE

Mountain Meadows Dogs

———✳———

DURING THE WINTER of 1856–57, Brigham Young's "Mormon Reformation" was the centerpiece of his fiery sermons throughout Utah. Key to the Reformation was the revival of blood atonement, which was never published or openly acknowledged by Young until this moment, when he felt he needed it to support his actions. Now Mormon elders were demanding that everyone be rebaptized and were encouraging Saints to inform against each other, all while Young advocated cleansing the wayward Saints through blood atonement.

The efforts to root out apostates spread panic through the Utah Territory, as Young's loyalists swept through the settlements, haranguing Mormons with a series of questions to test their purity and loyalty. Young sharpened his attack on the US Government, defiantly ordering his Saints to prepare to avenge the blood of Joseph Smith.

Into this atmosphere of suspicion came a wagon train of "Gentiles," crossing Utah Territory to start a new life in California. A few months before their arrival in the territory, the beloved Mormon apostle Parley Pratt was murdered near the Arkansas–Oklahoma border. Even though Pratt was fatally stabbed and shot by a man whose wife had left him to become Pratt's twelfth plural wife, Young used Pratt's death to inflame anti-Arkansas sentiment. Church leaders spread rumors from their pulpits about the "Fancher Train"—as it was called after its commander, Alexander Fancher—which had originated in Harrison, Arkansas, and was the wealthiest wagon train ever

Brigham Young at age 72—the "Prophet, Seer, and Revelator" and second president of the Church of Jesus Christ of Latter-day Saints. This engraving appeared in *Harper's Weekly* on January 27, 1872, five years before his death.

to traverse the continent. They claimed that the wagon train included Pratt's killers and was carrying the gun that had been used to murder Joseph Smith.

On September 7, 1857, in a meadow in southwestern Utah, a Mormon militia attacked the Fancher Train. After a five-day siege, the Mormons persuaded the emigrants to surrender under a flag of truce and a pledge of safe passage. Then, in the worst butchery of white people by other whites in the entire colonization of America, approximately 140 unarmed men, women, and children were murdered.

* * *

What became known as the Mountain Meadows Massacre began at dawn on a Monday, when the emigrants were sitting around their morning campfires. "While eating breakfast of rabbit and quail a shot rang out and one of the children toppled over," remembered one of them. A barrage of gunfire ensued from all directions, and within minutes, seven men were dead and the train's leader and twenty others were seriously wounded. The Fancher party had expected the verdant Mountain Meadows to be a peaceful oasis where their thousand head of cattle could fatten up on the belly-high grass for the final push westward. The Edenic spot between rivers emptying into the Great Basin and the watershed of the Colorado River, and between the arid plateaus to the east and the great Mojave Desert ahead to the west, was considered the best grazing tract in Utah Territory.

The Fanchers had one of the finest cattle- and horse-breeding stock operations in the American South, and they were taking their herd to sell in the gold-mining camps of the Comstock Lode. The train carried a staggering amount of gold and was armed with the most sophisticated rifles, pistols, and ammunition of the day. Elegant carriages, their panels emblazoned with paintings of stag heads, carried the women. In addition to the fine beef cattle, other animals in the train included a legendary racing mare descended from famous trotting-horse bloodstock and worth an untold fortune, and an Arabian black-satin stallion worth a million dollars in today's money.

The emigrants were stunned and confused by the war whoops of their assailants, for the Fanchers knew that the southern Paiutes of this region were a small, peaceful, and generally unarmed tribe. By the third day of the siege, their suffering was acute, as the wounded had died, their decaying carcasses attracting flies. The train was running low on food and water. In a tragic attempt to appeal to the humanity of their enemies, the emigrants dressed two little girls in immaculate white and sent them with a bucket toward the spring. Both were shot dead instantly. The emigrants finally understood that the forces arrayed against them were too disciplined and organized to be a pacific band of Indians. Still, the fact that it was a well-trained Mormon military unit, acting on orders from Mormon church officials, must have eluded them.

As the attacks continued, the emigrants hoisted a white flag in the middle of their corral, where it could be seen for miles. On Friday morning, September 11, dawn broke eerily silent, except for the crying of the wounded children. The emigrants had no food or water and were nearly out of ammunition. Many of their men had died. They knelt in a circle and prayed for a miracle. At midmorning, their prayers seemed to have been answered. On the horizon was a large group of white men heading toward the besieged camp, carrying an American flag. Ecstatic, the emigrants dressed a small girl in a white dress and sent her out, waving a little white handkerchief.

One man rode alone in front of the group, waving a white flag "held by all civilized nations and peoples, from time immemorial, as an emblem at once of peace, of truth, of honour." The man was John D. Lee—a prominent member of the church, one of Brigham Young's most trusted apostles, the highest-ranking member of the Avenging Angels, and a close friend and confidant of Benjamin Johnson. Lee gestured to the emigrant men with secret Masonic signals to convey camaraderie. He introduced himself as a federal Indian agent and a military officer of the American territory of Utah who had come to mediate between the emigrants and the Paiutes, whom Lee claimed were the aggressors against them.

Lee "said the Indians had gone hog wild but the Mormons would try to save us and take us all to Cedar City, the nearest big Mormon settlement if

John D. Lee was one of Brigham Young's most trusted apostles and would be the only Mormon leader who would be held accountable for the Mountain Meadows Massacre.

our men would give up their guns," a survivor would report more than eighty years later. But first they would have to turn over their provisions, arms, and livestock. Although Lee promised that their weapons and belongings would be returned to them, there was passionate dissension among the emigrants. In the end, the surviving men felt they had no choice but to accept the deal.

Once the Arkansans agreed to place themselves under Lee's protection, the Mormons moved swiftly. Lee directed his Nauvoo Legion men on horseback to move into a column, each walking next to an emigrant man. Suddenly, one of the Mormon guards on horseback fired a shot into the air and gave the order to his brethren: "Halt! Do your duty to Israel!" With that, each soldier shot the man next to him. The men died instantly, and the women and children began shouting and running. Then the order was given to kill them all, except for the children under the age of eight—the age of innocence in the Mormon faith.

The murders were carried out with swift and grisly precision. Twenty-four-year-old Nephi Johnson, a nephew of Benjamin Johnson and a second lieutenant in the Nauvoo Legion, was among the perpetrators. He would remember that the slaughter of 140 people had taken no more than five minutes, according to his pocket watch. Nephi was the son of Joel Johnson, Benjamin's brother and the prolific poet and hymn writer, and had been among the original Mormon colonists to settle the southern Utah area near Mountain Meadows. From the time of his arrival in Zion at the age of fourteen, Nephi began learning the local Indian languages, and his linguistic skills were noted by Mormon leaders. The Indians had great confidence in Johnson, calling him "the only man in the country that would talk straight." The father of a young daughter and with another child on the way, Johnson was working his own father's "harvest field" when church leaders enlisted him in a campaign to incite the Paiutes to take part in the killings. The Mormon leadership wanted to make it look like an Indian massacre instead of a Mormon massacre, and many of the Mormon men who participated painted their faces to look like Indians. Johnson was ordered to "Gather up the Indians And Distroy [sic] the train of Emigrants," he later wrote. He was told to "stir up all the other Indians he could find, in order to have a large enough force of Indians to give the emigrants a good *hush*."

After most of the killing had been completed, Lee assessed who might have been "old enough to tell tales," which led to several more executions of children. Nephi Johnson took part in these murders as well. After the massacre, two wagons belonging to the Mormon militia made their way to a stone-and-adobe ranch house in the foothills north of the site. The seventeen surviving children, ranging in age from nine months to seven years, were wailing and inconsolable, the blood of their parents and siblings still fresh on their clothes. "The children cried nearly all night," remembered the ranch's Mormon owner. Back in the meadow, the men left behind to guard the spoils went sleepless, as coyotes feasted on the unburied corpses, yipping with pleasure. A lone wolf stood on the treeline above the scene, recalled one of the killers, howling continuously under a crescent moon.

The next day, Nephi Johnson was in charge of collecting the booty. Women from Cedar City arrived to gather the clothing and jewelry of the dead, pulling off their shoes and removing earrings, brooches, watches, and rings. Johnson later expressed horror at what he had done, and said that the scavenging by pious Mormon men and women disgusted him. "Do you want to know my real feelings about it?" he responded to one of the leading officers when asked for his advice about distributing the emigrants' possessions. "You have made a sacrifice of the people, and I would burn the property, and let the cattle roam over the country . . . and go home like men." Johnson, a deeply religious man, did not want the Mormons to go down in history as having murdered people for their property. Like many others who participated in the massacre, he had been falsely led to believe by church officials that the Arkansans were to be blood atoned for their killing of Parley Pratt.

When the scavenging was finished, Lee assembled the officers under his command to settle on the story they would tell their fellow Mormons and the US Government, which would surely take an interest in the matter. "We *ordered* the people to keep the matter a secret from the *entire* world," Lee later confessed. "We also took the most binding oaths to stand by each other, and to always insist that Indians alone committed the massacre. This was the advice of Brigham Young too." Lee led the efforts to conceal any role that Young and church leaders had played in the massacre, knowing full well that the survival of the church depended on the Prophet's deniability.

THE MOUNTAIN MEADOWS MASSACRE.

This anonymous engraving of the Mountain Meadows Massacre is the most famous depiction of the event.

* * *

Though the church-owned *Deseret News* did not report the atrocity, rumors whipped through the Utah Territory and spread far beyond. "The whole United States rang with its horrors," Mark Twain later wrote, as word made its way to the East Coast press. According to Nephi Johnson, many of the Mormon men who took part in the killing were forced to do so against their will. Stories proliferated about alleged Mormon apostates in Utah who had joined the sprawling wagon train, hoping to gain safe passage to California, and who were singled out for blood atonement by the Mormon militia.

Gold plundered from the train was turned over to the church treasury, while the forty wagons were given to the church militia, and the fancy carriages were taken to Brigham Young. The Fanchers' cattle were branded with the church cross and driven north to Salt Lake City. The horses and the huge cache of weapons were divided among militia leaders in the southern colonies of Utah Territory. Soon enough, those passing through the territory remarked on the sudden prosperity of the local Mormons, previously known for their desperate poverty and threadbare clothing and now dressed in finery, the leaders of the massacre and their wives flaunting the possessions stolen from the dead.

By the spring of 1859, US military officials had found the surviving children living in the homes of local Mormons. They were traumatized not only by the massacre but also by living with the very men they witnessed killing their families, and with women wearing the dresses and jewelry of their mothers and sisters. Some of the older children identified the murderers as Mormons, not Paiutes, contradicting the official Mormon story. Christopher "Kit" Carson Fancher, five years old and named for the renowned mountain man and Indian killer, would say: "My father was killed by Indians. When they washed their faces, they were white men."

The military officials returned the orphans to relatives in Arkansas, and two of the older boys were taken to Washington to be interviewed by government officials. As evidence of Mormon culpability grew, a wave of outrage against the Mormons spread across the nation. President Lincoln compared the nation's problems with the Mormons to a big log. "It was too heavy to move, too hard to chop, too green to burn—so we just plowed around it." Yet soon the atrocity was eclipsed by the outbreak of the Civil War.

Just over a decade later, with the 1869 completion of the transcontinental railroad—the Central Pacific and Union Pacific rails joining in Utah—Brigham Young's Deseret became a crucial layover for the thousands of people trekking across the continent to California. Although Young had fought the railroad from its inception, he recognized the inevitability of American expansion. He thought that if Utah became a state, his realm would have more autonomy through its elected state government and he would thus be able to control the state's electoral politics. To that end, he applied four times for statehood—in 1849, 1856, 1862, and 1872—but was repeatedly turned down by Congress due to Mormonism's promulgation of polygamy. With his profile thus elevated, Young's role in the massacre brought even more national scrutiny. To appease antistatehood forces in Congress that were demanding punishment for the mass murder, Young sacrificed his closest friend and apostle, John D. Lee, claiming he was the sole perpetrator of the massacre, and

Young denied having any role in ordering it. Young excommunicated Lee, portraying him as an overzealous and renegade fanatic who acted on his own. At the same time, he ordered Lee and other guilty militia leaders—furtively called the "Mountain Meadows Dogs" by church officials—to move out of Utah. Some were sent to the wilds of the New Mexico Territory, present-day Arizona. Others went farther south, to Mexico, outside the reach of a US arrest warrant. "Make yourself scarce & keep out of the way," a church leader wrote to Lee.

For the next few years, Lee hid out at the confluence of the Colorado and Paria Rivers, which emerged from the Vermilion Cliffs in the upper Grand Canyon of northern Arizona. In 1872, the church sent lumber to his desolate exile so he could construct the first ferryboat to cross the raging Colorado. He founded the profitable Lees Ferry, believing that Brigham Young was protecting him in his banishment, unaware that a US federal grand jury investigating the massacre had indicted him on murder charges. In 1874, US marshals found him hiding in a chicken coop in Panguitch, Utah, while visiting one of his wives, and arrested him. The sixty-two-year-old father of fifty-six children—a high priest in the Mormon church who was now called "the butcher in chief" by the *Salt Lake Daily Tribune*—was jailed in Utah, awaiting trial. The following year, he was tried in the small town of Beaver, in what was dubbed the "Trial of the Century," attracting newspaper correspondents from around the country. While many expected that Lee would implicate Brigham Young, he did not, and the jury was deadlocked. But if Young hoped that the hung jury would settle the matter, he was mistaken. Following another public outcry after the trial, the massacre would continue to plague the Prophet and threaten Utah statehood until someone was held accountable for the slaughter. In an expedient move, Young made a deal with the federal government, in which he agreed to make available all witnesses and evidence necessary to convict Lee in exchange for limiting testimony that could implicate Young and the church. Lee's second trial opened on September 11, 1876—exactly nineteen years after the massacre. Previously unavailable witnesses appeared with vivid testimony that implicated Lee and absolved all high officials of the church.

Benjamin Johnson and his nephew Nephi had both been among Lee's closest friends, dating back to the exodus from Illinois. Now Nephi, who had killed women and children at Mountain Meadows, provided some of the most damning testimony against Lee. It took the jury just over three hours to reach a guilty verdict, and Lee was sentenced to death. The judge gave Lee a choice of execution method. Because beheading was Mormonism's preferred method for blood atonement, Lee chose to be executed by firing squad as a signal to the faithful that he was an innocent man.

On the morning of March 23, 1877, Lee wore a hat, coat, and muffler to the place of his execution, not far from Mountain Meadows. The rich emerald grass for which the landscape was famous had turned to brown scrub; gone were the huge cottonwoods that had once shaded the meadow. Paiutes claimed that the meadow, with its two tapered exits that had facilitated the ambush, was haunted. Long known as "a preferred location for the quiet execution of unpleasant tasks," the name Mountain Meadows became a Mormon euphemism for blood-atonement killings.

Lee sat patiently on his coffin and waited as a photographer set up his equipment for the official pictures of the scene. When the camera was ready and the five-man firing squad in place, Lee rose. "I have been sacrificed in a cowardly, dastardly manner," he said. Blindfolded, he raised his arms to the sky and gave the riflemen a final order: "Center my heart, boys. Don't mangle my body." At the volley, he fell back silently onto the rough-hewn coffin, his blood spilling onto the earth, giving the moment the symbolism he had wanted to avoid. He would be the only Mormon brought to justice for the massacre at Mountain Meadows.

Within days of John D. Lee's execution, the *New York Herald* ran an excerpt from Lee's full confession, which he had given to his attorney for publication after his death: ". . . Those with me at that time were ACTING UNDER ORDERS from the Church of Jesus Christ of Latter-day Saints. The horrid deeds then committed were done as a duty which we believed we owed to God and our Church. We were all sworn to secrecy before and after the massacre. The penalty for giving information concerning it was death."

Before his death, Lee predicted that if he was guilty, he would never be heard of again. "If I am not guilty," he told his sons, "Brigham Young will die within one year! Yes, within six months." On August 2, 1877—five

Official photograph of the execution of John D. Lee on the morning of March 23, 1877, not far from the site of the Mountain Meadows Massacre. Lee sat on his coffin, wearing a hat, coat, and muffler, facing the five-man firing squad that he instructed to "Center my heart, boys. Don't mangle my body."

months to the day after Lee's execution—Young fell mortally ill with cramps and vomiting after gorging on green corn and peaches. Six days later, he was dead. News circulated that he had cholera, then that he died of appendicitis. Over the next century, rumors persisted that two of Lee's sons had poisoned him—conspiracy theories that became part of Western folklore, especially among Lee's descendants. Whatever the cause of death, within days Brigham Young lay in state in a plain redwood box as more than twelve thousand Saints attended the Prophet's Tabernacle funeral.

* * *

Born in 1898 in Bunkerville, Nevada, and raised in a polygamous family, Juanita Leavitt Brooks had been fascinated from an early age by the history of her desert homeland. After attending Dixie Junior College in St. George, Utah, she returned to Bunkerville to teach school in Mesquite, Nevada, thirty-five miles northeast of the then-fledgling town of Las Vegas.

On her first Sunday home, in August 1918, Nephi Johnson, the community's church patriarch, sat next to her in the pew. She later wrote that she was "greatly attracted to this patriarchal old man, with his sharp black eyes and long beard." The two struck up a friendship—the eighty-five-year-old pioneer and the young woman he called "The Little Schoolteacher"—and Johnson gave her a blessing.

Soon after, he visited her at the schoolhouse, leaning on a cane outside her classroom until the bell released the children. "I want you to do some writing for me," Johnson told her, as he sat down in front of her desk. "My eyes have witnessed things that my tongue has never uttered, and before I die, I want them written down. And I want you to do the writing." Brooks replied that she would come to his home at a later date. But time passed and she did not visit him, and in the late spring of 1919, she learned that he was extremely ill and not expected to live much longer. She arose before sunrise and rode her horse to Johnson's ranch, where the old man lay half-conscious. Johnson's daughter thanked her for coming, saying, "He's been so restless about what he must tell you."

She stayed for two days, witnessing Johnson's tortured and delirious writhing, which she knew was related to the deathbed confession he was striving to tell her. "He prayed, he yelled, he preached, and once his eyes opened wide to the ceiling and he yelled, 'Blood! Blood! Blood!'"

Juanita watched in alarm. "What's the matter with him? He acts like he's haunted," she asked a family member at his bedside as he slipped into death.

"Maybe he is," answered one. "He was at the Mountain Meadows Massacre, you know."

While Nephi Johnson was the first massacre participant, after John D. Lee, to break his silence, contemporaneous historical accounts are rife with the tales of tormented accomplices. Many could not escape the dreadful memories of bloodshed that "withered and blasted their happiness," wrote Mormon apostate T. B. H. Stenhouse, "and some of them suffered agonizing tortures of conscience."

* * *

The Mountain Meadows Massacre was the decisive factor in Jean Rio's final break with the church, according to many of her descendants. The religious fanaticism that led to the massacre, and the overwhelming indications that the church, if not Brigham Young himself, had condoned it, undermined the faith of many Saints. Jean Rio set her sights on California, and the completion of the transcontinental railroad made that dream possible. It had become less risky for apostates to flee Zion. After the massacre, numerous stories surfaced about Mormon men who had refused to participate in the wholesale murder of civilians—those who did not believe in "killing to save"—and who fled westward with their families, settling communities in Nevada and California. Also in the aftermath of the massacre, US Army escorts began accompanying thousands of people to the West.

In 1869, Jean Rio would be among the first to travel by rail to California, where her sons, John and Charles, were prospering in politics and business, respectively. There she would live out the remaining fourteen years of her life in relative luxury, doted on by her sons. "I have every temporal comfort my heart can desire," she wrote. "My children vie with each other in contributing to my happiness." John, a prominent Republican state legislator in Sacramento, had become known for introducing antipolygamy legislation, and Charles had made a fortune as a lawyer and merchant in San Francisco.

After her nearly twenty years of poverty and disappointment in Utah, Jean Rio's life in the "Golden State" seemed a miracle. She shed her Mormonism and became a devoted Congregationalist. "I have lived in firm belief and faith in Jesus Christ, as the son of God, the only atonement for sin, and the only way of salvation," she wrote in her will. She died of cancer in 1883 at the age of seventy-three.

Her polygamist son William lived out his entire life in Utah, his allegiance to the church only increasing in reaction to what he saw as the persecution of the Saints by "Gentiles." Jean Rio had marveled at his unwavering faith, and though she disagreed with what she considered his extremist beliefs, she wrote that she was glad he honored his responsibility to his two wives and twenty-three children. "Plucked from the lap of luxury and set down in a frontier land of staggering toil and comfortless surroundings," wrote one of his children, "he tackled his job and made good without excuses or regrets. His brothers couldn't stand the privations and hardships and the dominance of the church in their lives and fled to California. But William stayed with the religion he had embraced as a boy." Despite the controversy surrounding the Nauvoo Legion, especially after its role in the massacre was exposed, William proudly donned the uniform of that militia—"epaulettes, sword, and all." He had been rewarded for his faithful devotion, receiving a high-salaried position with one of Utah's most powerful railroad contractors. Yet soon he and other polygamists were to face their most serious challenge yet, and many would believe they had no choice but to break from the church and resettle in Mexico.

CHAPTER FOUR

Zion in a Dry Place

———————————✦———————————

AFTER THE UNITED STATES had rejected Brigham Young's fourth bid for statehood in 1872 because of polygamy, Young looked toward Mexico, seeking land to colonize outside of America for his persecuted Saints. A "sort of safety valve for Utah polygamists," as early church narratives described Young's view of Mexico, "a place where family life and community building could continue unabated or undisturbed by legal restrictions placed on plural marriage by federal law." In the summer of 1874, Young sent two Spanish-speaking missionaries to the states of Chihuahua and Sonora to begin proselytizing, and a year later he sent several more emissaries in search of colony sites where his Saints could live the Principle.

The formal mission of 1875 consisted of eight men, among them prominent church officials. Young directed them to preach the gospel to Mexicans, while also keeping an eye out for suitable land for colonies along their route in Arizona, New Mexico, and Mexico. Another church leader told them to look for places where Saints could go to get out of harm's way, "in the event that persecution should make it necessary," referring to the anticipated next crackdown by the United States on participants in the Mountain Meadows Massacre, as well as to the ongoing conflict over polygamy. Some of the perpetrators had already relocated to Mexico a few years earlier, when John D. Lee had fled Utah. Young had solicited funds to aid the new expedition, raising not only cash but merchandise, food, "seven mounts and seventeen pack horses," and a spring wagon. The eight missionaries crossed the Colorado

River at Lees Ferry and made their way to Phoenix and Tucson before pushing east to El Paso, Texas, where they crossed the border into Mexico.

In Chihuahua, the Mormons were welcomed by the state's elite, including the wealthy and powerful Governor Luis Terrazas, who gave them permission to hold religious services in a large building called the "Cock Pit" in Chihuahua City. When more than five hundred people showed up to attend the services, the missionaries were ecstatic about the future prospects for the church in Mexico. After traveling from Ciudad Juárez (across the border from El Paso), to Casas Grandes (three hundred miles southwest of El Paso), and then northwest to Janos, the last Mexican town they visited before crossing back into the US, they returned to Salt Lake City with an optimistic report. Encouraged, Young dispatched another group in 1876 to explore the possibility of colonizing in Sonora. At the same time, some of the Mountain Meadows Dogs, as the killers had become known, sought sanctuary in northern Mexico. With resentment toward them building in Utah, these men became notorious fugitives, exiles fearing retribution from both US law enforcement as well as the Mormon church—from the latter for the knowledge they possessed. "I know that the church will kill me, sooner or later. . . . It is only a question of time," Mormon bishop and massacre whistleblower Philip Klingensmith would tell the *Salt Lake Tribune*. The *Tribune* later reported that his body was found in a prospect hole in Sonora.

Brigham Young had hoped that holding John D. Lee criminally responsible for the massacre would mollify Washington, DC, lawmakers, but it did not. Young would not live to see a Mormon kingdom established in Mexico. After Lee's execution and Young's death five months later, the American anti-polygamy campaign further intensified, especially after President Rutherford B. Hayes took office in 1877. Utah polygamists were under increased pressure to abandon their plural wives and families, both physically and financially. In 1880, Hayes even traveled to Salt Lake City to meet with John Taylor, Brigham Young's successor as the church's Prophet. Taylor, the erudite Mormon missionary who had converted Jean Rio and her family in Great Britain decades earlier, was even less conciliatory to the US Government than Young had been. "W[hen] they enact tyrannical laws, forbidding us the free exercise of our religion, we cannot submit," he proclaimed.

A polygamist hardliner, Taylor, along with Benjamin Johnson and a handful of others, was among the first men to whom Joseph Smith had revealed the divine Principle in the 1840s. "No other name in Mormon history is so closely linked to the defense and continuation of plural marriage as is that of John Taylor," wrote Verlan LeBaron in his 1981 biography of his family. Like Smith, Taylor fervently believed in a theocratic hierarchy, with God and men at the top and women and children at the bottom. Since God was greater than the United States, reasoned Taylor, the federal government had no authority to abolish polygamy. "I defy the United States; I will obey God," Taylor famously declared, forging his place in Mormon church history as the martyr for the Principle.

President Hayes was unimpressed, and, at his urging, Congress passed the 1882 Edmunds Act, prohibiting polygamists from voting or holding public office. "Lewd or unlawful cohabitation, the term used for plural marriage, was labeled a misdemeanor and made punishable by a $300 fine [equivalent to $10,000 today] and six months in jail," wrote LeBaron. Federal marshals traveled on horseback from community to community, raiding homes in the middle of the night, carrying out "cohab hunts" and scouting for "polygs." Polygamists were punished according to the number of plural wives they had, as well as how often they visited them.

Taylor "grieved over the outrages," according to LeBaron, and in 1885 the Mormon leader "concluded it was best for the Mormons to evade the law." He sent two parties to Sonora to explore the possibility of buying land there. The first of the official visits "resulted in an agreement of some kind with Cajemé, the chief of the Yaqui Indians, who occupied a large part of the state and had never been subdued by the Mexican Government," reported the *New York Times* on June 29, 1885. Taylor, then seventy-seven, preferred "a quiet life in Salt Lake City to the discomforts of a long journey through a wild country," but he thought it his duty to visit the nascent colony. Accompanied by three apostles, a private secretary, and a lawyer, he made a midwinter journey. Taylor's trip prompted speculation that he and his associates were "preparing to transfer the headquarters of the Mormon organization from Utah to Mexico," according to the *Times*, "or that they were at least beginning to build a city of refuge beyond the jurisdiction of United States courts where polygamist Mormons could find shelter."

After Taylor's return to Salt Lake City, Mexican troops attacked and slaughtered two hundred Yaqui Indians, capturing and executing Cajemé, taking control of Sonora, and forcing the Mormons to deal with the Mexican Government rather than the Indians. Fortunately for the Mormons, the newly installed Mexican president, Porfirio Díaz, welcomed them, making clear to the apostles that his government was eager for them to help settle the wild Mexican states of Sonora and Chihuahua, which were still dominated by Indigenous peoples.

Taylor then ordered thirty-three polygamist families in Utah and Arizona to leave their homes and colonize Chihuahua. Along with their hundreds of children, the Mormons took "all the plows, shovels, beds, chairs, flour and chickens they could fit into a horse-drawn wagon," according to an account published in 1985 to celebrate the one-hundredth anniversary of the diaspora. "It took them nearly a month to reach Mexico, fording rivers high with snowmelt and crossing steep mountains. Uphill, they doubled the wagon teams to pull the load. Downhill, women carried the children while the men tried to control the wagons and horses. An advance guard watched for Apache Indians; a rear guard watched for US marshals."

When they reached the mile-high valleys and plateaus of the Sierra Madre Occidental, three hundred miles southwest of El Paso, they began building the first permanent Mormon community in Chihuahua. Colonia Díaz, named for the Mexican president, was sited in the foothills, on the banks of the Casas Grandes River. The church had obtained control of three million acres of choice land, purchasing it through the Mexican Colonization Company, a creation of the church that acted as a land broker with the Mexican Government.

Meanwhile, John Taylor was forced into hiding to escape a federal arrest warrant, leaving the besieged church, whose assets had been seized, essentially rudderless. Church members' personal property was also impounded, prompting several LDS leaders to propose a manifesto outlawing polygamy in order to secure a détente with the United States. Taylor came up with a solution. Claiming two visitations—one from Joseph Smith and one from Jesus Christ—Taylor announced a revelation directing him not to sign such a manifesto, and instead to send church members to relocate to Mexico.

In January 1887, Congress passed even harsher legislation against the

Mormons. The Edmunds-Tucker Act was onerous, restrictive, and sweeping, and threatened the very survival of the church. It imposed severe penalties on the church for its failure to comply with the 1882 act, forcing even more members to go underground, including the church's most prominent religious and business leaders.

As polygamists faced the threat of lengthy prison sentences in the United States, Mexican colonization became urgent. Wives and children were even forced to testify against their husbands and fathers. By the late 1880s, more than a thousand Saints were in prison, some incarcerated as far away as Detroit. "The federal government then dealt its most crushing blow to the Mormons," wrote Verlan LeBaron, whose book about his family, though not reliable on every point, is rich with details of early Mormon history dating back to his larger-than-life great-grandfather, Benjamin Johnson. An eyewitness to the church's early dramas, from New York to Nauvoo to Deseret, Johnson was always at the right hand of Prophets Joseph Smith and Brigham Young, documenting his experiences for church historians. His original red-leather journal—an almost-four-hundred-page chronicle called *My Life's Review*—is now in the church archives in Salt Lake City. His descendants keep copies of the journal in honored places in their homes, despite the fact that he lived his final years in ignominy. All seven of his wives would leave him, and just a few of his forty-five children would remain close to him. "It says something about bounty and something about emptiness, and something about a man who perhaps was surprised that one did not prevent the other," wrote one of his thousands of descendants. "The church was disincorporated and the Supreme Court was ordered to wind up church affairs," wrote LeBaron. "The federal government took over church property," and many Mormons demanded that Taylor accede to the federal government.

But Taylor remained unyielding, and he died as a fugitive in July 1887. The eighty-two-year-old apostle Wilford Woodruff was installed as the fourth Mormon Prophet. An avid polygamist with nine wives, Woodruff realized that the Kingdom of God on Earth could only survive if the US retreated from its hostility and granted statehood to Utah. Woodruff claimed to have received a revelation from God that the church must stop sanctioning polygamy, and he wrote what would become known as the Woodruff

Manifesto. "I went before the Lord, and I wrote what the Lord told me to write," he told his stunned flock.

On October 6, 1890, the Manifesto became an official church declaration: "I now publicly declare that my advice to the Latter-day Saints is to refrain from contracting any marriage forbidden by the law of the land." Committed polygamists were horrified, accusing Woodruff of bowing to political expediency. Indeed, reconciliation between the federal government and the Mormon church began immediately, and Utah would become the forty-fifth state in the Union in 1896.

Before that happened, however, zealous polygamists broke away from the church, claiming their authority through their hero, John Taylor. Calling themselves "fundamentalists," they would await the arrival of "the One Mighty and Strong" who would "set in order the house of God," just as Joseph Smith had prophesied.

Incarcerated polygamists in the 1880s in front of Utah's first state prison, located in the Sugar House neighborhood of Salt Lake City.

* * *

Seventy-five years after the Woodruff Manifesto, seven male members of the LeBaron clan in Mexico would each claim the mantle of "the One Mighty and Strong," with tragic results. The LeBarons—as direct descendants of the apostle Benjamin Johnson—were a powerful force in the Mormon church in Utah in the late nineteenth century, and, like most devout male members, were passionate adherents of celestial marriage. Scorning Woodruff as a hypocrite and false prophet who had abandoned the true gospel of Joseph Smith, Johnson urged his family to emigrate to Mexico. Verlan LeBaron wrote that Smith taught "that a man will be judged more by how he governs his sexual powers than by any other thing." Abandoning the Principle was blasphemy to the true believers.

When warrants were issued for his arrest on polygamy charges, seventy-two-year-old Benjamin Johnson fled to Colonia Díaz, blazing a trail for his prolific progeny. A sturdy man with deep-set eyes, a high forehead, and a shaggy full beard now turned gray, Johnson had joined one of the early scouting expeditions to Mexico sent by President Taylor, whom he revered. By the 1890s, he had become obsessed with his family's relocation to Chihuahua, which he firmly believed would be the site of the Second Coming of Christ. Although Chihuahua means "dry place," it was rich with aquifers and streams and some of the most fertile soil in Mexico, all belied by its sandy roads and desert flora and fauna.

The lineage of those referred to as "the Mexico LeBarons" is an intricate maze of interrelated marriages among the Johnsons and LeBarons living on both sides of the US/Mexico border. The original mingling of the Johnson and LeBaron pedigrees dates to the 1842 marriage of Melissa LeBaron and Benjamin Johnson. In 1903, when Johnson claimed to have inherited from Joseph Smith the mantle as spiritual leader, he transferred that title to his favorite grandson, Alma Dayer LeBaron—firstborn son of his favorite daughter and her husband, Benjamin Johnson's nephew, Benjamin LeBaron. This is why the LeBaron surname, rather than Johnson, became synonymous with "the One Mighty and Strong" claims by LeBaron men in the twentieth century.

The tangled bloodlines of the Johnson and LeBaron clans are the result of generations of incest and polygamy. As members of a faith in which marrying one's first cousin was both acceptable and commonplace—if not outright encouraged in order to keep the bloodlines pure—the offspring of the original Johnson and LeBaron couplings numbered more than forty-four thousand by the end of the twentieth century, making it "the biggest family in the Americas," according to one account. Indeed, at a 2005 family reunion in Utah of Johnsons and LeBarons from Mexico and the US, twelve hundred cousins, dozens with identical names, lined up at the registration desk to receive color-coded stickers to wear—seven colors for Johnson's seven wives. The color green signified a descendant of Melissa, "the legitimate one," the family joked, referring to the fact that the first wife in polygamy is the only one with legal standing. They gathered in This Is The Place Heritage Park in Salt Lake City to honor their forebear, whom they credit with helping populate much of the American Southwest for both the LDS and the Mormon fundamentalist empire. One descendant called the quadrennial reunion "polygamy's last stand," at a moment when federal authorities were once again cracking down on the polygamous communities in Arizona and Utah.

The LeBarons were but one of several rival fundamentalist clans that fled to Mexico. "They have been taught that persecution is their heritage," Verlan LeBaron wrote about his own family. Tightly bonded by their outlaw status, the hard-core polygamists believed those Mormons who stayed in the United States had fallen under the sway of false prophets. The leaders of the massacre at Mountain Meadows, including Nephi Johnson, sought hideouts for the perpetrators in the wilds of western Utah and Nevada. Johnson founded a colony on the Virgin River, twenty miles west of present-day Zion National Park, and is reputed to have been the first white man ever to enter Zion Canyon. Several other Mountain Meadows Dogs were among those who went to Mexico with larger groups, though some had already decamped for Mexico in the early 1870s. Northern Mexico became a hotbed of runaway murderers and religious fanatics, all of whom felt they had been driven from their homes by violence or ostracism. All believed that polygamy was one of the most holy of God's principles, that the United States was a modern Babylon on the eve of destruction, and that their new Zion in the heart of the Sierra Madre was a paradise for God's modern chosen people. The LeBaron men in particular believed that they were main actors "in the end of the Times of the Gentiles," and the "direct descendants of Jesus and Mary Magdalene," as one of them once told a *Los Angeles Times* reporter.

In their new villages, the expats raised flagpoles and saluted the Mexican flag. They planted sycamore, walnut, elm, and weeping willow trees for quick-growing shade, cottonwoods and Lombardy poplars for windbreaks, hardwood locusts for making the handles of shovels and hoes, as well as peach, apricot, pomegranate, fig, plum, pecan, apple, pear, and cherry trees. Their vegetable gardens were abundant with squash, corn, beans, potatoes, onions, and carrots. They dug wells and canals, built irrigation systems, and constructed windmills and a dam on the Casas Grandes River. They erected churches and schools and homes that resembled those in the Mormon towns they had left behind in Utah and elsewhere. Their abundant farms, well-kept orchards and vineyards, and herds of well-bred cattle and warm-blooded horses were the envy of their increasingly alienated Mexican neighbors.

Polygamists such as Jean Rio's son William George Baker, who did not want to leave Utah, faced hard decisions about their families' futures. Baker bristled at being designated a criminal adulterer by the very church to which he had faithfully devoted fifty years of his life, and at the reality that his second wife, Nicolena, was now considered a concubine and their ten children bastards in the eyes of the church and the law. When the husband upon whom she was depending to "pull her through the veil" to everlasting deliverance went into hiding as a fugitive from US marshals, Nicolena struggled to take care of her family. "Husbands were expected to divide their property and cash among their several families and continue to take care of them financially," wrote one of Nicolena's daughters. "The results can be better imagined than described. It meant that many a wife with her brood was thrown almost entirely upon her own resources."

Nicolena had a milk cow, a team of horses, a good orchard, an alfalfa field, a garden, and a pasture. As she ventured into the millinery business and took in boarders, her sons made sure she had firewood and baled hay to feed the animals. All the while, the church continued to expect the annual ten percent tithing of her meager assets.

"Do not be uncaring about me, as I shall return soon . . . it is not wisdom for me to come home," Baker wrote from parts unknown, with instructions that her response to any of his letters should be sealed inside another envelope addressed to a nonpolygamist relative living in Utah. "Give my love and kisses to the children and be assured I am still lovingly yours—."

Yet, while Baker kept Hannah and their thirteen children well supported, Nicolena was forced to deny the paternity of her own children, whom she kept hidden from authorities.

A couple of years later, Baker returned to Richfield and moved in permanently with Hannah. Baker's 1901 obituary reflected his longstanding prominence in the community, but there was no mention of Nicolena or any of his children by her. Like the thousands of children of polygamists in Utah, they were disinherited and shunned by the very faith that had sanctioned and encouraged their births.

* * *

Brigham Young had led his people to the Salt Lake Valley precisely because it was a desert, a piece of land that no one else would want. Once there, his flock developed irrigation techniques and the other necessary survival skills to create a thriving society in that environment. The settlement of Utah set a precedent for the Mormons' expansion throughout the desert lands of the American Southwest where there were few other white people in the late nineteenth century. There were Indigenous peoples in the region, of course, and the Mormons would dispossess them when the opportunity presented itself. And just as they had tamed the desert of Deseret, they would do the same in their new lands to the south. The key, as always, was water.

The fundamentalist diaspora of the 1880s in Mexico faced many obstacles: extreme heat and cold, flash floods and drought, sandy soil and the strong seasonal winds. They planned their crops around rainfall and groundwater they pumped using windmills. In 1885, the first year of colonization, the Mormons' nine colonies—seven in Chihuahua and two in Sonora, including the first colony, Colonia Díaz—had planted two thousand shade trees, fifteen thousand fruit trees, and five thousand grapevines. In 1888, the Mormons built a canal, tapping the river four miles south of Colonia Díaz and turning the community's thirty-five-thousand acres purchased by the church into a fertile valley. The first shingled house built in Colonia Díaz—which was also the first of its kind built in the state of Chihuahua—belonged to Benjamin Johnson's grandson, William Johnson, who was also the church bishop for the Mexican colonies.

For all the adversity, the Saints persevered, and soon the tiny colonies were supplying the entire region with fruit and beef. But the colonists were secretive. Their farms, complete with orchards and vineyards, thrived behind walls. They had little contact with their neighbors, "who had known nothing but grinding poverty all their days and for whom the future held out no hope for better things," according to one newcomer, Thomas Cottam Romney, a historian and scholar of Mormonism. A son of Miles Park Romney—the great-grandfather of future US Senator Mitt Romney—Thomas Romney wrote the 1938 book *The Mormon Colonies in Mexico*, the first academic study of the founding Mormon colonies in Chihuahua and Sonora, where he was raised.

In the autumn of 1910, the Mexican Revolution erupted. Bloody class warfare pit impassioned agrarian insurrectionists against the country's wealthy autocrats and foreign capitalists. Indigenous natives and working-class Mexicans rose up against the government's military forces, and the insurgency spread throughout Mexico, especially into the northern states of the Sierra Madre Occidental, where rebels under the leadership of Francisco "Pancho" Villa called for the expropriation of land from the wealthy for redistribution to the peasants. Romantic stories proliferated around the globe about Villa, telling of a legendary revolutionary hero and his Robin Hood–like raids that saw him confiscate crops, livestock, and gold bullion from the rich and give the bounty to the poor. During the thirty-four-year reign of President Porfirio Díaz, land had been concentrated in fewer and fewer hands, with just three thousand families owning almost half of the country. In Chihuahua alone, the powerful Terrazas family owned seventeen million acres. Over the ten-year armed conflict, the revolutionaries seized land originally belonging to native Mexicans that had been taken by the Diaz government and wealthy landlords, and they created *ejidos*, or communally owned tracts of land to be used for grazing and farming.

As the revolution spread, inevitably reaching the Mormons, the colonists unsurprisingly received little support or understanding from local residents, who felt the Mormons had appropriated their land. Mormon church officials in Mexico declared neutrality, but the colonies still became targets of the rebel forces, and the Mexican president was unable or unwilling to protect them. When Diaz's government fell, and the new revolutionary government redistributed land and established the *ejidos*, the Mormons found that they had few friends. The revolutionaries coveted the Mormons' massive arsenal of American-made firearms and large brick-and-stone homes, with several of the new military leaders selecting the mansions they expected to occupy once they chased the Mormons out of the country.

"There appeared to be a concerted plan both on the part of the military forces and the nationalists to drive Americans from Mexico," according to a witness before a US Senate investigating committee. "This move led to acts of violence toward Americans and depredations on her citizens which were hitherto without precedent. . . . Innocent boys and girls were brutally beaten and killed. Officers of the Mexican Government took part in the numerous ravages to terrorize the American people . . . to drive the 'gringos' out of the country."

Pancho Villa demanded taxes from the Mormons and confiscated property from many of them. A "fearsome desperado, stealing guns and horses and leering at the women," as some colonists later described him, Villa was a heroic and exciting figure to some Mormons in Mexico, despite his actions against their coreligionists. The day that Villa's troop train stopped in Casas Grandes, "we went up close," remembered a resident of Colonia Juárez. "Everyone was shouting 'Viva Villa!' My father said Pancho Villa wanted a drink, so I gave him a drink of water. He was wearing a gray suit and polished boots. My impression was not of a dirty bandit. He looked so nice."

Any sense of common ground, however, was fleeting. On July 28, 1912, the revolutionary forces gave the Mormons twenty-four hours to prepare for their removal to the United States. "My mother was sewing all night. We were only allowed one trunk per person," recalled a ten-year-old girl. "It was a lark to us. We couldn't understand why the mothers were crying." The colonists, who numbered about four thousand in total, prepared for their exodus to Douglas, Arizona, and El Paso, Texas. A Los Angeles newspaper valued the property they were leaving behind in Mexico, including water rights and improvements, at nearly $8 million, describing them as formerly "the most well-to-do people in the church, possessing large tracts of the finest agricultural land in the entire country [of Mexico]." After they left, rebels looted many Mormon houses, smashing furniture and using musical instruments for kindling. A sign left on a demolished organ read, "Long live the Liberals and death to the Mormons," prompting the historian Romney to compare the scene to Oliver Goldsmith's 1770 poem "The Deserted Village," about an abandoned rural Ireland community whose residents were exiled to America. While it "is historically true that the immediate cause for the wholesale migration of the Mormons from Mexican soil was the demand made by the rebel forces for their firearms," wrote Romney, the "fundamental causes were to be found in the contrasting natures, traditions, habits and ideals of the colonists and their neighbors; in the envy and covetousness of the natives developed over a long period of years."

While most thought their arrival back in the US was the start of a brief interlude, few would ever return to Mexico. The LeBarons, though, were among those who did. "Scarcely had the whistle of the last train, bearing the refugees to safety died away," wrote Romney, then like "Israel of old in their flight from Egypt they longed for the 'leeks and onions' of the home land." None were more determined than Alma Dayer LeBaron to abandon Babylon's godless laws and return to Zion to restart his patriarchal kingdom-building.

* * *

Dayer, living in LaVerkin, Utah, after the flight north, received a vision from God directing him to lead his people back to Mexico, just as his grandfather Benjamin Johnson had prophesied decades earlier. The thirty-seven-year-old Dayer, Johnson's favorite grandson—whom Johnson had years earlier anointed as "the One Mighty and Strong"—had a newfound sense of urgency. His vision from God had begun with a visitation from Johnson, according to Verlan LeBaron, one of Dayer's sons. "Suddenly, a firm hand gripped him by the shoulder," and his grandfather's booming voice called: "Dayer, Dayer, my son, wake up!" As he sat up in bed, Dayer "beheld a vision which extended beyond the wall of the room. There seated comfortably on a beautiful throne was his grandfather, clothed in the white robes of the priesthood. In his right hand, he held a sceptre of gold, which rested at his feet and extended above his head. A crown with seven shining stars was on his head."

Dayer realized that the sceptre represented his grandfather's priesthood authority, and that the jewels in his crown signified his seven wives—a quorum. A man with two wives is considered a worthy male, while a man with a quorum of seven or more is destined for godhood. He then heard a "penetrating voice out of the heavens, the voice of God," as Verlan later described the divine encounter. "This shall be your destiny also if you abide my law," the apparition told Dayer, who interpreted the "law" to mean polygamy.

Dayer convinced his wife of fourteen years, Maud—"one of the well-respected McDonalds of Arizona"—that it was her responsibility to select a second mate. Maud, who was also his first cousin and mother of their eight children, obeyed the order and chose her teenage babysitter named Onie Jones as her sister-wife. Following their plural marriage, Dayer, Maud, and Onie, all three devout Mormons, were swiftly excommunicated by the church. Dodging an arrest warrant in the spring of 1924, Dayer, along with his wives and children, plotted how they could travel separately from southern Utah to Mexico. "Plans were hurriedly made," as a family member recalled, their escape "carefully orchestrated," and they all rendezvoused safely after crossing the border. They settled in Colonia Juárez, where Dayer, along with his parents, had spent his teen years before the Mexican Revolution. Founded on the Piedras Verdes River, 165 miles south of Deming, New Mexico, Colonia Juárez was fifteen miles east of the nearest Mexican town of Nuevo Casas Grandes and the famous archaeological ruins at Paquimé. Somewhere en route to Colonia Juárez, Dayer and Maud conceived their ninth child, Ervil, who would become the most famous offspring of their large family.

Colonia Juárez was much changed from the time when Dayer had lived there. The village was prospering as the cultural and religious center of the partially revived Mormon settlements in Mexico. With a population of 237, "prospects for crops are better than in years," as the *Arizona Gazette* reported, and millions of acres of fertile land were just "awaiting the magic touch of irrigation in the country," as another contemporary account put it. But the LeBarons were broke, according to neighbors, so Dayer was only able to buy two ramshackle brick houses on the poorer side of town.

The most notable change in Colonia Juárez was that the residents of the onetime bastion of fundamentalism and polygamy had turned "against the doctrine with reformist zeal." The returning settlers were mostly mainstream Mormons honoring the church manifestos that abolished polygamy, and the community ostracized Dayer as an excommunicated apostate. "Dayer was regarded in town as a crackpot. The local children would sometimes follow him down one of the town's tree-lined dirt streets, shouting and bleating 'B-a-a-a-a-h, b-a-a-a-a-h billy goat Dayer,'" alluding to the fact that Dayer, like the male goats he owned, had several mates. Yet Dayer was far from unique in this respect. Nearly all of the other families in the colony were polyga-mous. But the residents of the colony distinguished between the early polyga-mists—those who had taken up celestial marriage before the 1890 Woodruff Manifesto in which the church publicly denounced it (but implicitly con-tinued to encourage it)—and what they called the "new polygamists," like Dayer, who took up the practice after the church had made it grounds for excommunication. Dayer's neighbors believed, essentially, that they had been grandfathered in to the practice.

Nevertheless, for a brief time his family enjoyed their life in the col-ony. The children attended school, made friends, and participated in church socials, if not religious meetings. Benjamin LeBaron, Dayer's firstborn son by Maud, excelled at the prestigious Juárez Stake Academy. But their outcast status, combined with Dayer's loud and tireless proselytizing for polygamy, prompted the church to ban members from associating with the LeBarons, and the family was ultimately asked to leave Colonia Juárez.

The LeBarons deeply resented the ostracism and harassment from their polygamist neighbors, which they saw as hypocritical. "It broke Dayer's heart and he and his sons never got over it," as a family member said of the painful shunning. Those who saw themselves as tradititionalists, such as Mitt Romney's grandfather, Miles, himself a polygamist with four wives, regarded the excom-municated Dayer as an adulterer violating the tenets of the correct church. Romney led the attempt to expel Dayer from the settlement, telling him that the church was successfully stamping out plural marriage. "Father said that the church might as well attempt to stop the sun from coming up in the morning as to try to stop that practice," as Verlan wrote about the confrontation.

"The boys were as good young fellows as we had around here," a local said of the LeBaron sons, "but all through their lives they had a great amount of pressure. . . . That's what was wrong with the whole mess of 'em. Their parents had been excommunicated and they spent their lifetimes self-justifying themselves." But Dayer simply refused to leave Colonia Juárez, choosing instead to endure his low status and the social opprobrium (which he saw as persecution) for another twenty-five years before founding his own colony fifty miles southeast. Nearly all of the original Mormon colonies in Mexico had been broken up by the agrarian reform efforts during the Mexican Revolution. The eponymous Colonia LeBaron in Galeana—a ranch the family called the "New Zion"—was founded in 1944, one of the only new Mormon colonies established after the Revolution. To members of the other colonies, it would be known as the "bastard child" of Mormonism. Intermingling bloodlines and mythologies, the "hidden saints" of Colonia LeBaron, as they were called by Mormon leaders in the US, would live in isolation and mystery, along with what was said to be an intergenerational strain of insanity.

Dayer left behind in Colonia Juárez a successful fruit business and started anew with a fifty-acre allotment from the Mexican Government. In a move facilitated by a local patrón named Don Alberto Castillo, Dayer managed to acquire the *Galeana Ejido*—land that had been granted by the Mexican Government to the local farming community after the Revolution. From the start, members of the *ejido* accused the LeBarons of purchasing the land illegally and of dispossessing them. But Mexican judges sided with the Mormons, and despite warnings that the government could take away the land at any time, for any reason, Dayer "had implicit faith that the Mexican government would treat him right." He set about clearing the land of mesquite trees, building an irrigation canal and a ranch house, and planting groves of fruit trees as well as a vegetable garden. He instilled in his sons that the two most crucial elements of building the Kingdom of God on Earth were the return of the Jews to Palestine and the work being done in their New Zion.

Soon, fundamentalist friends from Utah moved to Mexico to join the colony, but leading members of the Mormon church began warning Saints to avoid the LeBaron family enterprise. The soil and the wives may have been productive, but the colony was far from a paradise. There was no electricity or running water, and for years Dayer's sprawling family would live in shacks and tents. Dayer's twelve-year-old daughter Lucinda, who suffered from psychotic episodes—and whom her family believed was possessed by evil spirits—was kept chained in a goat pen, spending much of her time in a fetal position. "The poverty and abuse was so depressing," recalled one family member. "Instead of the land of milk and honey promised by Dayer LeBaron," one daughter of a transplanted polygamist recalled, "my father had brought his wives and children to a land of saguaro cactus and scorpions and rattlesnakes," where there was nothing to feed them but "yams, yams, and more yams." A young daughter of another polygamist said the place swarmed with what she called "rattle day snakes."

* * *

Embittered by the rejection from their fellow Mormons in Colonia Juárez, those living in Colonia LeBaron "felt spiritually superior," according to a clan member, with Dayer claiming to hold the priesthood mantle of Joseph Smith that had been passed on to him by his grandfather, Benjamin Johnson. Shortly before his death from lead poisoning in 1951, Dayer "proclaimed he had had a vision" in which the "Lord told him that through his sons the whole world would be blessed." Its practical effect was to set his seven sons against one another as rivals for the "mantle." Maud had given birth to thirteen of Dayer's children, and six of their seven sons—Benjamin, Ross Wesley, Alma, Joel, Ervil, and Verlan—would compete to be "the One Mighty and Strong," leading to violence that would plague Dayer's descendants into the next century.

Benjamin LeBaron was the obvious heir apparent. Standing six-foot-two, he was charming, handsome, and intelligent. He once tried to prove his authority by jumping out of his pickup truck at a red light in Salt Lake City and doing push-ups in the busy intersection long after the light had changed to green, and with a police car behind him. As horns honked and the officer confronted him, he shouted that he was the "Lion of Israel," as his

sister-in-law Irene Spencer wrote about the event, and continued until he finished counting to one hundred. "That's more than you can do," he boasted to
the officer. "So that proves that I am the One Mighty and Strong."

In 1948, at the age of thirty-five, Benjamin was diagnosed with schizo-
phrenia, and later bipolar disorder. He was committed to the Utah State
Mental Hospital, leaving Dayer's other six sons to compete for the title. Four
years after Dayer's death on February 19, 1951, his soft-spoken, thirty-two-
year-old son, Joel Franklin LeBaron, suddenly declared himself "the true representative of Christ on Earth." That same year, 1955, Joel established the
fundamentalist Church of the Firstborn of the Fulness of Times, installing
himself as president, and appointed his brother Ervil as patriarch and spiritual
leader. Then the real trouble began.

"Seeing men vying for power is like playing 'Button-button, who's got
the button,'" Verlan LeBaron's second of ten wives would write in her 2009
book, *Cult Insanity*. She herself would know more than a dozen men who
claimed the title. "It amazed me how every leader seemed to use the same
scriptures to prove his right to wield power over other people's lives."

CHAPTER FIVE

"Am I About to Have a Cain in My Family?"

Their mother was grief stricken
Oh how she loved them both
Now one has killed the other
To kill more he's made an oath . . .
Should he be found guilty
And by law condemned to die
His blood spilt on the ground
May atone for him on high.

VERLAN LEBARON
AUGUST 21, 1979

MANY DOUBTED THAT the understated Joel LeBaron could convince followers that he was "the One Mighty and Strong," or that he was a prophet and
vessel for divine revelations. Many derided his new Church of the Firstborn
as the "Church of the Still-born." It was a family affair, with Ervil as the
scriptorian who "knew and interpreted the Mormon Scriptures forwards
and backwards up and down," according to one of the Firstborn members, as
well as patriarch of the new church, with the other brothers acting as apostles
under Joel's and Ervil's authority. Joel sent missionaries across Mexico and
the American Southwest; they announced his prophecies and called would-be

followers to Colonia LeBaron to live "the laws of liberty," based on the Ten Commandments and the "pure" teachings of Joseph Smith. Joel claimed that his divine ranking began with God and went down through Adam, Moses, Jesus, Smith (who received it from John the Baptist), to Benjamin Johnson, to Dayer LeBaron, and ultimately to him through the laying on of hands.

Joel summoned all "nations of Babylon" to gather in his kingdom, where "new converts' bloodlines would be fused with Joel's own royal blood," and where they were "dunked in the water of the beautiful baptismal Galeana Springs," as one described it. He also established an office in Salt Lake City, from which he directed bold and aggressive proselytizing among mainstream Mormons. The most significant boost to the church came in 1958, with the conversion of a group of Mormon missionaries from France. The French Mission, comprising the sons and daughters of prominent American Mormon families, was considered the most sophisticated of the church's missions anywhere in the world. "They not only preached the scriptures but had intensive explorations into the principles and tenets of the church," as one of their descendants described it. (Eight years after the group's conversion, Mitt Romney would become a missionary at the French Mission.)

The leader of the breakaway group of missionaries was a twenty-year-old Mormon convert named William P. Tucker, who had planned to enter a PhD program at UCLA when he was called to be a missionary in Paris and serve as counselor to the mission president—"the highest honor for any missionary." When a friend from Salt Lake City sent Tucker a copy of *Priesthood Expounded*—the fifty-six-page "Firstborn Bible" written by Ervil to set forth Joel's claim on the divine mantle—Tucker was intrigued. The pamphlet traced the lineage from Adam down to Joel as "the One Mighty and Strong," and Tucker became convinced that it was true, especially after the Mormon church excommunicated Joel, based upon what it considered his blasphemous assertions in the tract. Tucker soon apostatized and persuaded eight of his fellow missionaries in France to join him. All were excommunicated in a church trial in London, a case that unsettled the LDS establishment at the highest levels. "Such a thing had never happened before," said a member of the excommunication court. "It was astonishing, and the impact on the church was electric. All the leaders were in a state of shock, and it was regarded as a family tragedy."

The rebels returned to the United States aboard a Greek freighter, and most then made their way to the New Zion in Colonia LeBaron. They were "euphoric," according to one account: "Dedicated to their new ideals and anchored in their faith, they pursued their quest" to join Joel's church.

LDS authorities perceived the LeBarons as a "serious menace," if not an outright threat, and began monitoring their activities. LeRoy Hatch, a Mormon and the only medical doctor serving the Mexican colonies in the 1960s, became an informant for Salt Lake, telling church leaders he feared the Firstborners were racist and potentially violent against their Mexican and Indigenous neighbors, despite the fact that both were considered Lamanites and their conversion was central to Joseph Smith's original prophecies. "They used the term 'Lamanites' interchangeably, since they believed that all Mexicans have indigenous blood," said one Firstborn member, and, like all Mormons, they believed these Lamanites would lead the Army of the Lord during his Second Coming once they had become "white and delightsome people," as set forth in *The Book of Mormon*. Dayer LeBaron Sr. had directed all of his sons to marry Mexican women without worrying about the purity of their own bloodlines, which he said would continue through their plural marriages to white women. He believed, like his fellow Mexican Mormons, that the founders of the early colonies "represented some of the best blood of the Church," as historian Thomas Cottam Romney wrote, descended as they were from "the Nordic stock of northern Europe" who had "inherited a rich legacy genetically."

Their mother, Maud LeBaron, objected, not wanting her husband or any of her sons to marry the "heathen and take on the 'curse of the skin,'" according to one account, but each of them did marry Mexican women. Hatch reported that he had treated many of the Mexican spouses from the colony who were beaten by their husbands, especially by Ervil, who "beat both his Mexican wives, but never raised a hand to their American counterparts"— a fact that was challenged by at least one of Ervil's American wives, who claimed he abused her equally. She also claimed the LeBaron men routinely spanked all their wives to keep them in line.

Hatch also warned of likely violence within the LeBaron clan itself, which he described as "a cultish nest." Hatch had observed Dayer's seven sons competing to claim the keys to the kingdom and was especially concerned about Ervil's tempestuous personality.

* * *

Joel's Church of the Firstborn grew quickly and expanded into Baja, Mexico, and San Diego, California. New members consecrated their property, and soon the church was flush enough to invest in a cheese factory, a cattle ranch, a lumber business, and a gold-mining operation—"one ill-fated project after another" that resulted in bankruptcies and indebtedness that would haunt the clan for decades to come.

Ervil was the most passionate devotee, embracing his role as spiritual leader and eventually overshadowing Joel's position. The six-foot-eight, 240-pound, green-eyed Ervil had film-star good looks, the charisma of a con man, and appeared irresistible to women. The tallest of the LeBaron "boys," Ervil "could swing a grubbing hoe and rip out a deeply embedded mesquite stump with a force that brought admiration from the natives who worked alongside him," wrote his brother Verlan. Once he was named a patriarch in Joel's church, though, manual labor became a thing of his past.

Ervil's lifestyle was the inverse of Joel's humility and austerity. "Only a few days ago Ervil came into town driving a new car. He was well dressed. I'm sure he stayed in good motels," reported Joel's wife Magdalena Soto one day when her husband returned from preaching in Sonora. As she said to her husband, "You, the leader of the church, come home looking like this—exhausted after traveling two days and nights on a bus."

In the eyes of his brothers, Ervil's activities became increasingly problematic, his blatant white-supremacist stance leading to destructive conflicts with their neighbors. "Faded denim pants . . . were replaced by tailored pants, dress shirts, and well shined shoes." Ervil made plans to build a grand hotel, casino, and marina at Los Molinos—the Windmills—on the Pacific Coast, 180 miles south of the California border, where Joel's church was building a second Mexican colony. Ervil sold wells and land belonging to the LeBaron family to outsiders, and he was frequently seen gambling in Las Vegas, Nevada—the quintessential Babylon. Some of his personal acolytes were even picked up for drug smuggling in the Firstborn settlement of Los Molinos. He began speaking of his right to the priesthood to usurp Joel and announced that he was going to create "a great economic project" that would make millions of dollars—"*dollars not pesos*"—for the church hierarchy. "We will put signs on the highway so the gentiles will come here and leave their money with us," he told an influential apostle. During a water-rights dispute with Colonia LeBaron's neighbors, "Ervil talked about bringing in tanks, bazookas, and heavy artillery against the transgressors," recalled DeWayne Hafen, a fifth-generation Mormon and a Firstborn convert who became an ordained priest in Joel's church.

"There were deals for wives, women, money, land," said Hafen. "A lot of people told me I was a damn fool. Everyone . . . was dealing for something. I wasn't dealing for anything." Hafen later apostatized from the Church of the Firstborn to follow Joel's and Ervil's much older brother, Ross Wesley LeBaron, who claimed that he, in fact, held the priesthood keys and had started his own church back in Utah, in which the restoration of the gospel included talk of UFOs and extraterrestrial beings.

Ervil's justification of unethical, if not criminal, behavior alarmed Joel's inner circle. The most disturbing of Ervil's actions related to the domestic affairs of the Church's followers. He told young girls that it was his "sacred duty to place them with the man of his choice," wrote Verlan, and "far too often his choice was himself." Reports of his seduction of underage girls became ubiquitous. "Ervil reached the point that he could get a revelation to marry a girl faster and more often than anyone could imagine." He used his own daughters as gifts to reward his most devoted male followers, while insisting that his sons go to Babylon—the United States—to find wives rather than compete for young women with the colony's older patriarchs.

Ervil gave frequent speeches about "bleeding the beast"—the time-honored tradition among fundamentalists of bilking the US Government through tax evasion and welfare fraud. He also discoursed on blood atonement and the use of force against the church's enemies. He made a list of those condemned to die for breaking what he called "the Civil Law of God" that included President John F. Kennedy, along with the Prime Minister of Israel and the President of the Mormon church. The list would be kept secret for more than a decade. Ervil's preaching against the United States became more and more fiery; he spoke of his army of Firstborners assassinating top American government officials and made other terroristic threats. His rhetoric was so alarming that it even prompted the FBI briefly to consider some Firstborners as suspects in Kennedy's assassination. An FBI informant reported that a Firstborn leader known as the "Avenging Angel"—presumably Ervil—had discussed plans to disrupt civil authority and destroy communications systems and public utilities in the United States. Once that happened, as God's chosen people, the Firstborners would fulfill the White Horse Prophecy, and one of them would become the president, his followers told themselves. DeWayne Hafen later claimed that agents from the Salt Lake City Police, the FBI, and the Secret Service had approached him, seeking information about Ervil.

It seemed inevitable that there would be a break between Joel and Ervil, and in November 1969, Joel released Ervil from his role as second-in-command of the church. Ervil's removal as patriarch, and then his excommunication eighteen months later, split the sect's followers, who numbered approximately thirty families. Proclaiming that he, not Joel, was "the One Mighty and Strong," the messianic Ervil founded the Church of the First Born of the Lamb of God and named himself president, telling his followers that "we just might have to kill the sonuvabitch," referring to Joel. He advocated for officially reviving blood atonement—which Joel had disavowed in his Church of the Firstborn—and made clear to his flock that Joel had to be executed for his sins as a false prophet if he were to be saved in the afterlife. "The only way you can be forgiven for certain crimes is to shed your own blood," was Hafen's explanation for blood atonement. "Either take your own life, or volunteer to be killed. Thus, violent death is preferable over, say, hanging, because you can actually shed blood that way."

Ervil approached their sister Esther, a fragile widow who had suffered two nervous breakdowns and was trying to remain neutral in the family feud. And when he attempted to persuade her to invest in his projects in Los Molinos, telling her that he was buying fishing boats that could be used to dump the dead bodies of those he executed, she was horrified. He said he was also creating a business that would make sealed cement boxes for the bodies so they would sink, explaining to her "how the corpses would be taken care of so that no evidence or traces of them would ever be found." She was stunned by the delight her brother was taking in the bloodthirsty schemes, and she later recalled that, "at those words my blood ran cold."

In September 1971, Ervil's enemies in Colonia LeBaron began receiving death threats, including one sent to Joel's apostle Earl Larsen Jensen that was signed by "The Black Hand"—a right-wing Mexican death squad. Raised Mormon in Ogden, Utah, Jensen had had a distinguished intelligence and diplomatic career in the US Government, working for the FBI and the CIA and serving as the security attaché at the US Embassy in Tel Aviv from 1954 to 1956, before converting to Joel's church.

Wealthy, educated, and worldly, Jensen was considered a jewel in Joel's crown of converts. In 1958, he had been sent by the Mormon church to New York City to meet the freighter carrying the apostates from the French Mission, with orders to deprogram one of them—his own sister-in-law— but instead he was persuaded by the charming ringleader William Tucker to join the Church of the Firstborn. Jensen then moved with his wife, Carol, to Colonia LeBaron. "I'll never forget how stately she looked with her bleached blonde hair twisted and coifed and piled upon her head," recalled Irene Spencer, Verlan's second wife, of the moment she first saw Carol. "Her silk dress looked divine. I knew that her expensive high heels would soon be ruined from walking on the gravel roads. To me she looked like a fairy-tale princess. Most of us were dressed in secondhand, ill-fitting clothing, as were our Mexican members." Jensen built a sprawling two-story hacienda, stuccoed white with a red tile roof, complete with electricity and the first flush toilet in the primitive outpost. The showpiece of the colony, the house, guarded by a pack of purebred German shepherds, even boasted terrazzo flooring that Carol Jensen had so loved in Israel.

Jensen had been so high up in mainstream Mormon circles that the church brethren had been grooming him as a potential presidential candidate to fulfill the White Horse Prophecy. His defection to the LeBarons stung. "He was considered the goodwill ambassador to the Lamanites who welcomed the jobs he provided them," recalled a family member. "Thanks to him, all of the American wives in the colony had hired help, which improved their lives and those of the Mexicans." Within Colonia LeBaron, the fact that Jensen would be on the receiving end of Ervil's death threats elevated the seriousness with which they were taken. Ervil ordered two eighteen-year-old members of his church to hunt down Jensen and execute him. "God's speaking to me now," Ervil told them. "He's ordered you boys to use hot lead and cold steel."

"Each time we got a new threat, Mom would tell us to keep the doors locked," recalled one of Joel's young daughters. " 'And if I'm not home and you hear gunshots and explosions,' she always said, 'take your baby brother and run to the peach trees, cover him, and lie down in the dirt so no one can see you.' Uncle Ervil was like a ghost haunting us."

Ervil's mother, Maud, was distraught over the rupture among her sons and Ervil's verbal and physical threats against Joel. "Dear Son Ervil," she wrote on September 24, 1971, to the man thought to be her favorite son. "Your father came to my bedside and told me you were about to have inno-cent blood on your hands. . . . To imagine Dad gave you some authority is a lie. . . . I know who your father gave the authority to—He had no confidence in you. I'm afraid you have lost your mind—you have the spirit of revenge, and the spirit and desire to murder." Attempting desperately to dissuade him, she also revealed to him that her own father, like Benjamin LeBaron and now Ervil, had heard voices in his head that guided him down a dangerous and deadly path. "Maud had frequently blamed her husband Dayer for the streak of insanity that haunted the family," recalled a relative from the colony, "but everyone knew it came from Maud and Dayer being first cousins."

A month later, she appealed to Ervil again. "Your father has warned you and I am warning you. Ervil, be another Paul," referring to the biblical apos-tle who served as a peaceful interlocutor. Her letters fell on deaf ears, and Ervil continued on his path of vengeance. Appalled by his written manifestos promoting blood atonement, she wrote to him on November 3, 1971: "You know it's a lie that Joel is a fallen prophet! How are you going to live down the worst lie that ever was told. . . . Am I about to have a Cain in my family?"

Afraid for their lives, several of Joel's Firstborn families decamped from Colonia LeBaron and Los Molinos for the United States. Ervil declared Joel an apostate, and the intensity of his threats escalated as he published vitriolic pamphlets, including an eighty-two-page opus called *Priesthood Revealed*. "He was paranoid as hell," remembered his daughter Alice, one of his dozens of children. "Verlan and Joel will be put to death," Ervil ranted to his sister-in-law Irene Spencer.

On Sunday morning, August 20, 1972, Joel went to Ensenada, an hour's drive north from Los Molinos, to pick up his 1966 purple Buick sedan, which had needed repairs. He planned to retrieve his car from the home of his mechanic, Benjamin Zarate, a longtime Firstborn member who had recently shifted his allegiance to Ervil. When Joel arrived at Zarate's home, however, he found Zarate's son, who told Joel that Zarate had moved out and taken the key to the Buick with him. The son and another member of Ervil's new congregation then began arguing with Joel about scripture, while Joel was trying to attach a tow bar to the Buick. Zarate's son and the other man became increasingly agitated. "Why don't you come into the house and preach to me," one of them taunted Joel. Joel's fourteen-year-old stepson Ivan, who had accompanied him to Ensenada, stayed in the yard while Joel entered the home. About twenty minutes later, Ivan heard a fight going on inside. Then one of the men yelled, "Kill him," followed by two gunshots. Joel died instantly, shot first in his throat and then at point-blank through his brain.

There were no telephones in Colonia LeBaron, and only one in nearby Galeana, so word of Joel's murder didn't arrive until nine o'clock that night. A messenger carried the terrible and terrifying news of the Prophet's death to the home of his first wife, Magdalena. When the messenger appeared, Joel's eleven-year-old son Adrian was playing his guitar and singing in the moonlight. "Everyone knew it had been done by Ervil's orders," recalled Verlan. Ervil was the Mormon Cain, slaying his brother over a birthright that had been denied him. "Some people don't take me seriously until they see blood run," Ervil is said to have remarked during this period. The death brought panic to the community, as family members speculated about who might be killed next.

Joel's body was flown on a Cessna 410 to the Casas Grandes airfield for burial in nearby Colonia LeBaron. His namesake son, Joel Francisco LeBaron Soto, accompanied the bronze casket. "How solemn he was as he delivered the body of his slain father to his weeping mother and younger brothers and sisters," Verlan recalled. Joel's seven widows and forty-four children surrounded the casket at his funeral. "He stands with Abraham, Isaac and Jacob," said Siegfried Widmar, one of the church's more prominent members, addressing an overflow crowd in the small community church. "He stands with Abel. . . . He stands with John the Baptist and Jesus Christ, with Joseph Smith."

Verlan was chosen to take over as leader of the church because he had been its president, but everyone, including Verlan, recognized that he was merely a placeholder. He knew he had no legitimate claim to the mantle, nor any gift of prophecy. Despite his nine wives and more than fifty children, his leadership skills were lacking for a man of such bounty and responsibility. "He is a prince, not a prophet," as one of his wives said.

*   *   *

The killing of forty-nine-year-old Joel LeBaron was only the start of Ervil's ruthless campaign, the first of thirty-three known murders he committed; the actual number may have been as high as fifty. Ervil ordered Mafia-style hits on his many rival polygamist leaders and apostates from his church whom he called "the Sons of Perdition," invoking blood atonement and proclaiming himself "God's Avenger." To Joel's followers, their slain leader was the last Prophet before the Second Coming of Christ, and he was supposed to be immortal. The fact that the "Lord's hand came down on him," as one follower described it, emboldened Ervil to proclaim himself "the One Mighty and Strong." "Having successfully blood atoned Joel, Ervil figured that the bulk of the Firstborners would naturally just fall into his lap," as he had proven that Joel was mortal and therefore a false prophet. When that didn't happen, Ervil fled Mexico for the US to avoid arrest in connection with Joel's murder. Then he maneuvered to take over the fundamentalist branches of the Mormon church in both countries. "Everyone in the colony wanted revenge," said a family member in Colonia LeBaron.

With a hit list that included his remaining brothers and a rambling manifesto he titled *Hour of Crisis—Day of Vengeance*, Ervil also announced that not only his brothers, but also other adult men in Colonia LeBaron would be killed. At the top of his hit list was his brother Verlan. Joel's death had underscored the seriousness of Ervil's threats, and Colonia LeBaron went into high alert. On the day of Joel's murder, Ervil's thugs had gone to the homes of three of Verlan's wives, looking for Verlan. They didn't find him. Soon enough, Mexican law enforcement alerted Mormon leaders in Utah, as well as leaders of the numerous fundamentalist groups on both sides of the border, about Ervil's threats and deeds.

Verlan went into hiding, traveling among the US, Mexico, and Nicaragua while awaiting Ervil's apprehension by Mexican authorities. On the night of December 26, 1974, a convoy of Ervil's devotees staged a paramilitary-style raid on Verlan's bastion at Los Molinos, throwing Molotov cocktails into the settlement's adobe huts before pulling out their rifles. During the twenty-minute attack, the "Ervilistas" lobbed firebombs into the houses, leaving two dead and thirteen wounded. Verlan himself was out of town.

For years, Verlan would live with the threat of his own murder hanging over him. "Since Joel's death, my life has been one of constant movement," wrote Verlan in 1981, almost a decade after Joel's murder. "Knowing the threats against me, I have tried to avoid assassins' bullets while continuing to fulfill my duties as president of the church Joel started, and at the same time support my large family. . . . I've been told that over a dozen men and women were put under covenant and strict orders to kill me on sight. The lives of any around me are not to be considered when the assassins open fire."

Although Joel's murder was reported in American newspapers, it was mostly dismissed as the killing of a little-known leader of a tiny religious sect. The FBI was confused by the connections of the LeBarons to the Mormon fundamentalist colonies in Colorado City, Arizona, and Hildale, Utah, as well as other polygamist communities in the US. One agent said the "minute you step into this, you're in another world. . . . Everywhere you push, there's jelly." But in Utah, "far-sighted police officers viewed the attack as portentous," and church President Spencer W. Kimball was put under heavy guard. By this point, Ervil was proclaiming a plan to take over the LDS church, overthrow the Mexican Government, and then conquer the world. Ervil would make threats against every American president in the 1960s and 1970s—John F. Kennedy, Lyndon Johnson, Richard Nixon, Gerald Ford, Jimmy Carter—as well as against the famous evangelist Billy Graham, and the US Secret Service was on high alert.

In the United States, Ervil founded a front organization called the Society of American Patriots, ironically abbreviated as SAP, as an American newspaper pointed out, that distributed inflammatory literature parroting the

rhetoric of Neo-Nazis, the Ku Klux Klan, the Aryan Nation, and the Posse
Comitatus. SAP's published diatribes, distributed from a post office box in
South Pasadena, California, denounced "the wicked Babylon." The group
voiced the usual panoply of extreme right-wing grievances: government
taxes, welfare programs, the press, and gun control. Loyal American citizens
were called upon to "rise up and militantly throw off the bondage" of government corruption. SAP threatened an invasion of Mexico by the US Army,
ostensibly because "liberty and justice are being raped by depraved bigots and
corrupt [Mexican] officials." SAP then claimed the Carter presidency was
illegitimate, announcing, "We would rather have the death penalty placed
upon Jimmy Carter than to see him proceed further." Ervil's own writings,
suffused with prophecy and thinly veiled threats, were a grammarian's night-
mare. But there may have been a method to his madness, as Secret Service
agents were forced to admit that it would be difficult to convict him, given
the intentionally convoluted nature of his prose.

One journalist who immediately grasped the gravity and significance of
the story was Mormon columnist Jack Anderson. A legendary muckraker
who had inherited Drew Pearson's famous syndicated Washington, DC, column, *The Washington Merry-Go-Round*, had cut his teeth thirty years earlier
by exposing a Utah polygamist group unrelated to the LeBarons.

In 1976, four years after Joel's death, Anderson wrote about the murder
in his column, which appeared in nearly a thousand newspapers nationwide,
bringing the story widespread public attention. As Anderson later explained
in one of his memoirs, polygamist "cults" in the 1970s "seemed to demand
more from their members and give less. I heard stories about disciples disappearing, their leaders getting rich, girls being intimidated, and wives being
auctioned off." He wrote a series of columns about the "bloodbath" that followed Joel's death and dubbed Ervil LeBaron "the Mormon Manson," a refer-
ence to infamous American cult leader Charles Manson.

Rulon Allred, a popular Salt Lake City osteopath and leader of the
Apostolic United Brethren (AUB) in Utah, Colorado, and Arizona, the second largest group of Mormon fundamentalists in the US, was in Ervil's sights.
The Allred Group, as it was called, had been allied with the LeBarons for
decades. Joel and Ervil had been baptized into the group before breaking away

with their own churches, and some of Verlan's seven wives were related to the Allred Group. "We are living in the last dispensation in the fullness of times," Rulon Allred told one of his daughters, Dorothy Allred Solomon, in response to Ervil's threats against him. Some of the LeBarons have become "a law unto themselves," he said. "Satan is doing his utmost to thwart the elect before the Savior comes to call them home."

An apocalyptic state of mind took hold in the Allred Group. "Apparently threats on a polygamist were not important enough for law enforcement officials to provide my father with protection," Solomon later wrote. "So we steeped like the proverbial frog in the pot of water slowly heating to a boil, unable to tell when our fear took on immediate and dangerous implications."

Trying to tempt Verlan out of hiding, Ervil plotted the assassination of Rulon Allred with the idea that Verlan could be ambushed at Allred's funeral. On the morning of May 10, 1977, two women—two of Ervil's "Lambs of God"—disguised in wigs and sunglasses, entered Allred's waiting room at his medical office in suburban Salt Lake City and asked to see him. When the doctor appeared, nineteen-year-old Rena Chynoweth—known as the prettiest of Ervil's thirteen wives—shot Allred six times, fatally wounding him, and then the two women fled.

Four days later, Dr. Allred's funeral services were held in an auditorium large enough to accommodate a crowd of 2,600 mourners. Verlan slipped into the hall as inconspicuously as possible, only later learning that the members of Ervil's hit squad had lost their nerve in the face of dozens of television cameras and well-armed police officers. Jack Anderson wrote several columns about the sensational Allred murder at the hands of Ervil, focusing his attention on the continuing practice of polygamy throughout the Intermountain West and the difficulties faced by investigators. As one detective put it, "There are no drugs or drinking in this group—they are cold-sober people who believe in the rightness of their cause." A *Time* magazine story depicted Ervil as a deadly leader who exhibited "a new and bloodier brand of lawlessness—flagrantly criminal instead of quiet and covert." For the first time, a spotlight was shone on the complex web of polygamist groups that still existed in America, much to the chagrin of an official Mormondom eager to distance itself from the controversies of its past. Rather than accept Joel's view of a charitable, merciful Christ of the New Testament, Ervil's rebels focused on the wrathful God of the Old Testament. "He's always preaching this blood and thunder stuff . . . if people don't live the civil law [of Ervil's God], cut their heads off," a Utah polygamist from a rival church told *Time*. "He is very pugnacious but is also a smooth-tongued type." The neighboring villagers of Colonia LeBaron described Ervil as *loco* and *mitad diablo* (half-devil).

In 1980, Ervil was extradited to the United States after being arrested in the remote eighteenth-century Puebla town of Atlixco, a hundred miles southeast of Mexico City—the kind of hideout "Butch Cassidy loved during his Bolivia days . . . situated between a snow-capped volcano and an Aztec pyramid," as one account described it. After the most intensive and costly criminal case in the history of Utah to that point, he was tried for ordering Allred's murder and sentenced to life in prison. When he was first incarcerated, he lived with the general prison population. But after he began proselytizing successfully, he was moved to solitary confinement. While in jail, he wrote a 600-page "bible" called *The Book of New Covenants,* which contained an expanded hit list of enemies—including all of the descendants of both Joel and Verlan—for his disciples. A federal prosecutor described Ervil's cult as more like an organized-crime syndicate, citing the clues and details revealed by his covenants. Twenty copies were printed and distributed to Ervil's family members.

Ervil had a "mind that was in turn brilliant and deranged," and he "fashioned himself to be God's executioner," wrote Anderson. He "added a startling refinement to polygamy: He trained his women to kill for him." There was a method to his madness in creating a female "death team" composed of beautiful women, according to Irene Spencer, his sister-in-law and Verlan's wife. "Why did Ervil pick women for such a horrific task and perhaps the most visible murder [of Allred]? Women were more malleable and obedient to Ervil, and they were far more expendable in his scheme of things."

In the predawn hours on Sunday, August 16, 1981, Ervil, fifty-six, was found dead in his maximum-security cell at the Point of the Mountain state prison in Utah, apparently from a massive heart attack. The family hoped that Ervil's death would end the violence, but Ervil "made it his business to prolong the anguish," wrote Spencer. He ordained his firstborn son, Arturo, as his successor and "worldwide patriarch." Six other sons became high priests, and one daughter became a high priestess, leading to at least twenty more blood-atonement murders after his death. Verlan had spent nine years in hiding from his assassins, but if he experienced a newfound freedom, it was short-lived: Two days after Ervil's death, Verlan was killed in an automobile accident in Mexico when an oncoming car swerved into his lane and hit him head-on. His last words, spoken to the passenger with him, were: "Brother, it looks like we've been ran off the road." His family and followers were certain he had been murdered.

Just weeks before his death, Verlan had completed his family history. When he wrote at various points about Joel in Colonia LeBaron, it was "with a sort of misty-eyed reverence," as he put it. At religious gatherings in the colony, a ballad, "La Corrida de Joel," is still sung in Joel's honor. "Might Joel's people yet play some part in preparing citizens for God's kingdom here on earth, that He whose right it is to rule shall reign as King of Kings and Lord of Lords?" wrote Verlan in the final paragraph of his manuscript. "Perhaps then, shall another and vastly different volume be written of the LeBaron story."

* * *

After Ervil's death, his wives, children, and spiritual followers continued carrying out the murders of his designated enemies. Arturo assumed the mantle of "the One Mighty and Strong," claiming "the succession that began with Joseph Smith and Benjamin Johnson," as his father had designated, and he assumed responsibility for the killings. But Arturo was murdered two years later, and, after a power struggle among other sons of Ervil, William "Heber" LeBaron, Ervil's twenty-year-old son by his fourth wife, declared he was "the One Mighty and Strong," and he claimed leadership of the group in the summer of 1984. "When you have already decided that you are living in the last days, and you have preselected your team of good guys (you are on the good guys' team, of course) and when you fully believe you know who the bad guys are (anybody who doesn't agree that you are the good guys), then you're up against the entire world," wrote Dorothy Solomon, one of Rulon Allred's daughters.

For the next fifteen years, law enforcement in several US jurisdictions investigated Heber's own criminal syndicate, which was headquartered at *Rancho La Jolla*—"The Jewel"—in Sonora and encompassed a thriving car-theft operation in Phoenix and Dallas that became one of the largest in the

Heber LeBaron, one of Ervil's many children, covers his face with a Bible while leaving an extradition hearing in Phoenix, Arizona, on July 18, 1988. He was sentenced to life in prison for his role in the murder of four people in Texas who were on his father's "blood-atonement" list. *(Chad Surmick/Associated Press)*

Southwest. Heber reshaped the so-called Lamb of God Church into a tightly knit family business—"a Mormon fundamentalist version of the Mafia," according to one description. Phoenix authorities compiled evidence of the clan's theft of hundreds of automobiles in the US, mostly four-wheel-drive trucks and SUVs. The vehicles were retrofitted to be bulletproof and then sold, along with automatic weapons the LeBarons bought in the US, to Mexican drug traffickers. The income from this trade was, in turn, used to finance the murders of apostates named in Ervil's *Book of New Covenants*.

LeBaron family members, who were later convicted in connection with the murders directed by Ervil, also robbed banks and trafficked in narcotics, with the proceeds from these activities going toward blood atonement. "It was with the profits from this venture that . . . [Ervil] LeBaron's order to kill the 'Sons of Perdition' was financed," the FBI would report twenty-five years later. The LeBaron ranch and compound was "a bad scene" and "a veritable hotbed of hatred, militarism, and illegal activities" in the 1980s and early 1990s, wrote Rena Chynoweth, who left in 1979, after being acquitted by a jury for murdering Rulon Allred at Ervil's direction. It was "an arsenal for many types of automatic weapons" as well as stolen cars and motorcycles, she wrote eleven years later in her memoir, *The Blood Covenant*, in which she admitted her culpability in the murder.

"Because our legal business was not profitable enough to support the family and pay for the planned murders, it was decided that it should be abandoned in favor of fulltime criminal activity," Heber LeBaron himself would confess decades later. "We had connections in the United States and Mexico, so we started smuggling marijuana to finance the group."

Arizona law enforcement noticed the clan's increasing cleverness. "They had their hair cut short, dressed real well, wore Rockport shoes—just a very professional operation," wrote one detective. *Rancho La Jolla* sat just outside the town of Caborca, seventy miles south of the Arizona border. At the time, Caborca was the headquarters for the Sonora Cartel, led by the notorious Rafael Caro Quintero and his brother, Miguel Caro Quintero. The LeBarons, under Heber's control, operated their auto "chop shop" in a downtown Caborca building and associated with the Caro Quinteros.

Heber developed convenient relationships within the Mexican underworld, and with his dual citizenship, blond hair, and fluency in English and Spanish, he easily traveled back and forth across the border. By running marijuana and cocaine northward, and bringing cars, guns, and ammunition southward, Heber maintained total control of the money and distributed it as he saw fit to the "worthy male members." He designated Linda Rae Johnson, one of Ervil's widows, as the matriarch, and she served as bookkeeper, finance manager, and overseer of Heber's wives, sisters, and half-sisters. The only one of Ervil's wives who received any education, Linda gave "the impression of being a nice, pleasant middle-aged woman," said a Phoenix policewoman investigating the group. "The sort of woman who makes bread and takes care of the kids and that sort of thing. Yeah, and plans murders on the side."

The LeBaron women under Heber's control bailed out the men when they got arrested, produced fake birth certificates, created aliases and alibis, drove the stolen vehicles across the border, and rented safe houses in the US. "While planning the murders, the group stole pickup trucks and license plates. . . . They purchased suits, false beards . . . handguns, holsters, marine radios, and costume makeup," according to the FBI.

On November 5, 1986, Heber held up a bank in Dallas; he was arrested and then released on $50,000 bail. He immediately fled back to Mexico. His enterprise might have continued indefinitely, if not for his thirst for vengeance. While Heber was dabbling in bank robbery schemes, he failed to see that a powerful dissident in his ranks was gaining strength. He may have missed the threat because it came from someone who was not only one of his "female operatives," but who was one of his own wives (and also his half-sister): twenty-year-old Jacqueline "Tarsa" LeBaron.

A hardened zealot, Tarsa was the oldest daughter of Ervil's fifth wife, Lorna Chynoweth, who had recently been "blood atoned by her own son," Tarsa's brother, Andrew. A true believer in her father's covenant, "Tarsa was like a little Ervil," a Texas lawman was once quoted as saying. "If she wanted somebody to do something, she'd cozy up to them and it would be like honey coming out of her mouth. If that didn't work, she'd start in with the scriptures. . . . And if that didn't work, she'd turn to ice." All of the women and some of the men in Heber's operation were afraid of her, especially once she became known as the group's murderess and "high priestess," who was bent on turning the group into a matriarchy.

The murders of people listed in Ervil's manifesto continued into the 1990s. One investigator for the Salt Lake County Attorney's Office devoted more than fifteen years to the many killings committed by Ervil's offspring. "You can deal with a criminal who kills for greed," he told a reporter. "You can deal with a criminal who kills for anger. But how do you deal with killers who kill for God?" As a LeBaron family member put it, "Everyone is an infidel if they don't believe what you believe."

In 1992, six members of the LeBaron family were indicted by a federal grand jury in Texas on charges relating to what was called "The 4 O'Clock Murders" in Houston and Irving, Texas, on June 27, 1988—the 144th anniversary of Joseph Smith's murder. Four victims, former members of Joel's Church of the Firstborn, including an eight-year-old girl, died of shotgun blasts to the head. The slayings took place simultaneously at three different locations, at 4 pm, the same hour that Smith had been fatally wounded.

Of the six LeBaron siblings indicted—ranging in age from sixteen to twenty-two—three were convicted and sentenced to life in prison, including Heber. Another was sentenced to forty-five years in prison, and the youngest pleaded guilty and served five years in prison. Cynthia LeBaron, one of the sisters, whose testimony led to the convictions of her siblings, was granted immunity from prosecution and given a new identity in the Federal Witness Protection Program. She was relocated to an undisclosed American community and forbidden to have any contact with her extended family for the rest of her life. Tarsa, considered the mastermind behind the murders, was also charged, but she was hiding in Mexico, and American law enforcement received little cooperation from their Mexican counterparts in locating and extraditing her.

"We were taught that we were being persecuted because we were God's chosen people," said one of Ervil's fifty-four children from thirteen wives, many of whom he managed as his personal assassins. Investigators across numerous states and jurisdictions were relieved after the convictions, thinking that, finally, "this melodrama of the Modern West is almost over," as the *Los Angeles Times* reported, "more than two decades after an obscure religious feud between two brothers erupted into murder and sparked a killing frenzy." But even into 2021, the offspring of Joel, Ervil, Verlan, and Alma Dayer Jr.—their sons and grandsons—were still battling over who had the rightful authority to hold the leadership of the Church of the Firstborn in Mexico. These rivalries continued to play out in Colonia LeBaron and the immediate vicinity, and even though the murders have stopped as of this writing, the family's history of violence is never far from the surface, even though now complicated by the newfound prosperity of the clan.

Ervil's daughter Tarsa was still on the lam when, in 2008, Heber—in the sixteenth year of serving his multiple life sentences in Colorado's federal SuperMax prison—provided information to authorities regarding her possible whereabouts. In an articulate confession presumably made in exchange for better amenities in prison, Heber wrote that he was a fifth-generation Mormon "born to the most notorious and violent of the polygamous offshoots of the Mormon church." Heber described his father as a "madman," adding that Ervil was "not the only madman in Mormon history. Brigham Young . . . was also quite mad." Heber blamed Young's preaching of the doctrine of blood atonement for leading to so much violence in the church. "It was taught that some people's sins are so bad that Jesus' sacrifice on the cross could not atone for them," as Heber described the practice as imparted to him by his father when Ervil decided it was time to follow in Young's footsteps. "In order for those persons to be saved and go to heaven, their own blood had to be shed," he wrote, describing how when he was just eight years old, "my father and his followers went on a six-year killing spree in their efforts to subjugate the other polygamous offshoots of the Mormon church. Because of these murders, I spent the rest of my childhood in a bizarre nomadic environment where local, state, and federal law enforcement raids were common," while his parents and other members told him that the police and prosecutors and judges were "servants of the Devil, trying to stop God's work."

Heber claimed that he had renounced his fanatical beliefs after attending weekly Bible studies in prison and reading literature critical of the Mormon church, beginning with Fawn Brodie's biography of Joseph Smith. "I was brought to tears by *No Man Knows My History*," he wrote of Brodie's book. "It busted down to size all the legends I grew up with," and he converted to what he described as a more mainstream Christianity. "Now that I am a Christian, I am shocked and horrified by all the evil I did while in the cult . . . ," he wrote. "The Word of God clearly states that vengeance belongs to God and that we are to obey the laws of the land. I see my sin very clearly now and have asked God to forgive me."

Heber admitted to authorities that he had ordered numerous people killed between 1972 and 1980, and that he personally had led his group of followers in Sonora to carry out ten murders of rival polygamists in California, Denver, and Houston in a one-year period during 1987 and 1988. He wrote that, during his years of incarceration, he had come to realize that Ervil suffered from bipolar disorder and had passed it on to several of his children. "My father . . . taught me that the crashing lows came when God withdraws the Holy Spirit because of His anger and lets Satan attack you, and that the euphoric rapture was when the Holy Spirit was with you the most," Heber wrote. But after being treated in prison for depression, Heber said he came "to know that the euphoria has a clinical name, 'Mania.'"

Heber's testimony prompted the FBI to investigate the set of murder cases again, and it placed Tarsa on the Houston office's "Ten Most Wanted Fugitives" list, with the agency offering a $20,000 reward for information leading to her capture. The TV series *America's Most Wanted* featured her in its August 20, 2008, episode. Calling her the *consigliore* for the LeBaron crime family, assistant US Attorney Terry Clark of Houston described the "four o'clock killings" for which Tarsa was indicted as one of "the best planned murders I've ever seen in thirty years of prosecution," saying they "put the Mafia to shame." Clark described Tarsa as a forty-three-year-old woman weighing 135 pounds, standing five feet, eleven inches tall, and with brown hair and green eyes. She was fluent in Spanish and English, highly intelligent and articulate, known to wear disguises, and considered armed, dangerous, and an escape risk. "Authorities believe she may be teaching English to wealthy Mexican families," the report went on, and she was known to use at least fifteen aliases.

In May 2010, a tip led to Tarsa's capture in Honduras. She had been tracked to the city of Moroceli, according to the FBI, and INTERPOL arrested her with help from the US Consulate in Honduras and the Naval Criminal Investigative Service. She fought extradition, claiming that she was a Mexican citizen, but she was flown to Houston to face the fourteen outstanding charges against her: murder for consideration, conspiracy to commit murder, use of a firearm during a crime of violence, conspiracy to obstruct religious beliefs, and racketeering conspiracy (RICO)—charges that carried possible life sentences. She had been a fugitive for nearly twenty years. Standing before a US magistrate, wearing "a blue blouse and floor-length skirt, she told the judge she thought the judge and prosecutor are nice and she hopes her appointed attorney is nice as well," according to the *Houston Chronicle*. "She also asked for her psychiatric medicine." The prosecutor described her as a flight risk, so the judge ordered her to remain in jail pending trial. FBI agents told the *Chronicle* that more than fifty of Ervil LeBaron's children continued to follow their father's teachings, and that some of the people on his "hit list" still "live with the knowledge that they are vulnerable."

"Hallelujah!" exclaimed Irene Spencer, Verlan LeBaron's widow, upon learning of Tarsa's capture. "I am absolutely thrilled!" she told Fox News. "I basically think it's going to settle down. I myself feel a lot calmer and at peace just knowing that she is apprehended. Many people who still feared that someone would pick up Ervil LeBaron's mantle, ordering death to his enemies, will be relieved." Spencer also said that family members in Colonia LeBaron had become "more concerned about drug cartel violence in the region than the radical preachings of a dead polygamist."

In June 2011, days before her criminal trial was scheduled to begin, Tarsa entered into a plea bargain with prosecutors and was allowed to plead guilty to one count of conspiracy to obstruct religious beliefs. Her attorney claimed she was more of a victim than her actual murdered victims, citing the difficult life she had endured and her inability to refuse to play a role in the killings. She was sentenced to three years in federal prison—a surprisingly light sentence for someone charged with orchestrating four murders, including that of an eight-year-old cousin—and ordered to pay $134,000 in restitution to her victims' heirs. The last defendant to be convicted in the case, Tarsa was released on December 14, 2012, for "good behavior," after serving just fifteen months.

The sentence raised the question of whether Tarsa cooperated with federal law enforcement. "She should have gotten the death penalty," said Michael S. Vigil, former US Drug Enforcement Administration (DEA) Chief of International Operations. "If she cooperated, it had to be substantive. She would have to have provided the names of someone higher up involved in weapons, drugs, and murders," Vigil explained. "The government doesn't trade down."

Irene Spencer's elation notwithstanding, many descendants of Ervil's enemies still live to this day in fear of his progeny. "It's probably over, but I wouldn't count on it," the federal prosecutor in the case said in 2014 of the LeBarons' "reign of terror." Forty years after Ervil's death, observers within the mainstream Mormon church and the fundamentalist Mormon sects believe that the longstanding rivalries and tensions are very much alive. LeBaron family members have said the same. "It's a fact that the LeBarons have a tendency to be high-strung. We're highly sensitive, highly nervous and prone to crack up because of some family problems," one of Ervil's

Jacqueline "Tarsa" LeBaron, one of Ervil's daughters—a high priestess in her father's church who was called "a hardened zealot"—appearing in a Houston federal court on May 14, 2010. She was apprehended in Honduras on charges in the "4 O'Clock Murders" case, after being on the lam for nearly twenty years, and after her brother Heber provided information to authorities regarding her whereabouts. *(Steve Campbell File/ Associated Press)*

brothers remarked. "We became nomads, like traveling hordes, always hiding," recalled a church member and polygamous wife of the Ervilistas' rampage. "There was no refreshment of the scanty gene pool, and we just kept having babies. We were a society of secret keepers. We became desensitized to murder," she said.

"I think we are a most unusual family," Ervil's sister Esther once said. "There's no use any of us lying about the family. Facts are facts and truth is truth."

CHAPTER SIX

Saint Benji and the Vanguard

———— ✳ ————

FOLLOWING THE IMPRISONMENT of Ervil's criminal offspring in the 1990s, Colonia LeBaron appeared to settle into relative peace, even as numerous male descendants of Dayer LeBaron Sr.'s sons—Joel Jr., Verlan, and (Alma) Dayer Jr.—were still bickering over who should carry the mantle of "the One Mighty and Strong." The family of the murdered Joel LeBaron believed that Joel Jr., who, as firstborn son of first wife Magdalena Soto, went by the name Joel LeBaron Soto, was the rightful inheritor. Others believed that the torch had been passed to Verlan, the most recent living apostle, and that one of his many sons from nine wives should thus lead the community. The sons of Alma Dayer Jr. likewise thought they held the birthright.

By the end of the decade, the various factions had splintered along a different divide as they quarreled over whether "the One Mighty and Strong" was even currently on Earth. Two "basic camps" developed, according to one scholarly account. The "liberal side" contended that the holy priesthood was not on Earth at the time, and that they were awaiting the "right one to emerge, who will restore order to the family and help them prepare for the Second Coming of Christ." The "conservative side" believed that the modern-day Prophet existed and that "the laws of God should be physically enforced."

What both groups had in common was the undying belief that the time was nigh when the divinely inspired US Constitution would "hang like a thread." According to Joseph Smith's prophecy, a bloody civil war would destroy America, and Mormon elders would save the nation. (The actual

American Civil War had excited some Mormons at the time, but it was retrospectively seen as a false hope.) In keeping with their forebears' predictions that, as direct descendants of Smith, the LeBaron bloodline was the purest within the Mormon faith, both sides prepared in earnest for "the latter days." Despite familial disagreements, Joel LeBaron Soto (carrying his mother's maiden name, as was traditional), assumed patriarchal leadership of the extensive clan. Joel Jr., as he was known, designated his charismatic son, Benjamin, himself known as "Benji," as the namesake heir-apparent to his great-great-grandfather's spiritual mantle.

* * *

Early in the twenty-first century, the LeBaron community—consisting of the adjacent villages of Galeana and Colonia LeBaron—was still maintaining peaceful relations with the Sinaloa Cartel of Joaquín "El Chapo" Guzmán. Even though El Chapo—dubbed "the world's largest drug lord in all of history" by former DEA agent Michael S. Vigil, one of the world's leading experts on the Mexican cartels—was then serving a twenty-year prison sentence, he continued to oversee the cartel from his comfortable jail accommodations in a maximum-security prison in the Mexican state of Jalisco. He turned the prison into a private corporation, with the full cooperation of high-level military and political officials, regional law enforcement, and the prison staff. But in 2001, eight years into his sentence, when it seemed likely that he would be extradited to the US to face numerous charges and a life sentence, he escaped with the help of seventy employees of the prison.

For the next decade, the world's most wanted kingpin hid out in the sparsely populated Sierra Madre Occidental, while expanding his global drug empire to fifty countries throughout the Western Hemisphere and beyond. He bribed officials to protect him and moved between heavily guarded compounds in the "Golden Triangle"—the mountainous terrain of the states of Durango, Sinaloa, and Chihuahua, where most of Mexican marijuana, heroin, and methamphetamine is produced, and where El Chapo controlled local politics and employed thousands of farmers to cultivate the poppy and marijuana fields. Rarely seen in public, he sporadically dined out in Nuevo Casas Grandes, a city of sixty thousand located forty miles northwest of Colonia

LeBaron. These occasional outings to local restaurants in the territory he controlled were widely seen as taunts directed at law enforcement, proving that he was still *El Patrón*—The Boss.

As the Sinaloa Cartel expanded, the finite resources of the Sierra Madre, which had been redistributed to the locals during the Mexican Revolution, were in decline. The region famed for its veins of silver and gold, choice grazing sites on high grasslands, herds of game animals, and clear rivers and streams had been used up—overmined, overgrazed, overhunted, and dammed by domestic and foreign corporate giants exploiting generations of native Mexicans and Indigenous people who sold off what they had in order to survive. The region's massive old-growth forests had long since been logged to extinction, the deer herds and wild-turkey flocks exhausted, and the arid land turned to dust after decades of drought. Generations of peasant farmers had been left with only two choices: Join the Sinaloa Cartel and work its marijuana and opium fields or emigrate illegally to the United States.

Most chose to work for El Chapo, whom they saw as their salvation and who was glorified in drug-themed ballads known as *narcocorrido* tributes. Like many people in the region, El Chapo had been born into poverty, from which he had risen against all odds and become a billionaire by the time he was in his thirties. Rumors proliferated that he had a palatial compound east of Nuevo Casas Grandes, a massive farm and horse ranch in a verdant river valley where he planned to retire one day. So, in yet another sense, Chihuahuans claimed him as one of their own.

Somehow, the LeBarons had managed to coexist with El Chapo's drug-smuggling operation ever since he first rose to power in the 1980s. The family's presence in Mexico predated the cartel, and the two had achieved a détente, even as each carried out violent actions internally and against other enemies. But in 2006, when newly elected Mexican President Felipe Calderón declared war on drug smugglers and organized crime groups, the relations between the Mormons and the cartels started to shift. Appearing in public in military uniform, Calderón announced the deployment of forty-five thousand soldiers and twenty thousand federal police officers to fight the much-publicized Mexican war on drugs.

As a result, drug-related violence exploded, increasing in frequency and barbarity. Calderón went after the cartel leaders in what he called "the king-pin strategy," but it backfired. "Once he took down some of the leaders, frag-mentation happened, and violence increased. He didn't do a top to bottom clean out, so he created a Hydra," Vigil explained, referring to the mythologi-cal water monster with nine heads.

Calderón's approach led to fierce battles among rival cartels over terri-tory controlled by the Sinaloa Cartel. The Jalisco New Generation Cartel, the Zetas, the Tijuana Cartel, and the Juárez Cartel all set their sights on the hugely valuable smuggling routes near the Mormon colonies in Sonora and Chihuahua, where much of the violence took place. Calderón's strategy had little direct impact on El Chapo's organization. His cartel was the most difficult for the government to dismantle, given its distributed power struc-ture. The Sinaloa Cartel was a horizontal organization that functioned like a global corporation or international Mafia, with semiautonomous subsid-iaries throughout many parts of the world, each with the ability to make its own decisions. As violence escalated in the region, with El Chapo remaining untouched, Mexicans came to believe that Calderón's military was intention-ally eliminating El Chapo's competition, while leaving his syndicate intact.

As long as El Chapo maintained control of the drug routes in Chihuahua, the LeBarons seemed secure, even though the war around them increased in intensity. Their agricultural enterprises thrived, with their immense walnut and pecan orchards making them among the larger Mexican exporters of nuts to China and the United States. They were on friendly terms with those manning the Sinaloa Cartel's checkpoints on the roads to the US, and the LeBaron men traveled back and forth across the border with ease. "Two hun-dred miles south of Juárez," as a reporter once described the road from the border at El Paso to Colonia LeBaron, "is like *the* narco superhighway," with three hundred smuggling trails crisscrossing the terrain. "It's a straight shot to the Mormons, their guns, and their God."

* * *

With a population of approximately two thousand in 2006, Colonia LeBaron boasted a motel, two grocery stores, religious schools, and a church in the center of town. Family culture was still shaped by male supremacy, in which

A Mexican Army officer stops a car on July 16, 2009, in Colonia LeBaron. The military checkpoint was established after the murders earlier that month of Benjamin LeBaron and Luis Widmar. *(Adriana Zehbrauskas/New York Times)*

the man controlled the financial resources and spiritual salvation of his brood, and his many wives were expected to bear as many children as possible and defer to their husbands in all matters. This patriarchal structure often resulted in tension between women as they competed for husbands of standing who could "pull them through the veil," in accordance with polygamy doctrine, and between men as they competed for the most coveted women, often pitting mothers and daughters, fathers and sons, and siblings against each other. An example of what scholars have described as "elite" polygamy, the LeBaron community consists of a "small, powerful cluster of high-ranking males in the lineage" who exercise total control over women and resources. These prestigious, landowning men hold priesthood authority and also "marry all the young, reproductively viable women."

While the original Mormon colonists who settled in Chihuahua in the late 1800s—where they founded Colonia Juárez, Colonia Dublán, and other colonies—largely abandoned plural marriage during the twentieth century and returned to the fold of the LDS church, those in Colonia LeBaron were among the tiny minority who carried the practice into the twenty-first century.

Many of the men owned construction companies in the US, where some even contracted to build Mormon churches. Leading LeBaron men are known for their extensive network of American drywall businesses and for spending much of the year in the United States, from where they send money home to their families and return regularly to oversee the Mexican employees laboring in their fields. The younger men work as subcontractors for their many uncles and older cousins in the US, sending earnings home to their wives in Mexico. Other young men from LeBaron lay tile in Texas or work in the oil-and-gas industry in North Dakota, Louisiana, and the Permian Basin of the American Southwest. Their goal—often requiring a decade or more to attain—is to save enough money to purchase a lucrative pecan orchard back in Colonia LeBaron. The women and children generally remain year-round in the colony, where the average education is high-school level; those receiving formal educations are primarily boys, with girls homeschooled in female domestic traditions en route to becoming "stay-at-home moms," as they proudly post on Facebook.

Yet in recent years, a measure of liberalization has crept into Colonia LeBaron. Both boys and girls are increasingly seeking inexpensive community-college educations in Utah, Arizona, and Nevada. Young men become accustomed to their salaries and lifestyles in the US, as well as access to a larger pool of Mormon women, and young women are equally attracted to a modern version of Mormon fundamentalism, including polygamy, practiced primarily in the cities of the Southwest, such as Salt Lake, Las Vegas, and Phoenix. (This lifestyle has been portrayed by the television series *Big Love* and *Sister Wives*.) Still others are drawn to the enduring polygamous colonies of Short Creek and Hildale, where they have large extended families dating back generations. LeBaron women in their forties and fifties, including widows and common-law wives, often seek education and monogamy in the relatively more sophisticated Colonia Juárez, or move to the US to live with relatives.

Individual compounds in LeBaron are generally composed of five-acre plots surrounded on all sides by tall cottonwoods, elms, and fruit orchards, usually with two or three homes for separate but related polygamist families, where each wife has a home of her own with her children and the husband, who alternates overnight visits among the houses when in Mexico. The properties have expansive, landscaped lawns and expensive vehicles. Everyone is fluent in both Spanish and English, and the men swear and drink beer, unlike the vast majority of mainstream Mormons, who forswear alcohol. Traditionally, only Mexican-born LeBarons can own property in Colonia LeBaron, as the community was conceived by Dayer LeBaron Sr., and the most profitable land is held by the wealthiest LeBaron men, who own colossal walnut and pecan farms. Their land presently covers more than twelve thousand acres with 820,000 nut trees, according to marketing material from LeBaron Pecans. But that too has changed, as some of the colony's wives and widows have become powerful matriarchs in their own right.

It was during the three first years of Calderón's attempted crackdowns on the cartels that Joel LeBaron Soto emerged as a wealthy and leading patriarch of the clan, with his son Benji designated as bishop of the community church and the family spokesman. While drug-related violence ravaged much of Mexico, Colonia LeBaron appeared immune to it. Joel's personal agricultural empire grew and his fifty-two offspring from four wives—including one, Laura, who was a first cousin—proliferated. "A beautiful thing," as his son Julian once described his family to a television reporter. "There is no shame in it for us."

All of that was about to change.

* * *

On May 2, 2009, sixteen-year-old Eric LeBaron and a younger brother, two sons of Joel Jr., were hauling fenceposts to the family's Parapetos ranch near Colonia LeBaron. Suddenly, five armed men seized Eric and ordered his brother to run home and tell their father to answer the phone when it rang. According to the family's account, the kidnappers called and demanded a million-dollar ransom, or they would kill Eric. "The next day, 150 men gathered at the church house in Colonia LeBaron to debate what to do," reported the *Washington Post*. "One of their members, Ariel Ray, the mayor of nearby Galeana, reminded them that someone had put an empty coffin in the bed of his pickup. Some men argued that they should hire professional bounty hunters from the United States to get Eric back. Others wanted to form a posse."

Several family members spoke to the press. "If you give them a cookie, they'll want a glass of milk," said Craig LeBaron, one of Eric's brothers, referring to the cartels. "If we don't make a stand here, it's only a matter of time before it's my kid." Another brother, Julian, agreed, stating, "We knew the last thing we could do was give them the money, or we would be invaded by this scum." Eric's cousin Brent LeBaron said they needed to "sever the head of this monster right now."

The extortion attempts directed at the LeBarons had begun several months earlier, as the Mexican military presence on the US–Mexico border pushed the cartels into the once-tranquil countryside and drew the family into the government's war with the cartels. The Mormon communities in Sonora and Chihuahua—both the mainstream Mormons and fundamentalist colonies—were soon surrounded by violence. Kidnappings of Mormons became commonplace, along with other attempts at shakedowns aimed at the wealthiest among them.

While the community's men debated how to respond to Eric's kidnapping, a strange and distant figure—a businessman named Keith Raniere, based in Albany, New York—contacted Benji LeBaron and offered to help him secure Eric's release. Raniere, who led a personal and professional development company called NXIVM (pronounced NEHK-see-uhm), sent representatives to interview Benji and other LeBaron family members and invited several of them to Albany. The forty-eight-year-old Raniere had been involved in pyramid schemes since his twenties, including a stint with Amway and then as a founder of companies that were investigated and shut down in twenty different states.

It was not the first time the LeBarons had "latched onto self-help groups," according to a family member. Several LeBarons had joined the San Francisco–based Landmark personal development program founded by Werner Erhard, who had also created the EST program—the Erhard Seminars Training—which offered sessions on personal transformation in the 1970s. Raniere claimed to be one of the smartest people in the world, according to an esoteric IQ test, and he boasted that he had been able to speak in full sentences at the age of one, could spell the word *homogenized* by age two, understood quantum physics by age four, and had learned three years of college math and several computer languages by the age of thirteen. Billing himself as "one of the top three problem solvers in the world," the long-haired, bespectacled Raniere's latest scam had been prospering for a decade by the time he turned up in Colonia LeBaron. He was selling workshops called Executive Success Programs, or ESP, a motivational scheme under the umbrella of NXIVM. Raniere had thousands of followers who collectively had paid millions of dollars to NXIVM, which blended Ayn Rand, Scientology, the cosmology of Joseph Smith's early Mormonism about eternal progression, and other metaphysical doctrines.

"Raniere and the NXIVM community provided the LeBaron family with support and encouragement, assuring them that the only way the people in Mexico could stop the violence of the drug cartels and armed gangs was through peaceful protest," recalled yet another of Eric's brothers, Wayne LeBaron. Raniere convinced the LeBarons that the Mexican Government, especially at the local level, was corrupted by the powerful cartels, and that a peace movement was their only path forward. "Keith taught us much about violence, fear and apathy," said Wayne. "My experience of him was truly a bright, intelligent man who understands people and the world and its problems. I was especially moved at how deeply he wants to help the world be a better place."

Raniere dispatched a high-level NXIVM insider to Colonia LeBaron to document the family's crusade against the cartels. Mark Vicente, a South African filmmaker, had been recruited by Raniere four years earlier after Vicente had released a pseudoscientific documentary titled *What the Bleep Do We Know!?: Discovering the Endless Possibilities for Altering Your Everyday Reality.* The talking heads in the documentary included a New Age figure claiming to channel a 35,000-year-old Lemurian warrior named Ramtha, which was the name of the spiritual organization Vicente belonged to before joining NXIVM. The film became an indie phenomenon, earning almost $16 million worldwide, and served as an advertisement for Ramtha, based in Yelm, Washington. Its messaging was similar to that of NXIVM—that by changing your thinking, you could change reality.

Vicente had left Ramtha to join NXIVM and rose swiftly in its hierarchy. Soon, the attractive gray-haired Vicente, a born seeker, was sitting on the executive board, becoming so close to NXIVM's leader that he was widely considered Raniere's heir apparent. "His teachings are mysterious, filled with self-serving and impenetrable jargon about ethics and values, and defined by a blind-ambition ethos akin to that of the driven characters in an Ayn Rand novel," according to a *Forbes* profile of Raniere, described as a "corporate Svengali." The magazine's 2003 cover story, entitled "The World's Strangest Executive Coach," was the first to call NXIVM a cult. "Raniere's long, brown hair and beard make him look a little like Jesus, and his thoughtful demeanor could let him pass for a philosophy professor—or maybe a slacker poet."

When Raniere tapped Vicente in the summer of 2009 to travel to Colonia LeBaron, the latter had already been in Mexico since the previous year, filming testimonials about NXIVM's ESP workshops held there. Like Raniere, who had also traveled to the colony, Vicente was drawn to the LeBarons, as they seemed to be challenging cartel violence. Thirty-two-year-old Benji, as the spiritual head of the community, led the family's response to Eric's kidnapping. Raniere offered him advice on how to respond while refusing to pay the million-dollar ransom. Benji wholeheartedly embraced Raniere's counsel. "If we pay, we will make it so that tomorrow they will come to take the same money again from us," Benji said. "The easiest thing for anybody is to take your right to life. If we pay, we finance at least three more kidnappings."

Raniere convinced Benji that Colonia LeBaron was unable to keep its citizens safe, and that the LeBarons, as Mexican citizens, needed to take complete charge of their personal security. He said he could teach them not only how to stand up for themselves, but also how to be an example to all of Mexico. "What you want to do is you want to snuff out the motivation for violence in Mexico," Raniere told Benji. "So, what you want to do, you want to take the air out of it." He presented Benji with four options for addressing the fear created by the criminals. "The first was denial; the Mexican people could simply deny they were being terrorized and were in fear," he said. "Second was to embrace the fear, but this would mean giving into the fear. The third was to fight back, but this would lead to more violence. The fourth option was to meet the fear with a form of character, a strong

compassion that is resistant to fear." That fourth option, which Raniere himself advocated, was linked to Raniere's advice never to pay ransom money. "If
people stopped paying ransom, the kidnappings would stop."

But Raniere was wrong.

Raniere laid out a model for organizing against the cartels, and he
instructed Benji to create an organization called SOS Chihuahua—for
Sociedad Organizada Segura de Chihuahua, or Secure Organized Society of
Chihuahua. In just two weeks, SOS gained 4,200 members from communities throughout Chihuahua. Benji wrote a manifesto that urged SOS members
to stand up to the cartels, to arm and defend themselves, and, most notably,
to report crimes and pass along tips to law enforcement—encouraging dozens of local citizens to become informants and effectively painting the entire
LeBaron family as the same.

Benji organized a caravan of hundreds of Colonia LeBaron residents,
along with fundamentalist and mainstream Mormons from nearby communities as well as NXIVM members who had traveled from New York to participate. They marched to the state capital, Chihuahua City, to protest Eric's
kidnapping and demand that the authorities take action—a highly unusual
example of public posturing for the private and guarded LeBaron clan.
Vicente filmed Benji and the LeBaron family as their peace campaign gained
steam. Benji's slight stature belied his forceful nature. "What we are saying is:
Not a single kidnapping more!" he shouted to the wildly enthusiastic crowd
during the march to the state capital.

Chihuahua's governor and attorney general met with the group and
promised Benji they would conduct a thorough search for Eric and his kidnappers. They erected roadblocks and dispatched helicopters, police officers,
and soldiers to the Galeana area. Eight days after his abduction, Eric was mysteriously released. Family members insisted they had not paid a ransom, and
Eric reported that his kidnappers had simply told him to go home—a claim
contradicted by one of the confessed kidnappers, Carlos Andrés Butchereit,
who, when later arrested, told prosecutors the family had in fact paid $16,400
for Eric's release.

Julian LeBaron gave numerous interviews to the Mexican press, portraying the LeBarons as innocent victims and as morally exceptional. He

maintained that Eric was "liberated without payment because . . . he convinced his kidnappers to release him," Julian told Spanish journalist Lolita Bosch. But media skeptics doubted that the teenager's unique powers of persuasion had resulted in his release. "The Mexican people were amazed that we were able to get the government to react so quickly and with so much zest to resolve our problem," Wayne LeBaron recalled. "They came to us, dozens of families every day, to ask us how we managed" to get Eric released, he said, describing SOS as a "tremendous success."

Benji was elated and emboldened by this course of events, and he emphasized the role of Raniere's guidance. But the peace was short-lived. The following month, Meredith Romney—a seventy-two-year-old Colonia Juárez native and a distant relative of former US presidential candidate Mitt Romney—was kidnapped from his ranch near Janos, Chihuahua. A bishop in the Mormon church, Meredith Romney had served as president of the local LDS Temple. Gunmen shot out the tires of Romney's truck and forced him into their vehicle, leaving behind his wife and grandson. Held overnight in a cave, he was released the following day after his family paid an undisclosed ransom amount. In response, Benji became increasingly outspoken and further enmeshed with Raniere and NXIVM. "Keith, along with his team of people took us in and spent many days, much work and effort to teach us for 4-5 weeks what he believed would help us deal with our safety issues in an area of the country of Mexico that is overtaken by criminals, and do it in a nonviolent but firm way," Wayne LeBaron later wrote.

"People began to call us," an anonymous source from the LeBaron family told the *New York Times* during that summer of 2009. "They figured we could pressure the government on their behalf. We started to handle kidnapping and extortion cases. Then we felt we were going to begin to get into a dangerous situation. We were afraid that the family would be killed. But Benji said, 'I feel their pain. I can't let them down.' " Benji lived up to this promise. He was featured prominently in the local and national media, giving interviews about his anticrime activism. He had become a household name in the region for his outspoken advocacy in favor of relaxed gun laws and easier access to illegal weapons. The fact that peace was seen to go hand-in-hand with more guns was a sign of how most people mistrusted elected officials and law enforcement to keep them safe from the cartels. Benji gave high-profile speeches, and on July 1, 2009, he led a massive rally to the Government Palace in Chihuahua City to call for new gun legislation as a means of fighting the cartels. "We had to go to the government and say, 'Hey, you won't allow us to bear arms, but you're supposed to protect us," said Benji's cousin Brent. Benji "became a hero for the many in Chihuahua sickened by gangsters and violence," according to one account. "But fame made targets of both Benji and his community."

* * *

Soon after he arrived at Colonia LeBaron in the summer of 2009, Mark Vicente began filming Keith Raniere in conversation with the LeBarons for what would become *Encender el Corazon* (*Ignite the Heart*), about the LeBarons' struggle at the height of Benji's activism. The film was financed by Raniere and a wealthy venture capitalist (and NXIVM member) named Emiliano Salinas. A son of former Mexican President Carlos Salinas de Gortari, Emiliano was a member of one of the nation's most powerful political dynasties. He was also the founder and self-described "general coordinator" of the Inlak-ech Movement for Peace—named, according to him, for a Mayan phrase that means "You are me, and I am you."

Two years earlier, Salinas had launched NXIVM's Executive Success Program in Mexico City, and he was identified on the organization's website as a member of its executive council and "co-owner" of the group's center in Mexico. Salinas, who has a PhD in economics from Harvard University, described ESP as "like a practical MBA." He recruited many wealthy friends and business connections into the group and was instrumental in expanding its reach throughout Mexico. Now, he and Raniere were paying Vicente to highlight Inlak-ech and NXIVM's work in Mexico, while also encouraging Benji's pro-gun peace marches. Vicente had begun shooting his docudrama as a series of discussions about the drug-related violence in Mexico, in order to promote Raniere and NXIVM and to elevate Salinas's profile for a possible political career on a platform of nonviolence.

While searching for Mexican citizens who were "doing what they can to challenge a common enemy," Vicente, Raniere, and Salinas settled on the LeBarons as pivotal characters in their film and chose to emphasize the role

Raniere played in securing Eric LeBaron's release. The original objective of the film, according to Vicente, "was to awaken the country from its 'apathy' in the face of crime." But it soon veered into a thinly veiled recruitment tool for Raniere—who insisted that his followers call him "Vanguard," a title taken from a favorite arcade game—and propaganda for Salinas's movement. Eager to claim credit for Eric's release, and hoping to use it to burnish his brand in Mexico, Raniere decided that Vicente should become completely immersed in the world of Colonia LeBaron.

Despite his courageous public face, Benji's private fears began seeping into his interviews with Vicente after Eric's release. "Everyone tells me not to show my face, that it is dangerous, that I should be careful," he told Vicente in one interview. "But someone has to show their face, and I'm not doing it because I'm a hero. I'm really afraid." While Eric's release was heralded as a major success, it also provoked cartel leaders. A similar mix of trepidation and determination was also evident in the candid interviews with Benji's mother, the poised and elegant family matriarch, Ramona Ray LeBaron Soto. "If I have to sacrifice my life or my sons' lives, I will do so to uphold correct principles," she said, looking into the camera.

"Undoubtedly, the violent cartel members noticed that Benjamin LeBaron had gained influence and popularity as an anti-crime activist and community leader," according to a court document filed years later relating to a NXIVM criminal case in New York State. "It was critical, therefore, for the armed cartels, whose currency is terror, to instill fear and to re-establish control over the peaceful villagers and farmers."

Vicente's crew filmed Benji's brother Julian discussing the danger the family faced, often in conversation with Raniere. "The pressure we put on the government was so strong . . . that they responded immediately," he said, pointing out how much the Juárez Cartel was adversely affected by the sudden scrutiny. Julian spoke of witnessing one of its leaders calling Benji and saying, "If we realize that you are causing problems for us, we are going to kill you." According to Julian, Benji assured the drug lord that the family intended no harm to their business. But it was too late.

"My brother told him: 'They kidnapped our brother, we needed to defend ourselves.'" But the narco boss was not assuaged.

* * *

On July 7, 2009, at 1 a.m.—less than a week after Benji's large rally in Chihuahua City—four trucks carrying twenty heavily armed men arrived in Colonia LeBaron. Wearing helmets and bulletproof vests and dressed like police officers, the intruders began breaking the windows of Benji's expansive new home and wielding sledgehammers against the front door. Benji was inside with his wife Miriam ("Miri") and their five sons, all under the age of eight. The assailants demanded to be let in, saying they would use a hand grenade if he didn't open the door.

The men pried the front door open, and, once inside, they began beating Benji and threatening to rape Miri in front of the children unless Benji led them to his arsenal of weapons. Hearing the commotion, a neighbor called Benji's twenty-nine-year-old brother-in-law, Luis "Wiso" Widmar Stubbs, who lived nearby and who, along with his brother, Lawrence "Lenzo" Widmar Stubbs, rushed to Benji's aid. "A linebacker-sized martial arts devotee," as one account described him, Wiso tried to fend off Benji's attackers with his bare hands. Both he and Benji were bound hand and foot and thrown into one of the trucks, while Lenzo was wounded but managed to flee in his vehicle. Benji and Wiso were driven a couple of miles away, tortured, and each was shot four times in the head. Their bodies were left at the side of the road at the junction of the Casas Grandes–Flores Magón highway.

"Amid the blood and mesquite at the site of his last breath, Benjamin LeBaron's killers posted a sign that read: 'This is for the leaders of LeBaron who didn't believe and who still don't believe,'" according to a news story that Arizona Senator John McCain read into the *Congressional Record* as evidence of the rampant violence across his state's border with Mexico. "They taped a big sign right here that said, 'this is for messin' with Chapo Guzmán's people' or some stupid shit," Julian LeBaron told a reporter. A note next to Benji's body blamed him for the recent arrest of twenty-five cartel gunmen seized in the Chihuahua municipality of Nicolas Bravo. In Ciudad Juárez, three hours north of Colonia LeBaron, hand-painted banners threatening the LeBaron clan were hung from overpasses.

While Mexico's Federal Government had helped secure Eric LeBaron's release, it stood silent after Benji was murdered. A video camera at a highway tollbooth captured the attackers' departure from the area where Benji's body was dumped, clearly identifying the makes and models of their vehicles, as well as legible license plates. Federal law enforcement officials were quick to place the blame publicly on El Chapo's Sinaloa Cartel, which was fighting the Juárez Cartel for smuggling routes into El Paso. That claim was immediately contradicted by members of local law enforcement in the state of Chihuahua, which blamed the Juárez Cartel.

Within a few months, there would be arrests of at least two suspects in the murders, including Carlos Butchereit, a thirty-one-year-old native of Galeana and self-proclaimed *sicario* with the Juárez Cartel. Butchereit, a cousin of Benji's father, Joel LeBaron Soto, described the killing as "personal," explaining that he and Benji were "business partners in the US," and that Joel had threatened him. He told prosecutors that the murder was an act of "revenge" ordered by a cartel boss who had had a "falling out" with Joel. The State Attorney General Patricia Gonzalez announced that the murderers were members of *La Línea*—the armed enforcement wing of the Juárez Cartel, made up of former police officers and *sicarios*. Her credibility was challenged, though, since just a few months earlier, Gonzalez had portrayed *La Línea* as "an exhausted remnant of dead-enders whose ranks had been decimated by infighting and arrests." In response to Gonzalez, more banners appeared in Ciudad Juárez, reading (in Spanish), "Mrs. Prosecutor, avoid problems for yourself, and don't blame La Línea," and claiming that the murders were carried out by the Sinaloa Cartel.

The funerals for Benji and Wiso were the largest ever held in Colonia LeBaron, surpassing even that of the Prophet Joel LeBaron. More than two thousand people attended, including the state's governor, who had personally guaranteed to provide Benji and his family with security, as well as the state's attorney general. Eulogies included "multiple mentions of tears and blood," wrote Javier Ortega Urquidi, a scholar of Mormons in Mexican culture. Urquidi observed how the funeral brought together "the living, the formerly kidnapped, and the dead," writing that the "Mormons' blood smolders under the sun, under the surface."

A woman holds a picture of Benjamin LeBaron, left, and his brother-in-law Luis "Wiso" Widmar, during their funeral services in Galeana, Mexico, July 9, 2009. The two had been murdered two days earlier, while Keith Raniere of NXIVM was advising them and Mark Vicente was filming their anticrime activism. *(Associated Press)*

Nathan LeBaron, a relative, helped direct the hundreds of cars arriving for the funeral. Benji "was so outspoken, that was the reason for this," he told a reporter. "If we hadn't stood up, they wouldn't have bothered us." Brent LeBaron agreed, saying they were fighting kidnapping and extortion, not the drug cartels, but that "Benjamin had the savvy for speaking, so he did speak a little more than he should have." Still, he said no one in the community expected the killings. "We kind of felt we were a little at risk, but never thought these brutes would come in like this. It's been a community effort. We tried to make it so not just one person was the target."

Ramona LeBaron Soto, Benji's heartbroken mother, searched for meaning in her son's murder. "It's hard for me to understand, to see that there are people in this world that are so cruel and without feeling," she said in Vicente's film. "But within, I pity them. I pity them because they don't know how to live. They don't know or understand what happiness is."

Adrian LeBaron Soto eulogized his nephew Benji, and Wiso. "The men who murdered them have no children, no parents, no mother," he said. "They are the spawn of evil." All agreed that the two men had died valiantly while trying to protect the community. "They had a cause, they stood up for it, they were killed for it," said one relative about Benji's SOS movement. "And he's a martyr, as far as I'm concerned."

Eric LeBaron, whose kidnapping had set off this sequence of events, evoked the martyrdom of his grandfather, Joel the Prophet. "We aren't leaving. We are going to remain here and do what my grandpa said . . . that he would need to seal his testimony with his own blood." Julian agreed that Benji had followed in Joel Sr.'s footsteps. "He died trying to give us our freedom."

Inside the meeting hall where the service was held, small paper fans were handed out to attendees, quoting some of the last words spoken by Benji in his final interview with NXIVM filmmaker Mark Vicente: "I prefer to die a slave of principle, than to live a slave of men."

After the funeral, more banners appeared on highway overpasses in Ciudad Juárez, drawing attention to the LeBarons' wealth.

"Ask yourself," one said, "where did all his properties come from?"

CHAPTER SEVEN

NXIVM: Ignite the Heart

※

WHEN BENJI LEBARON was just fifteen years old, he had a premonition that his life would be cut short. His mother noticed one day that he was exceedingly sad, and she sat with him on his bed, imploring him to tell her what was wrong. "Mom, I have a feeling that I will not live many years," he told her. Ramona recalled the moment on camera for Mark Vicente's *Ignite the Heart* film. "He knew he had a mission to do something worthy. Something bigger."

To Ramona, Benji's vision revealed that he possessed the spiritual keys to the kingdom, inheriting them as a direct descendant of his grandfather, Joel LeBaron Sr., the founder and martyred Prophet of the Church of the Firstborn. "I know he is okay," apparently referring to her son in the hereafter. "We have to wake up. We have to think more about the future. . . . Is this how we want to live? It's hell in many places. And we ourselves as humanity are choosing that. We have to wake up."

Her son Julian, Benji's younger brother, reluctantly took up his sibling's "activist mantle," as one account put it. Egged on by Keith Raniere and motivated by the ideologies taught by NXIVM, Julian assumed Benji's leadership role within SOS. Agreeing to carry the family torch, while admitting to the press that he feared for his life, the husky farmer turned peace activist and freelance writer gradually embraced his new high-profile position. "They died like martyrs," Julian said of the two murdered men. He accused Colonia LeBaron's neighbors of colluding with the cartel against the family.

Following the bloody blowback to their counsel, Raniere and Vicente might have been expected to retreat back to Albany. Instead, they were undaunted. The murders only led them to further entrench themselves in Colonia LeBaron, and Vicente continued filming Raniere's meetings with the LeBarons. Vicente found the LeBaron story "moving and devastating," saying it had reminded him of experiences in his native South Africa. The atrocities he had witnessed in his homeland propelled him "to question certain fundamental assumptions at a very young age," he would write, and beliefs "about human behavior, morality, cosmology, existentialism and mysticism." Like Vicente, Julian LeBaron was also an easy mark for NXIVM's Executive Success Program recruiters. The two were introduced by Benji, who was killed just a few weeks after filming had begun, and Julian accompanied Vicente "dozens of times," according to one account, to meet with ESP executives in Mexico and with Raniere himself in New York. Raniere coached Julian on how to expand Benji's SOS protest organization across Mexico. "The main thing is, we want to be respected. And in Mexico, nobody's respected. We're not respected by the criminals and we're not respected by the government," would become one of Julian's oft-repeated laments.

While Julian and NXIVM were extending the SOS peace movement across the country, Julian was also trying to persuade the Mexican Government to give the LeBarons official permission to arm themselves, although surely the colony was well armed, dating back to the days of violence and threats from Ervil LeBaron and his followers, if not before. Alex LeBaron, a twenty-eight-year-old cousin of Julian's, was already dedicated to the cause of gun rights, and he now worked closely with Julian on the matter. A graduate of New Mexico State University—Las Cruces and a full-time pecan farmer, Alex had ventured into local, regional, and then national politics as a political adviser to Mexico's Institutional Revolutionary Party (PRI). As the owner of various agribusinesses, he was the leader of a movement focused on defending the rights of the agricultural sector and would soon join the administration of the PRI governor of Chihuahua, César Duarte Jáquez. But Alex would become a member of the federal congress primarily to push for legislation for the right to bear arms. A "burly and baby-faced politician," as NPR described him, Alex passionately argued for changing Mexico's gun laws because, as he told reporters, his father was murdered during a carjacking in Sonora in 2005. "We're Mexican citizens 100 percent," he said in 2012, "and we have the right to bear arms, and we're going to keep fighting for that right as long as it takes."

There is "really no law in Mexico that gives you the right to bear arms," Brent LeBaron told a reporter. One of the only legal ways to obtain guns was to prove membership in a rifle club or shooting range, an extremely convoluted process that involved months of background checks. There was only one official gun store in the entire country, and it was run by the Mexican Army from within a guarded fortress on a military base outside of Mexico City. So those who needed guns looked northward, to the world's most gun-obsessed nation. Mexican officials estimated that for every gun sold legally in Mexico, hundreds were being smuggled into the country from the US and ending up in the hands of the cartels. Targeted by the cartels, the LeBarons felt they had no choice but to take up arms in violation of Mexican law. Benji had been pushing for laxer gun laws, and his murder only increased the LeBaron calls for more guns. "We hit a real big low when they killed Benjamin," Brent said. "It was a real blow to our entire community." While waiting for permission to accumulate guns, the family began turning their colony "into a little fortress, using the same counter terrorist techniques the US Army uses in Iraq and Afghanistan," according to one account. Marco, one of Benji's brothers and a college student in the States, returned to Colonia LeBaron to organize a seventy-man militia to police the community.

The LeBaron militia patrolled the colony, setting up roadblocks and checkpoints as well as a watch hut on a hill overlooking one of the main drug-trafficking roads nearby. They were on the lookout for suspicious vehicles carrying well-armed *sicarios*. "We pretty much know everybody," Brent said. Their efforts appeared to be successful from the start. "Rumor got out that we had high powered rifles, snipers, and 50 cals [.50-caliber weapons] up here. You know how rumors can spread, which was a really good rumor for us, which was a benefit for us. I believe the watch tower is one of the key points in keeping the bad guys away from our town."

While waiting for the laws to change, the LeBarons would stockpile guns on their own. "It's very easy to acquire mostly American-made weapons here in our country," Alex told a reporter. "People in the drug organizations, including in the military, know that we have weapons because we've been saying it, that we have illegal weapons in our community. Come in and find them if you want. We buy them in the States, we know we traffic them illegally, but that's the only way to defend yourself in this country." Soon enough, Colonia LeBaron made clear it was "locked and loaded," though in an ironic and tragic manner. Less than three months after Benji's murder, on the moonless night of October 9, 2009, a squad of Mexican soldiers came to the front gate of the home of Alex's brother, DJ, and the family opened fire, reportedly fearing those outside were kidnappers. The LeBarons claimed the soldiers did not identify themselves and, as Alex put it, "in the middle of [the] dark, sometimes it's better to shoot and ask questions later." Shots were fired by both sides, leaving one soldier dead and another wounded.

The LeBarons watched as the two bodies were loaded into a military pickup. "My heart just dropped to the ground," recalled DJ. "I was, like, 'Oh fuck.' . . . 'We're in deep shit.'" DJ was charged with murder, but a judge dropped the case, apparently determining the shooting was accidental. As DJ was leaving the jail, a soldier gave him what he took to be a fateful message. "One guy looked at me directly in the eye. He's like, 'You're probably getting out right now. But we're going to fucking get you out there,'" DJ told the journalist Ioan Grillo. The military held a grudge for a long time, DJ claimed. "One of their guys got killed. . . . I did hear rumors for a lot of years that they were planning some retaliation," DJ recalled many years later. As for the cartels, Alex told a journalist at the time, "We got phone calls from the heads of the criminal organizations after that incident, and they told us they were proud of us."

Eventually, Julian's lobbying of the Mexican Government paid off, in the form of a new federal police and military base in Colonia LeBaron. After the shootout at DJ LeBaron's house, the kidnapping and the violence stopped. While some attributed the calm to the police presence in the colony, the LeBarons insisted it was their forceful message to the criminals that the family was determined to fight back. Already accustomed to living as outcasts after decades of familial civil war and bloodletting during the reign of Ervil LeBaron, "everyone became a watchman," said one of the community leaders.

Children riding bicycles in Colonia LeBaron on July 17, 2009, while a military patrol guards them. *(Adriana Zehbrauskas/New York Times)*

* * *

For the next eight years, Colonia LeBaron heeded the warning "in the clearest possible terms that they inhabited *tierra sin ley*—a lawless land," the BBC reported. The cartel's message to the LeBaron family was unmistakable: Don't interfere with our business or our transportation routes. Don't snitch to the police or draw attention to us. "To defy such a warning will cost you your life."

Vicente would spend those eight years, and several million dollars of NXIVM money, making *Ignite the Heart*, set in Colonia LeBaron against the backdrop of Mexico's raging drug war. "My brother and best friend were killed with a bullet in their heads," Julian says in the film. "I don't pay ransom and I ask you never to pay one for me."

That Keith Raniere's advice to the LeBaron family had resulted in the execution-style murder of Benji was conspicuously overlooked. Based on what Raniere said in a 2009 home video shot before Benji's murder and later leaked to YouTube, he may have understood that violence was one possible outcome: "I've had people killed for my beliefs, and because of their beliefs and for theirs. You might say . . . the brighter the light, the more the bugs." In Vicente's film, which overall was not nearly as forthright, Julian turned out to be a perfect protagonist, an empathetic character who had faced inconceivable suffering yet refused to be broken. Modestly educated but not unskilled—he had "built more than 200 houses since he was a child"—Julian's talent as a contractor and his steady call for justice were widely admired.

At a time when more than ten thousand Americans were enrolled in his various training programs, Raniere focused on expansion in Mexico, where leaders of NXIVM, including Salinas, promised "empowerment" and "self-actualization." The organization set out to train participants to break the cycle of violence in their country, using the LeBaron experience as an example, despite what that experience had actually entailed. Its "emphasis on 'readiness' resonated in a place where mass murder and kidnapping meant people always had to be on high alert," as a lawyer for Raniere would later describe NXIVM's appeal. But another observer thought that the "group's Randian emphasis on financial success as a moral good might also have had something to do with it."

Whatever the attraction, NXIVM's success was quick and extensive, especially within the Mexican ruling class. Salinas recruited his sister, Cecilia, and two other children of former Mexican presidents: Ana Cristina Fox, daughter of Vicente Fox, and Federico de la Madrid, son of Miguel de la Madrid. Rosa Laura Junco, the daughter of the man who founded *Grupo Reforma*, Latin America's second-largest print-media company, also joined. Raniere had been "playing and positioning his devoted follower Emiliano Salinas as his pawn for years while Emi's family groomed him to follow in his father's political footsteps," wrote actress Catherine Oxenberg, who took NXIVM courses herself but later became an outspoken critic of the organization, particularly after her daughter India left the cult in 2018. With Emiliano Salinas leading the way, the country's political elite embraced Raniere and gave him entrée into adjacent wealthy and influential circles.

Critical to NXIVM's reach was the financial support it received from two heiresses to the multibillion-dollar Seagram's liquor fortune. Over a period of fifteen years, Clare and Sara Bronfman invested more than $100 million into Raniere's organization. NXIVM's financial support would help launch

Julian LeBaron onto the national stage. Julian announced his new role leading the SOS organization with a "Petition to the Mexican People" that was
published in the *Dallas Morning News* in April 2010. "I am petitioning those
who are victims of murder, kidnapping or extortion, by people who force
the involuntary sacrifice of our good, so they can live further entrenched in
their evil and ruin the lives of those who know how to live, for the benefit
of parasites who do not," he wrote. "This year marks the anniversary of our
independence in 1810, as well as that of our revolution in 1910." He appealed
directly to the Mexican president. "President Calderón recently said: 'I have
the will, but I need men.' My response is: I love my country, Señor. Here in
Chihuahua, there is a man you can count on."

Lenzo Widmar, brother of Luis Widmar, who had been murdered by the
cartels alongside his brother-in-law Benji, echoed Julian's revolutionary tone
when interviewed for Vicente's film. "Two hundred years ago, Mexico had
to fight. One hundred years ago, Mexico needed to fight again. This time, we
just want to fight differently."

The following year, Julian yoked SOS to a new, larger, nationwide peace
movement led by Mexico's best-known and most-revered poet and author,
Javier Sicilia. Named "Person of the Year 2011," by America's *Time* magazine, Sicilia created the Movement for Peace with Justice and Dignity after
his twenty-four-year-old son was killed by drug traffickers in March 2011.
His son, along with six friends, was tortured and murdered by men who were
angry that two among them had informed on them—and to protest Felipe
Calderón's bloody "five-year-long military campaign against Mexico's narco-
cartels" that was aggravating the violence. In just three months, Sicilia's rallies
grew from a few hundred protesters to hundreds of thousands.

As soon as Julian heard the poet speak, he knew he wanted to join his
movement and surround himself with people like him. "He traveled and met
Sicilia, saw Javier and did not say a word, they just hugged, cried," reported
the high-profile newspaper *Milenio*. With Vicente there to document every
step of his journey, Julian "left his home, his wife, his children, his job, his
small business to join the movement with which he traveled thousands of
kilometers in the country, articulating a national movement of victims of the
war against drug trafficking during the administration of Felipe Calderón."

NXIVM: IGNITE THE HEART

Inspired by Sicilia, Julian began writing poetry. "I believe that poetry has a power to heal wounds and also to console," he said. The two men met with President Calderón for a historic series of conversations about the cartels. Julian was increasingly visible at events; his national profile surpassed that of Benji's as he became the movement's second-best-known public figure behind Sicilia.

Coached by Raniere, Julian was simultaneously an agitator who refused to hate his enemies and a loud voice demanding the right to bear arms. Several Mexican journalists focused on the jarring contrast, as well as Raniere's strange involvement with Mexico's political and cultural elite. Vicente's footage of Raniere showed him "slightly disheveled and mild-mannered—surrounded by adoring Mexican followers," wrote journalist León Krauze after viewing *Ignite the Heart*. "Raniere indeed offers a solution of sorts for Mexico's troubles: Follow his teachings to the letter. In his messianic scheme, the country would become an experiment."

Emiliano Salinas was certainly committed to following Raniere's teachings to the letter, proclaiming on his personal website that Raniere was a powerful voice against violence and corruption in Mexico. In 2010, he gave a TED-Ed talk about violence in Mexico, called "A Civil Response to Violence," which was filmed in San Miguel de Allende and was the first TED talk delivered in a language other than English. "Julian and Emiliano share the conviction that the world can be changed based on the modern and technological teachings of Keith Raniere," according to Mexican journalist Julio Hernández López, who described NXIVM as a "New Age sect that basically seeks economic enrichment through quackery for pretentious dupes."

Salinas's Inlak-ech movement financed Vicente's film and Julian LeBaron's activism. "What we are doing with Julian LeBaron is supporting him with his expenses, mainly his family. In order for him to carry out the mission he leads, he needs to stop working and we are also supporting him financially so that he can continue with this project, we are coaching him at all times," an internal Inlak-ech document revealed. The organization also tried to sponsor Javier Sicilia's Movement for Peace with Justice and Dignity, which apparently did not sit well with the poet who had founded the movement.

In February 2012, Julian LeBaron broke with Sicilia's movement just eight months after he had joined it, following disagreements evidently related to Raniere's and Salinas's involvement. Julian claimed that he left because Sicilia had "abandoned the path of citizen organization," and because Sicilia's movement had become "an interlocutor of an incapable government." The split seemed inevitable. While Julian was advocating for importing more guns from America, Sicilia was protesting against the flow of thousands of weapons coming into Mexico every year from the United States. A nonprofit called the Angelica Foundation, based in Santa Fe, New Mexico, stepped in to support Sicilia's "bi-national grassroots campaign" and financed a film called *El Poeta*, about Sicilia, at the same time Vicente was making *Ignite the Heart*, centered on Julian LeBaron.

Although Julian was offered positions in the Mexican Federal Government, he refused to join what he referred to as "the political class." His activism remained the cornerstone of the *Ignite the Heart* documentary, which became a marketing video for NXIVM and a vehicle for exalting Raniere, even as Vicente continued filming. Before there was a finished product, Emiliano Salinas, staff from his Inlak-ech organization, and Vicente traveled across Mexico promoting the forthcoming film, showing trailers and filmed testimonials from those appearing in it.

* * *

In early 2012, Shane Smith, founder of the media company VICE, brought a camera crew to Colonia LeBaron to film a nearly hour-long exposé called "The Mexican Mormon War: The Cartels of Ciudad Juárez, Mexico Are at War with a Group of Mormons, Some of Whom are Related to Mitt Romney." Romney, who was the Republican nominee for president that year, had taken a hardline anti-immigration stance, which Smith intended to reveal as hypocritical, given his family history in the Mexican Mormon colonies dating back to the late 1800s, with Romney's own father immigrating to the US in 1912.

Priding itself on gonzo journalism for the social-media era, VICE secured what seemed to be extraordinary access to the notoriously camera-shy polygamists. "Maybe one of the reasons that Mitt Romney is so concerned about the drug war that is taking place just south of the American border is because it affects him and his family personally," Smith explained to the camera between expletives, pointing out that one of Romney's distant cousins—Meredith Romney—had been kidnapped just three years earlier.

Despite the LeBaron family's decades of secrecy bordering on paranoia—and in contrast to their relationship with the press in Mexico and media from other nations—Julian, Alex, and Brent LeBaron eagerly welcomed the VICE team. The cousins all agreed to interviews and, not surprisingly, used the opportunity as a platform to push for relaxed gun laws. They spoke of how the narcotraffickers have state-of-the-art weaponry—"50 cals, assault rifles, military grade machine guns"—while the Mormons are not allowed legally to own guns. Still, they claimed that rumors of their own "50 cals" served the colony's purposes. Smith was quick to demonstrate that the LeBarons were not observant Mormons, his crew capturing them during a night of drinking at a bar in nearby Nuevo Casas Grandes, singing karaoke while taking shots of tequila while Smith drunkenly toasted the LeBaron family "because you guys fuckin' rock!" After a brief ride-along with federal police on a routine patrol, Smith and his crew quickly fled back across the border.

The VICE report was popular in the US, where it was viewed millions of times on YouTube, introducing the modern LeBaron clan to a broad American audience. Conspicuously missing from VICE's report was any hint that the NXIVM documentary crew was filming at Colonia LeBaron during the same period.

As the NXIVM movement in Mexico gained steam, Raniere and Vicente ramped up their work on *Ignite the Heart*. Though Raniere was still a relatively unknown figure in the United States, soon more than half of Raniere's closest associates were Mexican, many with a high profile. In February 2012, he came under closer scrutiny in the United States, when, under the title "Secrets of NXIVM," the Albany *Times Union* began an investigative series on the life and exploits of Raniere and the mystery surrounding his compound in that city. But the stories were not picked up by other newspapers and failed to gain national traction.

After a year of research, the Albany newspaper reported Raniere's boasts of having the highest IQ in the world and intellectual energy capable of setting off police speed radars. The *Times Union* estimated that NXIVM had ten thousand paying members in the US, at a time when Mexican newspapers suggested that the number was even higher in Mexico.

Forbes had previously drawn attention to NXIVM, finding that "some people see a darker and more manipulative side" to the would-be guru who ran "a cult-like program aimed at breaking down his subjects psychologically" while "inducting them into a bizarre world of messianic pretensions, idiosyncratic language and ritualistic practices." Like the *Times Union* series, the *Forbes* story was largely overlooked as NXIVM continued growing. Fueled by the seemingly inexhaustible Bronfman money, Raniere became what is known as a vexatious frequent litigant—a plaintiff who brings frivolous lawsuits solely to harass antagonists—managing successfully to sue his increasing number of critics and keeping negative publicity about NXIVM off the front pages of America's mainstream press.

In Mexico, the Inlak-ech movement continued to advertise *Ignite the Heart,* which was still in production. While Vicente and Salinas traveled across Mexico promoting the film and their organizations, they also showcased Julian LeBaron as a central figure in fighting rampant extortion, kidnapping, and violence by the cartels. Julian's so-called peace movement would itself raise nine million pesos for the film's production and distribution.

Vicente appeared before large audiences at exclusive hotels, black-tie events, and cultural centers during his fundraising drive. He told audiences that the completed film would premiere on July 7, 2016—the seventh anniversary of Benji's murder—in the small community of Galeana, and then it would be screened all across the country.

* * *

Keith Raniere was spending a significant amount of time in Colonia LeBaron, flying down on the Bronfman sisters' private jet and getting to know many family members. He was focused on helping the LeBarons in their stand against kidnapping and violence, but what was less known was his fascination with their polygamous lifestyle, which he furtively practiced, in his own way, back in Albany. Raniere had reportedly been married three times, not simultaneously, although it was unclear whether the women were legal or common-law spouses. But by this point, he maintained a harem of more than a dozen women drawn from the NXIVM membership, and he had developed "radical ideas about polygamy, incest, sociopathy, and power," according to one account. He taught his followers that women were to be monogamous, while men were to be polygamous, contending that it was in men's nature to "spread their seed."

"They were introducing the idea of polygamy, but with a soft sell, laying the groundwork," as a former NXIVM member described the way Raniere was slowly revealing the practice to his followers. After witnessing the polygamous LeBaron culture firsthand, Raniere was particularly impressed by the way male dominance was woven into every aspect of it. He was drawn to the docility and submissiveness of the colony's women, seeing them as the embodiment of true femininity. When he lost interest in one of his concubines, he directed his inner circle to find a "young virgin successor" as a replacement. He then used the women with whom he was involved sexually to woo additional mates, like the sister-wives he witnessed in Mormon polygamy culture. Women who had sex with Raniere said it was "billed as a spiritual experience, a transfer of his Godlike energy," and that he used sex to manipulate women.

Raniere mined early Mormon doctrine, admiring and attempting to emulate Joseph Smith's salesmanship and sexual prowess. A decade before he visited Colonia LeBaron, Raniere had recruited underage Mormon girls in the United States into NXIVM, luring at least one teenager from a fundamentalist colony based in Utah.

"My family . . . might best be compared to the deer herds that populate the Wasatch mountains above Salt Lake," wrote Dorothy Allred Solomon of the passivity of the polygamous female. "The mothers were vigilant and hardworking, raising the young and enduring every type of hardship with courage and grace." LeBaron girls were taught from childhood that it was their birthright and honor, as God's chosen ones, to practice the Principle, which was "all about future glory," according to a plural wife from the colony. Plural marriage embodied the entirety of women's aspirations: They were to provide men with as many children as possible during their time on Earth in preparation for the celestial kingdom. Most wives gave birth to a baby every eighteen months, until the women were no longer fertile, with twelve being the average number of children among polygamists in Mormon fundamentalist communities in both Mexico and the United States. Irene Spencer, who had thirteen children, eventually came to see childbearing as a means of control. "No mother with that many children would dare try to leave the group," she wrote, recalling a time when Joel LeBaron Sr. advised his brother—her husband—about how to keep a disgruntled wife from running away. "Just keep her pregnant," Joel told Verlan. "Soon she'll have so many kids she won't be able to leave.

Polygamy is illegal in Mexico, but the government has tacitly ignored the Mormons' practice of plural marriage since the 1880s, when Mormon fundamentalists settled the 100,000 acres of land the LDS church had purchased for them in northern Chihuahua. Mexico had "spread her protecting wings over a persecuted people," is how Verlan described it. While the Mexican Government now frowns upon polygamy, it has not conducted the kind of antipolygamy raids and criminal arrests that members of US law enforcement have undertaken. Today, those dual Mexican and American citizens who practice polygamy stay within the current law of both countries by only legally marrying one person. Because only one of the polygamist's marriages is legal in the eyes of the government, many plural wives and their children are left with few options to leave if they are unhappy with the arrangement, since nothing protects their status as wives except their husbands' whims. If raised in polygamy themselves, most wives and children don't have birth certificates or Social Security numbers. As Jean Rio Baker and her polygamous daughter-in-law, Nicolena Baker, both discovered in nineteenth-century Utah, neither an unmarried woman nor a plural wife had any legal standing as a spouse, and even less protection and support from the church. All children of plural marriages are extensions of their mothers and are therefore owned by their fathers. Today, older polygamists average three or more wives, with patriarchal leaders collecting even more. "There is more heated competition for wives who grew up in polygamous families as children . . . since it is felt they are more likely to be harmonious 'sister wives,'" as one account put it. "Men often also seek actual sisters as wives on the theory that a woman might be more willing to share her husband with her sister than a strange woman."

The memoirs of women who have left Colonia LeBaron in the twenty-first century have provided revelations about girls as young as twelve becoming wives and delivering babies every other year well into their forties. Reports proliferate about men marrying underage girls and sometimes first cousins. LeBaron defectors have written about complex family dynamics in which the male patriarch dictates every move of the wives and children, including how the wives are expected to travel across the border into the US to pick up monthly welfare checks to support the family, while the husband's earnings in the US are brought home to Mexico tax-free—part of the enduring covenant of "bleeding the beast." One polygamist wife described the pervasive "welfare racket" of defrauding the US Government, saying, "All things are justified in the eyes of the Lord, as long as you're building up the Kingdom."

In this patriarchal system, every woman is expected to bond with her husband's other wives, as well as with all of the other women in the community who have also been raised in polygamous families. For them, motherhood is a patriotic and religious duty to bear and raise children for the Kingdom of God in these "latter days," though it is rarely practiced as preached. Jealousy between wives is taboo, but it cannot be extinguished, because women and their children are in constant competition for resources and affection. Polygamy is "patriarchy spun off into its furthest possible extreme," wrote a scholar who specializes in the physical and emotional abuse often caused by the practice. "Women are the commodity and the exchange rate . . . for the lord and master who reigns supreme over them."

Not all the LeBaron women today suffer their oppression quietly, or see themselves as oppressed in the first place. Many of the young daughters and wives of Colonia LeBaron resemble typical American teenagers and young adults, or even social media influencers, much more than the women in their fundamentalist sister communities in Arizona and Utah, who dress like nineteenth-century pioneers. The women of LeBaron wear miniskirts and heels and post glam shots and selfies on Facebook and Instagram. "This began in recent years when they wanted to be attractive to their husbands who are constantly exposed to the young women of Babylon," said an older plural wife from the colony, referring to the seasonal migration practices of the LeBaron men. "The girls want to be accepted. And slowly the devil crept in. From Puritans to flesh pots." Another daughter of a polygamist spoke about "date night shopping." The sister-wives go on shopping excursions together to boutiques and department stores in Phoenix and Las Vegas, after which "they dress each other up sexy for their scheduled night with their husband." Some of the women, though, are envious of the monogamous relationships they witness while visiting their husbands in the US. Just as the men drink and curse, some of the women in this fundamentalist community are more liberated, at least in some superficial respects.

* * *

Keith Raniere studied the LeBarons' polygamous lifestyle closely. The pretty young wives with their feminine clothing and modern hairstyles were polite to strangers, deferential to the men, sweet with the children, and affectionate with each other. The teenage girls were as fresh and lovely as young coeds everywhere, glued to their cell phones, trying out cosmetics, and flirting with the boys. In 2015, Raniere decided to create his own elite group of women followers, which sources said was based on the LeBaron model and, especially, on the cohesive unit of sister-wives who worked together on behalf of the patriarch. He chose a fake Latin name for his new secret sorority: *Dominus Obsequious Sororium*—translated as "Lord/Master of the Obedient Female Companions"—shortened into the acronym DOS. The group—Raniere's latest pyramid scheme—was also known as "The Vow." It consisted of successive levels of female "slaves" led by female "masters." Over the next three years, at least 102 women would be inititated into DOS, which one of Raniere's female masters described as "like the Freemasons but for women wanting to build character and change the world." Many of the recruits believed they were joining a women's mentorship program, and only later did they learn they were being groomed for sex with Raniere. The sisterhood was presented as a "force for good, one that could grow into a network that could influence events like elections," one recruit told the *New York Times*. "To become effective, members had to overcome weaknesses that Mr. Raniere taught were common to women—an overemotional nature, a failure to keep promises, and an embrace of the role of victim."

Raniere recruited eleven girls from Colonia LeBaron, ostensibly to work as nannies and teachers in a NXIVM offshoot program, a group of international schools called Rainbow Cultural Gardens, which was operating in Mexico, the United States, and the United Kingdom. Telling their fathers that the jobs would take them far away from Chihuahua's drug violence, Raniere flew them to Clifton Park, a mostly white suburb of Albany where NXIVM owned a compound that its members dubbed "the mothership." He had created Rainbow Cultural Gardens as an experimental institution for the children of wealthy NXIVM members, whose parents paid as much as $120,000 annual tuition for their prekindergarten-age kids to learn several languages. Raniere promoted the experimental schools as "breeding a new, more evolved generation that would speak more languages, live according to higher principles, and score higher on intelligence tests." Called Multidisciplinary Specialists, or MDIs, girls were hired from various countries, including those from Colonia LeBaron, to work as babysitters and to teach different languages, including Russian, German, Mandarin, Spanish, and Arabic, to children as young as three months old. The curriculum was built on Raniere's teachings and claimed to immerse children in nine languages at the same time.

In 2016, eleven girls, aged thirteen to seventeen, traveled from Colonia LeBaron to upstate New York and stayed in a mansion owned by Rosa Laura Junco, who operated the program in Mexico and arranged for the girls to teach Spanish. Within DOS, Junco was known as a "first line" slave of Raniere, and she answered directly to him. No teaching experience was necessary for the LeBaron girls, and the only screening process involved Raniere scrutinizing photographs of them. Once in Albany, the girls were "exposed to Raniere's pedophilic and misogynistic teachings," according to later court testimony related to sex-trafficking and child-pornography charges brought against Raniere. They were "being groomed to have sex with Raniere." Federal Prosecutor Moira Kim Penza argued that the LeBaron girls were "targeted specifically because, having been raised in a polygamist sect, they were more vulnerable to Raniere's teachings on sexuality, including that it is natural for women to be monogamous and for men to have more than one partner—a philosophy that served Raniere's own sexual preferences."

When the LeBaron "nannies" arrived in upstate New York, they found that several members of another wealthy and well-known family from central

Mexico had been ensconced at the compound for the previous seven years. This family's NXIVM members included a mother and father and one son, as well as three daughters who were simultaneously part of Raniere's sexual harem, with one of the underage sisters held in captivity and isolation against her will for nearly two years. The LeBaron girls were assigned to become "Delegates," a separate group created just for them within the Rainbow Cultural Gardens. India Oxenberg, the twenty-five-year-old daughter of the actress Catherine Oxenberg, was in charge of them. She put them on diets— only five hundred calories a day, virtually a starvation regime—explaining that Raniere had a preference for ultrathin women, and she strictly monitored their eating habits.

* * *

True to his word, Mark Vicente premiered *Ignite the Heart*—"written, produced, and directed by ESP," and "Presented by Inlak-Ech [*sic*]"—on July 7, 2016, in the small Nuevo León town of Galeana, to honor the memory of Benji LeBaron. "This felt like the right thing to do, to honor his sacrifice," Vicente wrote on social media. "The whole community rallied to see it. They (and we) were filled with pain, memories and pride for what Benjamin LeBaron had done. He had challenged criminals in a way no one had ever done before. His story will now be in the books." Vicente said the film was the result of more than seven hundred hours of footage shot over an eight-year period. "The perspective from which the questions were asked, and the sensitive approach of the filmmakers, brings to the screen a unique mosaic of deep emotionality and human honesty," Vicente posted on the film's Facebook page. During the summer of 2017, Vicente's team—including his codirectors and his NXIVM and Inlak-ech coproducers—showed the film in 120 venues throughout Mexico and in a few US cities. Vicente claimed that hundreds of thousands of people saw it.

While Raniere was the centerpiece of the film, Julian LeBaron had the key supporting role, his monologues underscoring Raniere's arguments about antidotes to fear and his conviction that NXIVM would transform Mexico's culture of violence. He spoke of the increasing anger he felt after the murder of his brother but said he was redirecting his rage toward solving the underlying hatred in the country. Seated at a table with Raniere, Julian spoke of "humanization and consciousness" as the path forward toward peace, and of "millions of people acting consciously," rather than depending upon a political leader to end the violence.

At the premiere, Vicente recalled filming his last interview with Benji before the latter's murder in 2009, saying, "His words have echoed in our hearts for years." On screen, "Raniere is presented as a messiah of Ayn Rand's radical individualism, and he offers the only solution to Mexico's pain: by Mexicans adopting his system, his 'values,' his philosophy through NXIVM and ESP," Mexican journalist León Krauze wrote of the film. "The film takes you on a journey from darkness to hope," said Vicente before one of the showings.

Behind the scenes, however, Raniere's relations with the residents of LeBaron, and the lessons he took from the colony about the role of women, were creating tension. Vicente later claimed he became alarmed when Raniere began advocating openly for polygamy within NXIVM. His discomfort increased, he said, when members of NXIVM's executive board, including Clare Bronfman, became angry at him for minimizing Raniere in the film and failing to accentuate Vanguard's supremacy. Yet many who saw the so-called documentary had the opposite reaction, seeing it as blatant hagiography of Keith Raniere intermixed with images of gratuitous violence conducted by Mexican cartels. "The film's oversimplified and risky diagnosis of Mexico's inequality and the country's convoluted 12-year war on crime could have been harmless if it weren't a thinly veiled disguise for something different: a massive propaganda effort to raise Raniere's profile in Mexico," wrote León Krauze, who "came away disgusted."

Vicente, though responsible for what was, in essence, a glorified advertisement that he spent millions of dollars and eight years producing, claimed to be appalled by the final product. Suddenly, and at first mysteriously, in early October 2017, he halted all showings and pulled the film from distribution. Vicente's reasoning became clear in the middle of that month, when the *New York Times* reported that there was a federal criminal investigation into Raniere for running a sex ring with enslaved women who were being branded with Raniere's initials. Vicente claimed to be "devastated" by the revelations about his boss and leader, and shocked that his film was being used as a recruiting tool for DOS, which was targeting underage girls in Mexico, including from Colonia LeBaron. Vicente announced that he had learned that "the film was being used to support an alleged criminal enterprise," implying that he had become a whistleblower for American law enforcement.

Vicente bemoaned that his film about the LeBarons and cartel violence had been co-opted by people involved in a sex cult—a lament many found disingenuous, given his decade-long total immersion in NXIVM and his daily proximity to both Raniere and the LeBarons. "This film, although it showed a beautiful story of bravery, also by association was supporting, without our intention, NXIVM, a criminal business," Vicente said, admitting that he was embarrassed and ashamed. "I ask myself, 'What the Hell did I do?'"

Learning of the federal criminal probe in New York, Raniere fled Albany and moved into a luxury villa, with high security, in Puerto Vallarta, Mexico. "One would think that given the number and nature of Raniere's Mexican associates, the story would have caught fire in Mexico," wrote Krauze. "In fact, the opposite happened. Raniere's deep Mexican connections have been conspicuously underreported by the country's press."

For his part, Emiliano Salinas, who had once called Raniere "heroic," denied knowing about the sex ring within NXIVM. He went on a press tour, distancing himself from the scandal and claiming that the stories published in the US were unfounded. "My name does not appear in the aforementioned article, nor is there a link with what I do in Mexico," he said in a statement, referring to the October 2017 *New York Times* story. After Raniere was arrested in Puerto Vallarta and deported to New York in 2018 to face federal criminal charges of racketeering, sex trafficking, conspiracy, forced labor, identity theft, sexual exploitation of a child, and possession of child pornography, ESP Mexico issued a statement expressing confidence that Raniere would be found innocent.

Julian LeBaron said that he had never agreed for Vicente's film "to be used as a recruiting tool of any kind," adding that he had been convinced that the documentary was a "good way to promote citizen participation in response to violence."

As for the eleven girls from Colonia LeBaron taken to Clifton Park, New

York, Vicente would later testify that Raniere "mentored" the teens in the basement of Junco's mansion and in his primary library. "And though we may never find out exactly what type of mentoring Raniere was doing with the young girls, we do know they all considered him to be 'creepy,'" said a federal prosecutor, "and that they all abruptly returned to Mexico."

CHAPTER EIGHT

"Water Flows Uphill to Money"

WHILE THE NXIVM scandal finally made headlines in the United States, and with its conspirators headed toward justice, the LeBaron clan waged another battle hidden in plain sight. This fight had deeper roots and even greater stakes. In the spring of 2018, the family's decades-long struggle with its Mexican and Indigenous neighbors for precious water resources in the arid land of Chihuahua erupted into violence.

With a population that now has swelled to approximately five thousand, Colonia LeBaron stretches six miles long by four miles wide. It is bounded by the family's fields, which are, in fact, within the *Ejido Galeana* and the *Ejido Constitucion*, the communally owned tracts of land dating from the Mexican Revolution. Since the 1970s, the LeBarons have been at odds with disaffected members of the *ejidos*, who have accused them of illegally purchasing land and stealing water from them. After judges repeatedly sided with the LeBarons, "whom they saw as productive members of the local economy," according to one scholar, the distrust and accusations simmered for several decades, but it had increased around 2015 as the LeBarons began encroaching further.

The use and control of water was a defining theme for most of Mormon history, beginning the day after Brigham Young's vanguard reached the Great Salt Lake Valley in 1847, when the Mormons immediately set to work damming and diverting what would one day become known as Emigration Creek. When Young sent bands of the faithful deeper into the American West after the Great Salt Lake area was largely settled in the 1850s, and decades later into northern Mexico, they arrived intent on securing springs and streams that would allow them to cultivate the land. Like other white newcomers throughout the history of the North American West, they seldom paused to consider the ramifications of depriving Indigenous tribes and game animals of access to the water that had sustained them for hundreds of years, if not millennia.

But the Mormons were building the Kingdom of God on Earth, and they justified their excessive water use by invoking biblical prophecy, believing that they were destined to transform the desert. Their efforts were central to their self-understanding as "stewards over these earthly blessings which the lord has provided [to] those of us who have this soil and this water," according to Mormon scriptures.

Some neighboring communities believe the LeBarons have long been associated with the dominant political and economic forces of the region, operating as a small empire that has, over the years, negotiated special terms with various government leaders. They are thought of not only as land-hungry foreign occupiers but also as allies of the right-wing Mexican political elite and "Prianist governments." Some in Mexico called them "American invaders," or "the Galeana Cartel." While Julian LeBaron had been busy with his peace movement, the rest of his family appeared to be busy acquiring more land and water. Julian's father, Joel Jr., had owned La Mojina Ranch since 1977. In 2015, almost forty years after the initial purchase, the ranch suddenly—and suspiciously, according to critics—began expanding immensely in acreage. The new land was divided up among at least seventeen family members, all direct descendants of Joel Sr. A frenzy of real estate transactions between 2015 and 2017, which involved dozens of newly issued deeds, included essentially priceless water rights to the new land. Mexican news reporters drew attention to the fact that, at the time of the transactions, Alex LeBaron, the pro-gun activist and PRI operative who had served as a delegate on the National Water Commission, was "a close collaborator of former [Chihuahua] Governor César Duarte Jáquez, who promoted him as local deputy and federal deputy, always in charge of water commissions." Also closely involved was his brother Max, who was Duarte's "private secretary." Alex had won a seat in the federal Congress in 2015 as a PRI representative for District 7 of Chihuahua, his goal ever since Benji's murder.

Of the seventeen owners of land within the expanded family ranch in the *Ejido Constitucion*, the oldest among those identified were Joel Jr. and his four brothers from Joel the Prophet's first wife, Magdalena Soto: Leonel Armando LeBaron, Luis Carlos LeBaron, Ricardo LeBaron, and Adrian LeBaron. The other owners identified were three of Joel Jr.'s sons, including Julian, and Julian's son Diego. "The rest of the owners are also from the LeBaron family," according to one press account. Alex LeBaron reportedly "registered 153 properties in the Public Property Registry, between September 29 and October 9, 2015, which were granted to him at no cost, through a different *ejido*, the *Ejido* Galeana." Just days before he acquired these properties, some had been changed from "common use lands" to "human settlement lands." The group of landowners in the *Ejido Galeana* had originally obtained the land in 1778. The land was taken from them during the Revolution and then re-granted to the *ejido* by the Mexican Government after the Revolution. The 2015 registry named Alex LeBaron the new owner, identifying him as a thirty-four-year-old unmarried farmer from Galeana.

After Alex LeBaron's term as water commissioner and PRI party congressman ended in 2018, the commission initiated a lawsuit concerning the "Illegal wells of Joel Francisco LeBaron and Ellen Nadine Jones [Joel Jr.'s second wife]." The case was filed at the beginning of January of that year, and just weeks later, the LeBaron family was ordered to legalize their permits.

A group of ranchers and activists mobilized against a well being drilled by the LeBaron family. Calling themselves *El Barzón*, the collective originally formed in the 1980s identified itself as "a plural and inclusive organization, socially and politically committed to the fight for social and economic equity, the fight against corruption, the defense of human rights, land, territory, as well as family and social heritage; the preservation of the environment and natural resources to reverse the effects of climate change." Eraclio "El Yako" Rodríguez, Alex LeBaron's replacement as Mexican Congress deputy from Chihuahua, was the local leader of *El Barzón*, which was involved in several political struggles in the state against miners and corporate ranchers. Rodríguez, a federal lawmaker with the National Regeneration Movement (MORENA) party that replaced the PRI in Chihuahua, reported that he and other *Barzonistas* had received death threats from the LeBaron family.

On April 30, 2018, more than five hundred farmers from five different communities stormed Joel Jr.'s La Mojina Ranch to protest the diminished water table and to document the land clearing and well drilling. They accused the family of drilling hundreds of new wells in nearby municipalities—wells that siphoned water from the rivers and aquifers for the LeBarons' commercial cultivation of their massive walnut and pecan farms. Whole communities were left without drinking water, their small agricultural fields suddenly parched and barren. Thousands of citizens were affected, according to the *Barzonistas* and other *ejidatarios* (*ejido* members). The LeBarons were also accused of diverting water by bulldozing and damming reservoirs meant for Indigenous communities downstream.

During the decade since Benji's murder, the LeBaron community had fortified itself with an arsenal of weapons, an armed and trained family militia, and apparently a fleet of drones. Now, the situation turned violent. The protesters, driving a convoy of pickup trucks, ran over walnut seedlings, destroyed eleven wells, burned down a house, crops, and some vehicles, and used their own drones to document the skirmish, which showed the ranch employees firing shots, including .223-caliber live ammunition, into the unarmed crowd. The protesters took control of the waterlines that they claimed the LeBarons had illegally diverted for growing agave for tequila production, while "shouting racist and xenophobic remarks," according to Julian LeBaron. When it was over, at least one LeBaron and five protesters were wounded. The LeBarons claimed to have suffered a loss in property of more than a million dollars from the destruction of three thousand walnut trees and fires set to a winery, heavy machinery, pickup trucks, and homes.

El Barzón reported finding a dozen illegal wells with diesel-fueled pumps, along with evidence that Joel Jr. was illegally watering approximately 247 acres, when he only had the authority to water about forty-four. "We're tired of this situation," said a rancher who was a member of *El Barzón*. "We wanted to do things formally: we filed complaints to the prosecutor, the environmental authorities, and nothing has happened. They're just delaying things or avoiding taking action." In addition to alleging the larger LeBaron family enterprises have drilled more than two thousand water wells on their ranches without permission, "by obtaining permits through the payment of bribes," according to a report in *Mexico News Daily*, the *Barzonistas* also complained that Joel Jr. had cleared hundreds of acres of common ground to grow nineteen thousand walnut trees, which are notorious water consumers but popular for their high market value. They also accused the LeBarons of attempting without permission to connect to the power grid controlled by the *Ejido Constitucion*.

"If the LeBarons connect it makes it easier for the Terrazas to do so," an *El Barzón* leader told the Mexican press, referring to another of the most powerful and prominent Chihuahua families who had been in a century-long battle with the peasants in the region. The Terrazas clan had held the largest privately owned domain in Mexico before the Revolution. Pancho Villa had confiscated their property (along with that of the country's other oligarchs) and distributed it to the *ejidatarios,* and the Terrazas have been fighting with the *ejidos* ever since. For generations, the Mormon colonies in the region— the LeBarons and others—were considered allies of the powerful Terrazas empire, and they "were hated thrice over" by the Indigenous people because "they practiced polygamy, were hostile to Catholicism and had bought up expropriated land," according to a historian of the Mexican Revolution.

Julian LeBaron countered that *El Barzón* was a criminal anti-American gang associated with Chihuahua Governor Javier Corral, a LeBaron nemesis, that was trying to take over the LeBaron lands. *El Barzón* disputed Julian's characterization, stating that they were fighting the privatization of communal natural resources and telling the prominent Mexican daily newspaper *La Jornada* that the Chihuahua state government "protects" the LeBaron family with forty agents of the state police. "*El Barzón* and the government are the same," Julian said, declaring that all of the wells at La Mojina were registered with the National Water Commission and that all of the land was legally acquired. The previous year, the commission had identified a dozen illegal drainages on La Mojina Ranch. A high-profile investigation by *La Jornada* reported that Alex LeBaron used his influence when he was a delegate of the National Water Commission to give "395 concessions to family members and illegal strawman companies." Those concessions "allowed the enrichment of [the LeBaron family] at the expense of the water shortage affecting 900 families in *Constitucion ejido*." Alex denied the allegation, but his successor on the commission accused him of "having granted false permits, not formally registered and without following the regular procedure, in favor of the Mormon community to which he belongs."

At the time, the state of Chihuahua ranked third in the nation, behind Sonora and Sinaloa, in irrigated agriculture, with the number of agricultural wells increasing in recent years, especially in the areas where the LeBarons' former cattle ranches had been turned into more profitable farmland. Those running the giant, water-guzzling marijuana and poppy fields and avocado groves of Chihuahua were also vying for these ancient waters, pitting drug cartels, subsistence farmers, industrial growers, and Mormon colonies against each other—or sometimes in collusion with each other—in pursuit of the rapidly dwindling resources. In the near future, the wells for agricultural use are expected to dry up, due to both overuse and climate change.

After the protests at La Mojina, Julian LeBaron told the press that the family had fired shots in self-defense. Both sides were quick to broadcast their versions of events on social media. *El Barzón* claimed that the LeBarons had "put a price on the head" of two high-ranking *Barzonistas*, including the state's director of agricultural development. In response, Julian accused the Chihuahuan government of arming *Barzonistas* with machine guns and providing them with state police protection, vowing that his family would "take justice into our own hands" if the government and the activists did not stand down. Julian told a television interviewer that he was "quite worried" that *El Barzón* would return "and finish destroying everything."

El Barzón leaders announced publicly that they had received death threats from the LeBarons, and one newspaper described the Mormons as "very aggressive." In June 2018, a few months after the confrontation at La Mojina, two *Barzonistas*—Ramon and Anselmo Hernandez—were murdered in Chihuahua, reportedly for "protecting water rights." The father and son—corn, oat, and bean farmers—were agrarian activists who "participated in the demand that the overexploitation of the river basin be stopped." The double homicide went unsolved, and the media stopped short of blaming the LeBarons.

The *Barzonistas* were already reeling over three other unsolved murders of its members, including the group's revered cofounder. In October 2012, Ismael Solorio and his wife, Manuelita Solís, were killed, presumably in retaliation for their high-profile activism against the overexploitation of resources in the state of Chihuahua. For three generations, the Solorio family had farmed chile peppers and raised cattle on *ejido* land near the rural town of Benito Juárez, not far from Colonia LeBaron. The beloved Ismael Solorio had helped form the *El Barzón* movement, originally organizing against predatory banking practices. Manuelita was a primary school teacher and fellow activist, and the couple was murdered while driving from their farm to a medical appointment in Chihuahua City. They were found seated in their truck, Ismael shot twice in the back of the head and Manuelita in the chest. Then, in February 2015, one of their colleagues, Alberto Almeida, was gunned down in a Sam's Club parking lot in Juárez, just across the border from El Paso. A defender of human rights and the environment, Almeida was shot in the head in front of his daughter and wife, joining a long list of politically motivated murders compiled by one international environmental organization.

* * *

A July 2009 aerial view of the town of Colonia LeBaron, with its sprawling, profitable, and water-intensive nut orchards. *(Adriana Zehbrauskas/New York Times)*

The year 2019 began ominously for Colonia LeBaron on numerous fronts, and events brought unwanted attention to the state of Chihuahua from US federal law enforcement, especially the DEA. The first significant development was the guilty verdict delivered on February 12 for Joaquín "El Chapo" Guzmán Loera in Federal District Court in Brooklyn.

The sixty-one-year-old El Chapo was the highest-profile Mexican drug-cartel boss ever to stand trial in the US. He was accused of masterminding the importation of thousands of tons of cocaine into the US and conspiring to make and distribute heroin, methamphetamine, and marijuana. He was known to have used hit men to carry out hundreds of murders, assaults, kidnappings, and acts of torture over nearly three decades of his reign in Mexico's Sierra Madre region, though he was not charged for those crimes, allegedly due to a lack of evidence.

During his three-month trial in New York, key associates, including a top lieutenant, testified against him, shining a spotlight on the activities of his Sinaloa Cartel and its many years of political corruption in Chihuahua. Prosecutors presented "a mountain of evidence against him" that included dozens of surveillance photos, hundreds of intercepted text messages, and the often-chilling testimony of fifty-six witnesses in what was described as a "circuslike extravaganza," wrote Alan Feuer in the *New York Times*. The heart of the government's case was "the operatic cast of cooperating witnesses who were called to testify," and who provided an in-depth portrait of El Chapo's Sinaloa Cartel.

Among the witnesses against him were fourteen men who had worked as top lieutenants in his organization. "I've never faced a case with so many cooperating witnesses and so much evidence," one of El Chapo's lawyers told the press. It was the first time that details about the financing and history of the world's largest drug cartel were heard in an American courtroom, with bomb-sniffing dogs and police snipers surrounding the building.

The trial and El Chapo's conviction were followed closely in Mexico, including in Colonia LeBaron; the Sinaloa Cartel and its billionaire drug lord had been a central figure in the colony's world for thirty years. Of particular relevance to the LeBarons was testimony relating to the hundreds of millions of dollars in bribes paid by the cartel to the Mexican police,

military, government leaders, and numerous political officials in the state
of Chihuahua. One witness claimed that El Chapo paid off Genaro García
Luna, Mexico's former head of public security and one of the country's
most powerful officials, who had connections at the highest levels of the
US Government. Forty-nine-year-old García Luna had accepted millions
of dollars in bribes, often stuffed in suitcases, according to the testimony,
"all while working hand in glove with US law enforcement and intelligence
agencies." García Luna had relocated to Miami and started a private intelligence agency, whose advisory board included a former head of one of the
CIA's covert operations wings.

Several high-ranking associates of El Chapo spoke of the historic relationship between the Sinaloa Cartel and PRI political figures in Chihuahua
state and elsewhere. The evidence at the trial included references to César
Duarte Jáquez, governor of the state from 2010 to 2016, who had complete
control of the PRI party in Chihuahua, and with whom Alex LeBaron was
closely allied during his six-year term as a local deputy and National Water
Commission delegate. Duarte left Mexico at the end of his term, decamp-
ing to Florida amid informal allegations that he had been embezzling public funds. After Duarte left office, the incoming Chihuahua governor, Javier
Corral, discovered a budget deficit of more than $2.5 billion. He opened an
investigation, ultimately accusing fifty-six-year-old Duarte of overseeing a
vast network of corruption: of bribing government officials, politicians, and
businessmen, as well as amassing a multimillion-dollar fortune that he used
to buy expensive houses, ranches, and exotic animals. Charges were brought
against Duarte for distributing more than a hundred million dollars to relatives, friends, and associates under the guise of government contracts, purchases, and farm subsidies. Duarte remained in the US, beyond the reach of
the Mexican Government, but when testimony about the Chihuahua bribes
surfaced in El Chapo's trial, there was widespread speculation that the trail
of Sinaloa Cartel corruption led not only to Duarte's office but also to the
PRI and its operatives in Chihuahua, including Alex LeBaron. (Duarte was
finally arrested in Miami in July 2020 and is facing charges in both the US
and Mexico that prosecutors have claimed could amount to fraud exceeding
$6 billion.)

* * *

On the heels of El Chapo's dramatic conviction following historic and sensational testimony about corruption in Chihuahua came another lengthy trial that focused attention on Colonia LeBaron itself. The six-week trial of NXIVM founder and leader Keith Raniere—also in Federal District Court in Brooklyn—began in May 2019. Charged with seven counts of racketeering, sex trafficking, production of child pornography, and conspiracy, Raniere was accused by prosecutors of masquerading "as a self-help guru to gain the trust of his followers, and then exploit[ing] them for his own financial gain and sexual gratification."

The key witness against Raniere was Mark Vicente. Days of testimony from Vicente and others about the secret society of DOS within NXIVM, and its recruitment of underage sexual partners for Raniere, made for a media spectacle. A national American audience was once again introduced to Colonia LeBaron, particularly in relation to the eleven girls recruited to work as what NXIVM leaders called "nannies" at his compound near Albany. Several LeBaron family members wrote the judge, vouching for Raniere's character and urging leniency.

On June 19, 2019, fifty-eight-year-old Raniere was convicted on all counts and faced a likely sentence of life in prison. "He is not sorry for his conduct or his choices," his attorneys would tell the court. "He remains proud to have been permitted to play a part in helping citizens and residents of Mexico strive to bring peace to a country beset by violent gangs, kidnappings and murders, a struggle that continues to the present and that will continue into the future." Emiliano Salinas finally severed his longstanding ties with NXIVM.

A month later, on July 17, El Chapo received a life sentence, which he would serve in the infamous SuperMax prison in Florence, Colorado. At the "Alcatraz of the Rockies," as the nation's highest-security penitentiary is called, the escape artist El Chapo would spend twenty-three hours a day in solitary confinement in a seven-by-ten-foot cell. El Chapo and the Sinaloa Cartel had, ironically, been a stabilizing presence in the region where the LeBarons had thrived for decades, and his life sentence threw Chihuahua into chaos, with various rivals vying for the Sinaloa empire.

The LeBaron family faced still more scrutiny in Mexico during that summer of 2019. In August, a Chihuahua court ruling in favor of the *Barzonistas* directed Joel Jr. to restore land confiscated by the family from small farmers in Chihuahua. When it seemed clear to the *Barzonistas* that the LeBarons were ignoring the order—and in fact were planning to excavate fifty new wells—the conflict between the parties escalated rapidly. That month, members of *El Barzón* accused the family of "drying up the desert" and completely exhausting the *ejido* well that served a community of three thousand, and once again the *Barzonistas* raided their property. A story in a Mexican newspaper reported that Julian had "unleashed a smear campaign on social media to 'create an atmosphere of animosity' against *El Barzón*," which the family was criticizing as a socialist organization (stating the obvious). In this sense, the LeBarons were similar to their right-wing, heavily armed Mormon counterparts in the western US who were engaged in land-use conflicts against the federal government, which they likewise accused of being socialist.

Joel Jr. adamantly denied that he had benefited from his nephew Alex's position as head of the National Water Commission, implying that there was a rift within the family. "I can't tell you what Alex LeBaron did or didn't do in CONAGUA," he told a reporter, referring to the commission, "but I, Joel LeBaron Soto and his family, neither here nor in Galeana do we have a single well that he has given or authorized us. If other LeBarons have, well, let them get theirs. I don't have wells like that here in Mojina."

The cartel violence and clashes over water offered a contrast to the billboards advertising the golf club being built by Eleazar LeBaron Castro, Joel Sr.'s son with his third wife, Isabel Castro, and who had taken on Benji's widow, Miri, as a plural wife. Like Eleazar's father, Miri's father, Siegfried Widmar, had been a leader in the Church of the Firstborn, and had also been on Ervil LeBaron's hit list, targeted for blood atonement. The billboards announced the construction of a new subdivision around the club: "panoramic view lots, farm lots (horses, chickens, sheep . . .), lots next to the clubhouse and private lots with security." As president of The Springs Golf Club Association, Castro had also recently announced that, in exchange for drinking water, the nonprofit association would build "the long-awaited municipal public swimming pool construction project" for Galeana. Websites promoted other LeBaron enterprises, including Galeana Vineyard and Winery—offering one variety called "Desert Rose"—Chateau LeBaron, and LeBaron Pecans.

"There is no church organization anymore," said a family member who lived in the colony during the early days of the Church of the Firstborn, through Joel's murder and Ervil's reign of terror. "If someone is claiming leadership, or the keys to the Kingdom, that is a lie. There are no longer any guiding principles. They are all homegrown kids who don't know the history or the doctrines. It's now all financial, not religious. They've become so wealthy so fast, and the cult mentality, that they are God's chosen people, has really taken root in the community. The holy Galeana Springs we all held sacred and where we were all baptized has dried up." In a reminder of how near the past is to the present, the family member agreed to be interviewed only when granted anonymity, out of fear of violent reprisal.

Even polygamy itself—the reason for the colony's existence—has a tenuous hold on the women. "The men pretend it's doctrinal," said an older plural wife who managed to escape decades earlier, "but they're really just 'converted below the belt,' as we used to say." Another family member, who had been on Ervil's hit list and left the colony many years ago to raise her children in the US, agreed with this assessment. "The colony is a magnet for trouble," she said. "They have a good racket. Many of the women are not there by choice. They are scared shitless."

In the fall of 2019, elegant mansions dotted the foothills overlooking Colonia LeBaron, as did the frame of the luxury home that Rhonita LeBaron and Howard Miller were building for their young family, not far from the homes of two of Rhonita's wealthy, entrepreneurial uncles, Matthew Jensen and Bart Tucker, and that of her mother, Shalom. From Jensen's ridgetop showcase on the mountain summit, one could see mature nut orchards and crops covering the land in three directions, all the way to Blue Valley in the distance. The autumn harvest was at its peak and the community's inaugural Pecan Festival would soon be underway. But first there was a wedding scheduled in Colonia LeBaron, with most of the La Mora community—just across the spine of the Sierra Madre—expected to attend.

CHAPTER NINE

"Innocence Is Shattered"

KENDRA LEE MILLER was busy making wedding plans on November 4, when the column of black smoke was spotted. As details of the murders of her sister-in-law, Rhonita, and eight other members of her extended family became clear, the twenty-seven-year-old emerged as a family representative amid the wave of press that rolled into the isolated area of northern Mexico. With her November 11 wedding date fast approaching, the bride-to-be demonstrated impressive poise as she was interviewed by CNN's Anderson Cooper.

She described how the family was preparing for the funerals of the three mothers and six children who had died the previous week at the hands of people she had called "terrorists and evil mobsters." She spoke frankly about how Rhonita, along with four of her seven children—Kendra's nieces and nephews—had been shot and set ablaze during the late-morning attack. She talked about the victims' essential goodness and the sorrow she and so many others felt in now turning their backs on fifty years in La Mora. "We have beautiful homes and pecan farms," she said, but more than a hundred members of the community had decided it was not worth staying in a place where there was no security.

"We've fought hard to get media attention," she told Cooper, revealing that the family had received "confirmation" that they were targeted "in order to stir up trouble and start a war" between the Sinaloa and Juárez Cartels. Working from notes, she closed the interview on a subject seemingly as important as any other to the family's future: the right to bear arms, given the apparent lack of police and military protection. "I don't know where you're standing on the whole, people-trying-to-take-away-guns-in-America right now, but I say, fight for those guns. These things are happening here in Mexico because the people can't protect themselves, because by law they're not allowed to own these guns."

In another interview with American media, Miller described Rhonita as "a light that shined and wanted to give her whole life for God and family." She spoke of how their large clan was being sustained by the prayers of "thousands and thousands of people" from all over the world. After the interview, she announced on social media that she was soon to become a plural wife, a fact that few outside of the LeBaron and La Mora communities were aware of to that point, as most polygamous marriages are kept secret except within the clan, given their illegality in both the US and Mexico. As the *Deseret News* put it, the announcement added "to confusion for the world's media trying to sort out the intersection of a horrific drug-related crime, religion and the family's unique faith."

Acknowledging that the world was "horrified and shocked at this atrocity," Miller still moved forward excitedly with her wedding plans. She then posted more details on social media about her marriage, saying that she would become the second wife of Zack Laub of Stockton, Missouri, and she had created a wedding registry on Amazon's "The Knot" site. "I'm taking this step with eyes wide open, aware of the challenges and also the blessings living in a plural marriage can bring, and I choose all of it," she wrote on Instagram.

Almost from the moment the news of the attacks broke, the Mexican Government claimed that it was a case of mistaken identity. That the victims were caught in the crossfire between rival cartels would have been a plausible claim if not for the eyewitness accounts offered by the surviving children who had seen "their brothers and sisters shot to hell and back," as Rhonita's father-in-law, Kenneth Miller, described it to an American reporter. In a strange echo of the Mountain Meadows Massacre 160 years earlier—which might have gone down in history as a slaughter by Indians had a five-year-old survivor not told American soldiers that the "Indians" were white men once they washed off their red face paint—the facts of the ambushes might have remained a mystery if not for the testimony from the oldest of the eight children whose lives were spared. "Mom told us all to duck," Dawna's fourteen-year-old daughter, Kylie, recalled. They could see "three guys on the hill," wearing black masks. They came down "to finish the job," her thirteen-year-old brother, Devin, said. "Then [they] saw little kids and told them to get out and go home."

Alex LeBaron told CNN that "they were attacked separately but simultaneously," contradicting the government's claims, including the official timeline that the three vehicles were assaulted independently and hours apart. Reports that there were more than a hundred gunmen at the scene indicated a highly sophisticated operation that probably included not only cartel forces but also Mexican military and state police, further ruling out the mistaken-identity theory—on the assumption that a trained force would have been able to recognize women and children. The families were infuriated by the government's obfuscation, claiming they were targeted intentionally by the Juárez Cartel in retaliation for their relationship with the Sinaloa Cartel. "We need to know who did it and why," Julian LeBaron told an interviewer.

After Benji's murder in 2009, the families had coexisted with both the Sinaloa and Juárez Cartels, almost as though all sides agreed that it was in everyone's interest not to bring attention to the region. Residents of both La Mora and LeBaron rolled down their windows at the Sinaloa Cartel's checkpoints. "They nodded to the sicarios at local horse races and shared pomegranates during the harvest," reported the *Washington Post*. "When the cartel vehicles needed repair, La Mora's American mechanic fixed them for the same fee he charged his neighbors," as former La Mora mayor Adam Langford described the communities' interactions with the traffickers.

But by the summer of 2019, with El Chapo out of the way, tensions had been mounting between the two cartels—or between the Sonora and Chihuahua sides, as Kendra's thirty-two-year-old brother, Kenneth Miller Jr., put it. "The Chihuahua side is trying to move in because this is a huge smuggling route through here," he said. Still, "We thought the same thing we always did—they won't come after Americans," said Amber Langford, Adam's relative and a forty-three-year-old midwife who had overseen the births of some of the murdered children. "They would stop us at a checkpoint and ask what we had. We'd say honey or potatoes, and they'd let us go." Many in the community even believed that the Sinaloa Cartel served as "a kind of shadow police force" for them. "The fact is," said Adam Langford, "that the state didn't provide law and order, but the cartel did." Kenneth Miller said the men at the checkpoints were often respectful and apologetic. "They would say, 'Sorry guys, we are just guarding our territory.'" Residents would nod at cartel gunmen whose names they knew, describing the drug gangs "as simply an accepted part of daily life in Sonora." One family member called it a "gentlemen's agreement"; basically, it's "We won't bother you, if you don't bother us."

After the killings, hundreds of relatives traveled from the United States for the funerals. On the LeBaron side, many were descendants of Benjamin Johnson and the nineteenth-century settlers of Chihuahua; on the La Mora side, most were descendants of the American polygamist colonies from the twentieth century. "LeBaron is a generic term because we are all intertwined, hence there are mixtures of Langford and Johnson with LeBaron in Chihuahua, Sonora, Baja California and Quintana Roo," said Alex LeBaron. They all shared facts about the murders and rumors about the motives and perpetrators. Alex regretted that the prosperity of the Mormon colonies was "overshadowed by the issue of organized crime," and he defended the fact that the LeBarons' ranches stood out amid what a reporter described as "a panorama of poverty" and a lack of infrastructure in the municipalities to which they belong. "People here tell us all the time that we are rich, that we are gringos . . . but none of this is possible without hard work," said Alex's nephew Daniel LeBaron.

* * *

Douglas Johnson drove to Phoenix from La Mora on the afternoon of November 4, crossing the border and heading for the Sky Harbor Airport to pick up Rhonita's husband, Howard Miller. That morning, Howard had been in his apartment in North Dakota getting ready for a late-afternoon flight to Phoenix, where he was scheduled to rendezvous with Rhonita and four of their seven children. When he received word that Rhonita's vehicle was found shot up and burning, and that his wife and children were missing, he rushed to the airport and tried, unsuccessfully, to get on an earlier flight. Then he received a phone call that his wife and the four children were dead. Late that evening, Howard landed in Phoenix and was met by Johnson.

A large, bearded man, the forty-year-old Johnson described the return to Mexico with Miller as one of the loneliest trips he had ever taken in his life. Mexican border agents initially didn't want to let them cross from Arizona into Mexico. When they arrived in a town in Sonora to buy coffee, the locals were astonished that they were driving down to Bavispe in the middle of the night to the site of a likely cartel massacre. "Howard didn't speak the whole way," Johnson said. They arrived in La Mora at 10 a.m. on Tuesday, and Howard and his mother, Loretta, went immediately to the site where Rhonita and the children had been attacked. Coming upon the scorched Chevy Tahoe, "Howard nearly passed out. He didn't want to see." But he was obsessed with the possibility that his wife and children might have been kidnapped. "Are we sure no one got out of the car?" he asked. "The grandkids' heads were teeny, burnt to a crisp," Loretta later said to a reporter.

By this point, the residents of La Mora and LeBaron were already preparing for the funerals. Amber Langford, the La Mora midwife, helped embalm the bodies while the boys and men on the ranch built wooden coffins, both tasks taking place only in La Mora, even though some of the victims would be transported to Colonia LeBaron for burial. César Rodríguez, a Mexican photographer on assignment for the Spanish newspaper El País, arrived in La Mora on Tuesday afternoon and was granted intimate access to the affected families. "I was at home in Xalisco, west of Guadalajara, at around 10 p.m. on Nov. 4 when I saw the news," Rodríguez later wrote. He was getting ready for bed when his editor asked him to go to Sonora. He caught a bus to the Guadalajara Airport and boarded a plane to Hermosillo the next day. There he met up with reporter Pablo Ferri, and the two rented a car to drive to La Mora. Rodríguez's photos, and Ferri's reporting—the first, and most vivid, images and accounts of the massacre—would be distributed throughout the world. "I tried to take photos that meant something," Rodríguez said. Ferri was at the kitchen table in Rhonita's home, interviewing Rhonita's father, Adrian, while Rodríguez sat in stunned silence. "I was just sitting at the table, not taking pictures. At one point, I asked Adrian, 'Do you mind if I just take pictures while you're talking?' And he said, 'Take as many pictures as you want. We need this to be known.'"

Adrian stood and led Rodríguez to his dead granddaughters' bedroom. "It was so powerful; you could see their toys, you could see a little dress that belonged to Krystal, who was ten. You could see their bed; you could see a toothbrush and toothpaste. You could see a sign that read *Daughters of the King*. It was hard to see all of that," Rodríguez wrote.

"Lashes of rage scatter across the table," was the way Ferri described the scene. "More than sadness, anger. And the desire to talk, to tell everything, for everything to be known . . . a nursing baby who waited there, alone, in the car, with her dead mother lying on the ground ten feet from her, for hours, in this damned fold of the Sierra."

The funerals started on Thursday, November 7, in La Mora. "The day La Mora buried its dead began like many others," with the daily chores of feeding the chickens and milking the cows, reported KJZZ, the NPR station in Phoenix.

Christina's mother, Amelia Langford, said La Mora had always been idyllic. But no longer. The village's young men hastily making hand-carved coffins wept as they sawed, assembled, and sanded the wood. "I don't want to think about it, but I'm building the coffin of my sister," said one. As they completed each humble pine box—one for Dawna and smaller ones for her two children, Trevor and Rogan—they covered it and loaded it onto a truck. A single larger box was made to hold Rhonita and her twin infants, Titus and Tiana. The five children of Dawna Ray Langford who were injured in the attack had been transported by a Mexican Air Force helicopter to Tucson, Arizona, where they were taken to a Phoenix hospital. Just days later, they were accompanied back to La Mora to attend their mother's, brothers', and cousins' funerals.

The funerals took place in quick succession, starting in La Mora for Dawna and her two children on Thursday, and ending in LeBaron on Friday and Saturday for Rhonita and her four children and then Christina. Overwhelmed by the number of bodies, morticians in La Mora were unable to keep up with the embalming—which was why Amber Langford was helping with the work—leading to a rush of memorial services. "We're just trying to gather and be there and offer our love and support," said fifty-year-old Joe Darger, the American polygamist considered the inspiration for the HBO series *Big Love*. Darger had two children who married into the Langford family, and he traveled to Mexico to pay his respects. "Innocence is shattered right now," he said. Hundreds of mourners assembled under white tents set up on the thousand-acre ranch and farming community. Mexican security personnel packed the village as National Guardsmen patrolled the area in trucks. Sonora's governor arrived in a helicopter.

"The eyes of the world are upon what happened here, and there are saints all over this world whose hearts have been touched," Jay Ray said as he eulogized his forty-three-year-old daughter, Dawna, who was among the first buried. "God will take care of the wicked."

Dawna, eleven-year-old Trevor, and two-year-old Rogan were laid to rest inside a single grave. Dawna was remembered for her lively storytelling, Trevor for his love of waffles, and Rogan for his ever-present smile. Dawna had grown up in LeBaron in a prominent Mormon fundamentalist family that had settled there in the 1950s. Jay Ray's grandfather had been one of Joel LeBaron Sr.'s earliest converts. Dawna had moved to La Mora in 1995, at the age of eighteen, when she married La Mora native David Langford, and raised thirteen children. "She was a devoted wife and devoted mother," recalled her brother, Justin Ray. She had loved the beautiful little hamlet, with its population of just over 150 full-time residents—and as many as three hundred part-time residents with dual citizenship who regularly traveled back and forth across the border—most of them interrelated. She adored the "cypress trees that grew on the edge of brick walls, the yellow leaves of pomegranate trees teasing the skyline, the handsome, custom-built homes," as one account put it.

"She was the favorite of the whole family," said Jay Ray. "I just felt a helplessness for my family," said Ryan Langford, one of Dawna's eleven surviving children, in his tribute. Her husband, David, was comforted by his plural wife, Margaret, who sat beside him at the service. After Dawna's funeral, four generations of women congregated in her large home for tamales and chicken soup. But for the husbands of Christina and Rhonita, Tyler Johnson and Howard Miller, "La Mora had been tarnished," wrote Azam Ahmed of the *New York Times*, who attended the funeral. "Their faces swollen and eyes blank," both were determined to take their loved ones to Colonia LeBaron for burial the following day, in what was described as a "five-hour, bone-jarring drive" that passed by the sites of the murders. "I don't know if I'll ever come back here," said Johnson. "Not after everything that's happened."

Rhonita LeBaron Miller was a more central figure in the LeBaron family than either Dawna or Christina, given that her paternal grandfather was Joel the Prophet, and her maternal grandfather was Joel's devoted apostle, William Tucker, who had defected from the Mormon church and led the group of missionaries from France to Colonia LeBaron in 1958 to join Joel's church. Rhonita's father, Adrian, was a son of the martyred Prophet, and current self-described presiding elder in the Church of the Firstborn. Her living grandmother, Rhonita Tucker Jensen, mother of Shalom, was a formidable matriarch in Colonia LeBaron.

During Rhonita's funeral ceremony in LeBaron on Friday, November 8, family members were led in reading Mexico's national anthem—including the little-known, revolutionary and controversial "hidden stanzas" that were sometimes prohibited at official events:

> Homeland! Homeland! your children swear
> to exhale their breath on your behalf,
> if the bugle with its warlike accent
> summons them to deal with courage.
> For you the olive garlands!
> A memory for them of glory!
> A laurel for you of victory!
> A grave for them of honor!

As the coffins of Rhonita and her four children were lowered into the grave, her cousin, Julian, asked the mourners to throw flowers and a little dirt onto the coffins.

In North Dakota, the LDS church where Rhonita worshipped, and where many relatives were also members, held a memorial service that same day for her and her children. More than 150 mourners gathered in the heart of Williston—home to nearly a hundred relatives of the LeBaron, Langford, Miller, and Johnson clans—for a candlelight vigil.

Although Christina Langford Johnson was reared in La Mora, her husband Tyler Johnson had deep family ties in Colonia LeBaron. On Saturday morning, November 9, Christina's funeral was held there. The community was shrouded in fog as more than three hundred people crowded into the LeBaron community church. "LeBaron showed its roots, with some aging buildings appearing to be straight from a Wild West movie set," wrote a reporter covering the funeral for Reuters. It is "scattered with signs touting religious life but also advertisements for rodeos featuring alcohol, hinting at traces of secularism." Amelia eulogized her daughter, Christina, as a "mama hen" who was fiercely protective of her six children—as epitomized by her giving up her own life to save that of baby Faith's. On the altar, white flowers spelled out MOMMY, next to a heart made of roses. A nature lover, Christina saw Mexico as "her paradise," according to her mother.

* * *

Many family members in Mexico and the United States posted on their social-media accounts an image of a black ribbon inscribed with the text *Oremos*

The young daughter of one of the murdered mothers in the backyard of the Miller home in the community of La Mora on November 6, 2019. *(Meghan Dhaliwal/New York Times)*

por LeBaron-La Mora—"Let's pray for LeBaron-La Mora." The massacre also spawned a logo, a ballad titled "Justice for La Mora," an Instagram account, the *narcocorrido LeBaron Familia*, Facebook and Twitter accounts, numerous hashtags, a YouTube video honoring the fallen, posters and T-shirts reading "La Mora Nine" and "La Mora Strong," and a GoFundMe account that quickly raised nearly $200,000 for Dawna's husband, David.

Within a week of the attacks, dozens of friends and relatives had changed their profile pictures on Facebook to a painting of a woman holding a child. Rhonita's sister-in-law, Kendra, explained the symbolism and significance of the graphic: A mother "with her back against her enemies," who is pierced by nine arrows representing the three mothers and six children who were killed. There are eight bandages signifying the survivors, US and Mexican flags denoting the victims' dual citizenship, and "a symbol of both countries uniting to end cartel rule."

There was little mention of the LeBarons, as the La Mora contingent made a concerted effort to disassociate themselves from that more famous, controversial, and powerful branch of the family. "One name is being used much more than others," Emily Langford told a reporter, complaining that she was "hearing the name LeBaron everywhere," when in fact all of the victims, except for Rhonita, were Langfords, Millers, and Johnsons. "Everyone is not a LeBaron." Dawna's mother wrote on a relative's page: "This is *my* family as much as theirs." Another Langford relative underscored that feeling, posting on Facebook that, while the LeBarons are "good people," La Mora and LeBaron are "completely different communities, different beliefs, different politics, and different cultures, 140 miles and a state away."

As they mourned, relatives also reevaluated their lives in Mexico. "The question we all have here," Adam Langford said, "is how does this thing end?" Unconvinced that Mexican authorities could guarantee their protection, most of the immediate family members of the slain women felt they had no choice but to leave their homes and the nation of their birth.

Not the Millers. "You will not find a more peaceful place," said Kenneth Miller, describing what happened to his family as "one of countless massacres." His wife Loretta agreed. One of Verlan LeBaron's fifty-six children by ten wives—"twenty-eight girls and twenty-eight boys"—Loretta said they intended to keep the family tradition alive in La Mora. "We have fourteen kids and thirty-three grandkids, minus the four from the massacre," she told a reporter. "We usually have a pretty full house but that's how we like it. We would like to see that with our own kids carried on." (As Verlan LeBaron's daughter, Rhonita's mother-in-law, Loretta, was also the first cousin of her father, Adrian.)

The three new widowers quickly turned their backs on their native Mexico. Just days after burying Dawna, David Langford led a mass family evacuation from La Mora to the United States, accompanied by his plural wife Margaret and his numerous children by both mothers. He left behind "millions of US dollars invested in pecan orchards around La Mora," according to one of his brothers. Tyler Johnson left Colonia LeBaron with his and Christina's six children—including the baby, Faith—to live in North Dakota, where he could count on the support of the many LeBaron family members already based there. Howard Miller returned to North Dakota, leaving his three surviving children to be raised part-time by Rhonita's parents, Adrian and Shalom, in Colonia LeBaron, and part-time by his own parents, Kenneth and Loretta, in La Mora.

Undaunted, Adrian LeBaron also vowed to remain in Mexico to avenge his daughter's killing. "I owe it to Rhonita and my grandchildren to stay and fight. If I have to tell their story a million times for the next twenty years in order to live in peace, I will. We are being persecuted." Adrian described himself as both indignant and powerless, but he refused to be run out of his home. "If I leave this town, I'm going to die of sadness in some other place in the world," he told a reporter. "I'd rather die here for the cause of liberty and freedom and life. That's my point. There's no other place. There's no other option." Local historian John Hatch, a descendant of the original Mormon colonists in northern Mexico, also insisted he had no intention of ever leaving his ancestral home in Colonia Juárez, Chihuahua. "I've always felt safe here," he said. "We've been very blessed, and we've even heard it stated that the cartels have been told, 'Hey, don't mess with those people [the Mormons]. Leave them alone.'"

"What my family has all said is that they're done. There's nothing worth staying here for," Kendra Miller told the *Deseret News*. Yet in one of her media appearances, she made an appeal to the world to help the family stay in La Mora. "What happens if we leave the people in these towns?" she asked, referring to the nearby villagers who worked on the Mormons' farms and ranches. "I personally want to keep fighting for these people. I want to use this media attention to say to the cartels, 'Your day of power is over. You're done.' That's what we want. That's why we want to ask for the help of the United States."

Numerous family members posted videos on social media about "the grand exodus of La Mora," revealing that many were abandoning their homes in Mexico to resettle permanently back in the US, giving up lucrative orchards, herds of cattle, and beautiful homes. Some said they planned to build a new community somewhere in the US, while others expected to join the American polygamist colonies that were once called the Short Creek Community—or Short "Crick," as they pronounced it—in Arizona, and the adjoining colony across the Arizona–Utah border in Hildale, Utah.

"They're scared for their lives," Leah Langford said, referring to the full-time residents of La Mora. She spoke of a "paradise lost." For more than seventy years, they had lived there in "absolute peace and prosperity," with confidence, fearlessness, and trust, another Langford family member said. Now they were frantically packing, and La Mora would soon be a "ghost town." Lafe Langford, Kenneth Miller's nephew, who lives and works in Louisiana, had hoped to bring his seven children to Mexico to raise them in his native La Mora community. But that dream was now dashed. "Right now, I cannot," he said.

During the weekend of November 9, some one hundred members of the La Mora families fled their homes, traveling in a caravan of eighteen vehicles. They headed north toward Arizona, with as many belongings as they could pack, praying for safety in numbers in the daylight hours and hoping the military presence left over from the funerals would make any potential attackers wary of approaching them.

Those dismayed to see so many people leave La Mora included, as Kendra Miller had suggested, the workers who depended upon them for their livelihoods—a noticeable contrast to the feelings of the LeBarons' neighbors, who wished they would leave Mexico. The village closest to La Mora, San Miguelito, founded in the seventeenth century by Jesuit missionaries, was almost entirely dependent on the Langford and Miller families. "Why should our family have these soldiers around us for protection when other people have nothing?" Kenneth Miller asked a journalist. The La Mora landowners were the sole sources of income for most villagers, whose lives had been enmeshed with theirs for decades, laboring on their farms and ranches and in their orchards. Without that income, meager as it was, the surrounding communities feared a slip into dire poverty. Guadalupe Retana, who lived in a nearby town and who had worked for the Langford family for many years, said that the La Mora families employed nearly all of the town's inhabitants as babysitters, housekeepers, carpenters, and farmhands, and they would be forced to seek work elsewhere after the exodus. Unfortunately, moving north to the US was not an option for these locals. "They are American citizens; they can return to the United States, but we are Mexicans, we have to deal with this whole situation," said Retana. A woman named Yanely Ontivelos, mother of a young son, feared for the future of her family with no jobs left at La Mora. "They, thank God, can go, but we stay. If nobody helps us, we are lost."

A graphic logo created to honor the "La Mora Nine." In November 2019, it was distributed widely among mourners and members of the international press.

Kendra Miller went through with her wedding but afterward relocated to the US. After the move, she recorded a song titled "Fire on Fire" that was mixed and engineered by her new husband and appeared as the soundtrack of a promo video called the *LeBaron Singout! The Blast Off*, featuring thirteen members of her extended family.

* * *

Even observers who knew about the violent history of the LeBaron clan were shocked by the attack of November 4, 2019. Images of Rhonita's burned-out SUV on a forlorn mountain desert road quickly spanned the globe. The sheer brutality of the act, and the courage of injured young children cowering in the cold night of the Sierra Madre waiting for help, were covered as far away as Europe and Australia.

The heinous attack ignited the long-simmering issue of violence in Mexico and America's role in it. Yet President Donald Trump apparently saw a problem only on the Mexican side. When Trump vowed, on Twitter, to send in the US military, he ignored (or was unaware of) the fact that the victims were dual citizens whose families had been living in Mexico for a century or even longer. "A wonderful family and friends from Utah got caught between two vicious drug cartels, who were shooting at each other," Trump tweeted early on the morning of November 5, when neither the motive nor the facts had been sorted out—nor had Mexican officials even arrived on the scene. Just moments later, he tweeted again. "This is the time for Mexico, with the help of the United States, to wage WAR on the drug cartels and wipe them off the face of the earth." He added: "We merely await a call from your great new president!" referring to Andrés Manuel López Obrador ("AMLO").

López Obrador responded, thanking the American president for "his willingness to support us," and, in a phone call later that afternoon, he told Trump that Mexico would handle the investigation and would "ensure justice will be done." He told the press that he was not going to change his security strategy and would not counter violence with more violence. AMLO's non-confrontational policy approach to the drug cartels—dubbed "hugs not bullets" ("*abrazos no balazos*")—was, as his administration described it, designed to avoid an all-out war. He demanded, however, that America do something to stop the arms trade to Mexico, since the cartels had acquired nearly all of their weapons from the US. Trump was correct, in a sense, that the attack was the result of a policy problem, but he did not acknowledge that the problem was, at least in part, on the American side.

The LeBarons were not persuaded that López Obrador had the commitment or ability to investigate and prosecute those involved, so they continued to press the US Government for help. For decades, the LeBaron community had navigated turf battles with the neighboring cartels, but "the cunning murders of their relatives" now led them to approach the American president. Alex LeBaron told a Mexican newsmagazine that the family had let its guard down over the years, "largely because we got tired of being afraid." His nephew Daniel explained that he was eager to accept help from the US, because "this is out of control and the Mexican Government has shown that it is beyond its capabilities. . . . [T]his discourse of national sovereignty is ridiculous." Kenneth Miller, Rhonita's father-in-law, agreed. "I'm not saying I want the U.S. to come down here to revenge my family," Miller said, "but to help all of Mexico."

Proud of their sovereignty and angry about Trump's ongoing barrage of often-racist insults as a candidate and then as president, Mexicans were outraged by the threat of US military intervention in their country. Undeterred by López Obrador's snub, Trump and his congressional allies doubled down. Republican Senator Tom Cotton of Arkansas suggested that US troops "might invade Mexico or take some form of unilateral action" in response to the murders. "If the Mexican government cannot protect American citizens in Mexico, then the United States may have to take matters into our own hands."

The LeBarons further aggravated Mexicans by lobbying US Government officials—going beyond the petition they addressed to the Trump administration—to designate the cartels as terrorist groups so that American forces could launch strikes against them. They reached out directly to Republican Senators Rick Scott of Florida and Mike Lee of Utah, the latter a Mormon. "We are just pissed off," Rhonita's sister, Adriana LeBaron Jones, said, telling the press that the petition was launched because of frustration with López Obrador. Christina's baby Faith "could have starved to death and died," Jones said. "Those kids could have bled to death," referring to the survivors and the delayed response of Mexican law enforcement. The petition brought the desired attention in the United States, prompting Trump to tell Fox News host Bill O'Reilly on November 26 that he didn't want to reveal details of his plan, "but they [the cartels] will be designated." In fact, Trump claimed that he had been working on the terrorist designation for the previous ninety days—starting more than two months before the massacre—and planned to put them "in the same category as al Qaida, ISIS, and Boko Haram."

The LeBarons' pressure on the US Government to intervene drew outrage and stoked anti-Mormon sentiment in Mexico. "Many feel that might lead to US boots on the ground in Mexico," said one reporter. Trump's tweets and the LeBarons' request "fell like a bomb," according to a Mexican news account. "Classifying the Mexican cartels as terrorists would allow the United States government to intervene unilaterally, that is, without requesting permission in the national territory." On December 10, Trump announced that he would postpone the cartel's "terrorist" designation at the request of López Obrador, leaving some LeBaron members furious—not at Trump but at AMLO. "I would have stood up and applauded if he had taken the step, but he'd much rather put the onus on Trump," Adrian LeBaron Soto said. "I am playing the role of Benjamin Franklin when he went to France to ask for support so that the United States could stand up to the boot of the English," the grieving fifty-eight-year-old father told a reporter. "Mexico is now under the boot of terrorists and cartels. And we need help." Adrian vowed to continue fighting for a formal designation of Mexican cartels as foreign terrorist organizations, meeting that week in Washington, DC, with several Republican legislators to plead on behalf of the family.

* * *

In late January 2020, Julian LeBaron led a march of LeBaron family members to the Capitol building in Mexico City, calling for "truth, justice, and peace." Javier Sicilia, whose peace movement Julian had joined eight years earlier after the death of his brother Benji, "was once again on the road" with his former partner-in-activism. Sicilia had not planned to organize another national protest. But, as he put it, "I just couldn't take so many more deaths, especially what happened to the LeBarons—women and children murdered in such a repugnant, outrageous way."

The marchers each walked part of the way wearing only one shoe, to honor the nine-year-old survivor McKenzie Langford, who lost a shoe while attempting to find her thirteen-year-old brother, Devin, after the November 2019 attack. Hundreds of extended family members of the LeBarons and Langfords took part. "We can blame and complain about what the government does all day long, but that will never fix our problem. We have to act," Julian said of the reason for the march on the nation's capital. They had intended to leave a letter for López Obrador, and they were disappointed when the president refused to grant them an audience when they arrived in Zócalo Square.

The LeBarons' critics were growing tired of the family's increasingly outspoken cries of martyrdom. The journalist Ioan Grillo spoke to what he described as "a gaggle of counter protesters" who were shoving the LeBarons and shouting, "Leave the Country" and *Fuera LeBaron!* (LeBaron Out!). Asked why she opposed a family that had been attacked by the drug cartels, one protester responded: "Because the LeBarons just come to take land from indigenous people. It was a settling of scores."

López Obrador made several Cabinet-level security officials available to Julian, Sicilia, and other family members, but he was critical of the march during a press conference the next day. He accused the activists of suffering from "amnesia," saying they had been "silent as mummies" in the face of the flagrant corruption of high-level government officials in the previous administrations dominated by the PRI. Now they were yelling "like town criers." The president specifically drew attention to former Security Minister Genaro García Luna, who, according to testimony in El Chapo's trial, had received millions of dollars in bribes from the Sinaloa Cartel. "Enough hypocrisy," he told reporters, blaming the violence on his predecessors' use of military force to fight the cartels. Some observers even suggested that the conservative LeBarons sought to undermine the López Obrador administration because of their historic and longstanding ties to the PRI, under which the LeBarons had prospered from the 1950s into the twenty-first century. In opposition to the PRI, López Obrador, who was most often described as a center-left progressive democrat, had founded MORENA, the party that had launched him into the presidency in 2018.

"There are a lot of powerful and heavily armed people on all sides fighting desperately for control of the resources," a resident of a community next to Colonia LeBaron said in late 2019, referring to the charged atmosphere that had, by that point, led to the violent murders of the Mormons that year. "They are fighting for land, for water, and to oversee the smuggling and distribution routes into the US."

Julian believed that the anger directed at the LeBarons focused on their relative privilege. "We have dual citizenship. We have the protection of the FBI and Donald Trump's tweets that scare the bejesus out of some people." In February 2020, Julian survived an attack when a group of fifteen gunmen surrounded his home in Casas Grandes. His pack of Belgian Malinois guard dogs were not enough to protect him, and he hid behind a concrete wall and called for help from the federal police posted in Colonia LeBaron, who came and accompanied him to the US border. He traveled to Seattle and stayed there for a couple of months. Asked by a journalist why he thought the cartel wanted to kill him, he answered: "Because of everything. We are a thorn in their side." Julian's father, Joel Jr., became ever more paranoid, according to family members, a recluse living in a walled compound protected by police and bodyguards. Since Benji's murder in 2009, the LeBarons "have had a federal police escort of fifty agents and twelve armed units to protect them," according to the *Yucatan Times*—a fact denied by Julian.

Adrian announced the creation of "Wild West–style volunteer militias, to take on the cartels," because he had no trust in the Mexican Government. "Why are they raising an army?" asked a LeBaron relative who says the police presence in the colony and the idea of a burgeoning private militia is "polarizing the family. If people would study history—the history of the blood feud between Ervil and Joel—they would know that that history will repeat itself." The former DEA agent Michael S. Vigil also thinks the posses would be a disaster. "Creating a militia is tightening the noose around their own necks," Vigil said. "They'll create human rights abuses and run sideways with the cartels who will wipe them out." Adrian's call to arms suggests a comparison to another powerful Mormon family, this one in southern Nevada. Its patriarch,

Rhonita Miller's parents, Adrian and Bathsheba "Shalom" LeBaron, along with Julian LeBaron and Javier Sicilia, take part in the "March for Truth, Justice, and Peace" on January 26, 2020, in Mexico City. The four are walking barefoot to honor nine-year-old McKenzie Langford, who walked nearly ten miles wearing one shoe while seeking help for the surviving children from the November 4, 2019, ambush. *(NurPhoto)*

Cliven Bundy, claims sovereignty from the US Government and encourages right-wing militias to support the family's antigovernment protests.

Adrian again vowed to fight, saying "traffickers want to get rid of the gringos. They want to turn our communities into ghost towns." But now he went further, advocating on social media and in a community-wide forum for Colonia LeBaron to become a sovereign entity within Mexico.

"They killed the wrong daughter," he told *The Washington Post*. "And we will not stop."

CHAPTER TEN

"An Eden in Contention"

"ALL EVENTS IN Mexico go through three stages," Charles Bowden, the legendary borderlands journalist, once said. "First there is the event. Then there are the rumors and theories about what happened. Then comes the final stage. It never happened." And so it was with the murders of Rhonita LeBaron Miller, Christina Langford Johnson, Dawna Ray Langford, and six of their children.

When, in the immediate aftermath of the killings, Mexican officials announced that the massacre was a case of mistaken identity, the initial theory was that the Mormon caravan had been attacked by an offshoot of the Sinaloa Cartel that mistook women and children for members of the Juárez Cartel. "The press ran with the story, and it seemed the case was solved," according to one of the earliest journalistic accounts.

A series of conflicting stories and official statements followed. Mexico's security secretary, Alfonso Durazo, laid out a confusing timeline, putting the attack several hours later than it actually occurred. Durazo's chronology challenged LeBaron claims that the women were targeted, and he backed the government's claim that they were caught in the crossfire between two cartels. Then a Mexican general voiced another theory that had been raised—a variation on the first, with the roles reversed: It was the Juárez Cartel that had deliberately attacked the vehicles, wrongly believing they were carrying Sinaloa *sicarios*. The scenarios were mirror images. These theories, and others proposed in the early days after the attack, involved some version of cartel confusion, as if experienced killers acting in broad daylight had failed to identify the people in the SUVs as women and children.

Of course, the family rejected this line of thinking from the start, insisting that their relatives were the intended victims, that the Mormons were well known in the area, that they had untinted windows and must have been visible to the attackers, that some were shot at point-blank range, even after emerging from the vehicles, and that the surviving children bore witness to a deliberate attack.

Two days after the attacks, former Mexican Foreign Minister Jorge Castañeda steered the speculation in yet another direction, contradicting the official narratives in telling CNN that Rhonita was the primary target of the massacre because she was a prominent activist in the family's clashes with both the cartels and the *Barzonistas*. Reporters began speculating about whether the murders were related to drug trafficking, or whether the family's conflicts with their neighboring *ejidos* over water might have been the motivation—or even that the *Barzonistas* and the cartels had joined forces. Suddenly, it was no longer a case of mistaken identity, and the cartels weren't the only suspects. While the LeBarons welcomed Castañeda's claim that they were targeted, some disputed the characterization of Rhonita as an activist, either against the cartels or for the LeBarons' water rights. "The only thing she was an activist for was her children," one relative said. Other family members did not argue with the label, just with what it meant. "My sister thought it was worth fighting for Mexico," Adriana LeBaron Jones wrote about Rhonita. "We are not fighting the cartels; we are fighting for our right to life, freedom, peace and prosperity." Taking up Rhonita's mantle, Adriana addressed the "Mothers of Mexico" with a page-long petition. "We want unkidnapped paths, crime free, and unmanipulated gasoline," she wrote.

"The Barzón connection is the theory du jour in the Mexican press," according to a news account a week after the attacks. This account described "parched land and rising violence" in laying out the LeBarons' long-running dispute with their neighbors. "Both sides appear to have acted violently." *El Barzón* spokesman Joaquín Solorio was outraged at the conjecture that the farmers would be involved in such a horrific act. "Now I am immersed in speculation and accusations about the LeBaron case and I demand that the prosecutors clarify the case," Solorio told a Mexican news site. Solorio was still grieving over his brother and sister-in-law, who were slain because of their activism, their murders unsolved. "I am a victim too," he said. "I find it distasteful, this finger pointing and speculation. It's up to the authorities to determine [who's responsible]. The murder of women and children is reprehensible." Jeremy Kryt, who reports on the drug war from Mexico and Colombia for the *Daily Beast*, quoted cartel sources as saying the attack was intentional, suggesting that it was meant to drive the LeBarons out of Mexico altogether and that it had been approved at the highest level of the criminal organization. "Kids? Little babies? Mexicans don't kill a bunch of white kids for no reason," he wrote.

* * *

What was not in dispute, and what all sides agreed upon, was that the decades-long, uneasy peace that the Mormons shared with the Sinaloa Cartel had begun fracturing in the months leading up to the massacre. The expansion of drug trafficking and therefore violence—across the region and other states in Mexico—was one factor in the escalating friction. But the primary reason was El Chapo's removal from the scene following his 2016 capture. His three drug-lord sons, *Los Chapitos*, faced competition in the region from kingpins who might not have challenged El Chapo himself, such as Nemesio Oseguera-Cervantes, the head of the imposing and vicious Jalisco New Generation Cartel (CJNG). "El Mencho," as Oseguera-Cervantes is called, is "far more intelligent, savage, hyperviolent, cunning, and powerful than El Chapo," according to Michael S. Vigil, who says El Mencho has built a mini-state in Mexico with a private army and paramilitary force equipped with machine guns, rocket launchers, and a fleet of armored vehicles. Standing five feet, seven inches and weighing 150 pounds, the fifty-five-year-old billionaire is as disciplined as El Chapo was reckless, and "deadlier than a rattlesnake." The war he was fighting with the Sinaloa Cartel, from which he had broken away years earlier, was marked by a brutality shocking even for Mexican drug violence, including beheadings, public hangings, and the murders of pregnant women.

El Mencho's ascendancy occurred after El Chapo's apprehension by US authorities. The US Department of Justice has described CJNG as "one of the five most dangerous transnational criminal organizations in the world, responsible for trafficking many tons of cocaine, methamphetamine and fentanyl-laced heroin into the United States, as well as for violence and significant loss of life in Mexico," and has put him on its Most Wanted list with a $10 million bounty for his capture.

In the months before the massacre, the Sinaloa Cartel demanded, for the first time, that the La Mora families stop buying cheaper fuel in Chihuahua, which was controlled by the Juárez Cartel. "Unfamiliar men manned the usual checkpoints," according to La Mora family members. "They appeared jumpier, sometimes pointing guns at passersby. Rumors spread about the intensifying turf war between criminal groups" in the neighboring states of Sonora and Chihuahua. Julian LeBaron later told CNN that his family had received threats from a criminal group that is dedicated to stealing fuel. "Our family has an interesting mix of mysticism, predictive dreams, and revelations," said another LeBaron family member, "and we had a lot of premonitions before the attack." The LeBarons, like many in La Mora had already done, started asking each other whether it was time to pick up stakes and leave for the US. They began taking more precautions, including traveling in convoys and carrying weapons. From the start, Rhonita's father, Adrian, sought to place blame for the murders on the Juárez Cartel, which he claimed had instructed *La Línea* "to carry out the deadly assault as a tactic to block off the Sinaloa Cartel's drug-trafficking route to the United States."

Such speculation was dismissed by Michael S. Vigil, who described the Juárez Cartel as "nothing more than a horse with one leg." The Sinaloa Cartel is the "King of Cocaine" that controls the "trafficking of drugs and precursors from South America. The Juárez Cartel and *La Línea* are no threat to them," he said, describing how El Chapo had tried to structure the Sinaloa Cartel as a quasi-matriarchy, with more women in leadership roles than any other drug organization in the world—a matricentric configuration that was now being challenged internally by the three *Chapitos*.

In 2007, when El Chapo married Emma Coronel Aispuro, an eighteen-year-old, American-born beauty queen, he brought her into his organization as a full partner and confidante. Thirty-three years her senior, the international drug lord had suffered horrendous abuse at the hands of his father as a child. "His father beat his mother and his sisters, and when Chapo tried to protect them he was severely beaten as well," according to Vigil. "His only protection was his grandmother, so when he obtained his own power, he shared it with the women in his world." As a result, Emma Coronel, with whom El Chapo has twin daughters, knows the inner workings of the cartel, including the smuggling routes and, especially, all of the US and Mexican Government officials it has bribed. Any challenger to the Sinaloa Cartel would need to factor in her knowledge and participation after El Chapo's incarceration and her association with current cartel leader Ismael "El Mayo" Zambada—who is on the FBI's Most Wanted list—as well as the *Chapitos*, whom she's known all of her adult life. In February 2021, the thirty-one-year-old Coronel was arrested in Washington, DC. Facing a life sentence, she pled guilty to federal drug-trafficking and money-laundering charges in the US, and in November 2021 she received a paltry three-year prison sentence. The "Narco Princess has been in the drug trade since she was a little girl," says Vigil. "As the mother of two nine-year-old girls, she was highly motivated to cut a deal with investigators. Her cooperation could bring an end to the Sinaloa Cartel's $11 billion drug empire." She has no loyalty to Zambada, after two of his sons testified against El Chapo. Evidence she could provide US prosecutors about Zambada—as well as information about Genaro Garcia Luna and Cesar Duarte Jaquez, high-level Mexican officials incarcerated in the US on drug trafficking and corruption charges, respectively—is expected to have a dramatic impact on the Mexican cartels.

The only significant rival to the Sinaloa Cartel is El Mencho, who has made inroads deep into their territory, including in Chihuahua and Sonora. While CJNG is more violent, Sinaloa is more powerful. The *Chapitos* own most of the fentanyl laboratories, and cocaine trafficking is their main business. Ivan Guzmán, who is considered the smartest *Chapito* and heir apparent to El Chapo's domain, has been targeted by the US Government for smuggling cocaine, heroin, methamphetamine, and marijuana, using trucks, boats, and tunnels. Theirs is a global empire, with chemicals imported from Asia and cocaine from South America. By comparison, Juárez and *La Línea* are minor players. The smuggling route into Arizona to which Adrian LeBaron refers is inconsequential compared to the Pacific Ocean ports of entry, and overland routes, and tunnels from Baja

California through Tijuana to San Diego that the Sinaloa Cartel and CJNG are fighting over.

In addition to battling El Mencho, the *Chapitos* are aligned against their internal rival, Zambada, described as "Mexico's version of Carlo Gambino," who is angling for one of his own sons to take over the cartel. Called "the most powerful capo in the Sonora-Chihuahua corridor," Zambada was "supposedly deeply upset over the [LeBaron] massacre." He gave orders not to "rock the boat" following the cartel's attack on federal forces during the failed attempt just two weeks earlier to capture one of the *Chapitos*, Ovidio Guzmán. That botched operation brought enormous law-enforcement and media attention to the area. If Zambada had wanted to lie low, as was reported by Jeremy Kryt, then shooting up "a bunch of blond-headed children" and putting it all over the news had the opposite effect.

"Why were there so many shooters?" one DEA informant, with specific knowledge of the forces at work, said to me. "Because it was intensely personal. It's very complicated and dark, with both historic and current elements. [The Mormons] dammed their water, stole their land, and that's just part of it. It's a blood feud and a money feud. Someone had real intel from inside the Mormon community on the women's movements. It was not an accident that none of their husbands accompanied them."

What is clear to at least some US drug-enforcement officials is that the killings got out of hand. "Certain shooters didn't know there were going to be children," said one, explaining why one of the gunmen who was driving a red truck approached Dawna's bullet-riddled SUV and, surprised at seeing the kids, told them to run home. The massacre, both intentional and not, sparked subsequent gun battles among *sicarios*—many of whom "were pissed off, coked up and carrying machine guns"—that continued throughout the afternoon.

American drug-enforcement agents dispute Adrian LeBaron's theory that rival cartels were intentionally bringing attention to the region, as doing so would be counterproductive to the interests of all of them. The attack might well have been "a vendetta against the family who was encroaching on their territory. They had been warned and didn't take heed, so a kill team was sent in," said Vigil. "The message the Sinaloa cartel traditionally sends is 'if they can't get to you, they will get to your family, which will hurt you more,'" said Vigil. The fact that the cartel sent more than a hundred shooters, in two ambush teams, when it would normally send in twenty or thirty hit men, was "overkill," and further evidence of intent. "They knew exactly who they were shooting," said the DEA informant, dismissing any suggestion of mistaken identity. "They used a fucking RPG-7 rocket-propelled grenade," he said.

* * *

Adrian LeBaron did not waver from his conviction that the Juárez Cartel and *La Línea*, not the Sinaloa Cartel, had murdered his daughter and four grandchildren. He spearheaded efforts to hold them accountable when it seemed that López Obrador's administration, which claimed to be aggressively pursuing criminal investigations, was making little progress. In a highly unusual and unprecedented move, Adrian joined twenty-four family members in a civil lawsuit filed in a US federal court against the Juárez Cartel, accusing it of international acts of terrorism. Howard Miller, Rhonita's husband, and Tyler Johnson, Christina's husband, were lead plaintiffs in the case. In addition to Adrian and Shalom LeBaron, Rhonita's parents, the plaintiffs included other relatives of the victims from the LeBaron, Johnson, Miller, and Langford families.

The lawsuit was filed on July 31, 2020, in North Dakota. It charged the cartel with seven claims, including international acts of terrorism, assault and battery, wrongful death, and negligent and/or intentional infliction of emotional distress, and asked for punitive damages. Believed to be the first suit of its kind ever brought against a Mexican cartel in the US, the complaint asked for compensation for the families under the US Anti-Terrorism Act, in an amount to be determined at trial. The Anti-Terrorism Act allows any American citizen to seek damages within the US if they are victims of terrorist acts outside the country; all the plaintiffs had either American or dual citizenship. Michael Elsner, a South Carolina–based attorney representing the family, said the lawsuit was intended to hold the cartel financially accountable for its actions. Elsner, a member of the Motley Rice law firm, one of the nation's largest plaintiffs' litigation firms, has a history of pursuing cases with international implications. He represented victims of Hamas suicide bombings in a lawsuit filed against a Jordanian bank that financed the terrorist group, as well as American citizens in litigation brought against Libya for the 1988 bombing of Pan Am Flight 103 over Scotland.

The lawsuit claimed that during the last week of October 2019, a hundred men from the Juárez Cartel went to a Chihuahua ranch in Buenaventura—a community near Colonia LeBaron that was owned by a *La Línea* leader—where they divided into two groups for a planned attack in Sonora designed to seize territory from the Sinaloa Cartel. The next week, armed with automatic weapons and dressed in civilian clothing, the two groups had set up staging areas eight miles apart in the mountains near La Mora. The legal team's investigation, which Elsner said relied in part on a "confidential informant" embedded with the Juárez Cartel, revealed that the hit teams intentionally tracked the vehicles of Rhonita, Christina, and Dawna. From their hilltop outposts, they watched the women's cars with binoculars; in Rhonita's case, the gunmen videotaped their attack on her SUV, complete with a chilling audio narration. Her SUV, which the lawsuit mistakenly identified as a black Suburban rather than the blue Chevy Tahoe that she had borrowed from her mother-in-law, as described in all previous reports, came under heavy gunfire for ten full minutes from automatic and belt-fed machine-gun rounds. The video showed the assailants approaching her vehicle while the shooting continued.

The litigation was largely seen as symbolic, with little chance of success. It did, however, have one immediate effect: It pushed the narrative that the motive behind the murders was that the LeBarons were "vocal, public critics of the Juárez Cartel," with staged anti-cartel marches, and presented the family members as "symbols of Mormon resistance to the cartel." It also deflected attention away from the Sinaloa Cartel, other drug-trafficking organizations, the Mexican military, the LeBarons themselves, and the family's other enemies.

As the Mexican Government's investigation dragged on, Adrian LeBaron began focusing, almost to the point of obsession, on Rafael Caro Quintero as the mastermind behind Rhonita's massacre. The infamous drug lord is one of America's Most Wanted criminals, having begun serving a forty-year prison sentence in Mexico for the 1985 killing of DEA Agent Enrique "Kiki" Camarena before obtaining an early release in 2013 on a legal technicality. Caro Quintero—with whom Ervil LeBaron's homicidal children, including murder suspect Jacqueline "Tarsa" LeBaron, were associated in the 1980s—reportedly found refuge in the Sinaloa Cartel. Based in his native Sonora, Caro Quintero went into hiding to avoid capture by US officials who were outraged by his release. The FBI is still offering a $20 million reward for information leading to Caro Quintero's capture on charges of kidnapping and murdering a US federal agent. According to Adrian, Caro Quintero had recently switched sides, leaving the Sinaloa Cartel and forming an alliance with *La Línea*. Adrian would claim that it was Caro Quintero who had met with *La Línea* leaders in the municipality of Buenaventura a month before the massacre. That scenario had been laid out in the lawsuit, but now Adrian identified Caro Quintero as the key figure in the meeting that was held near the LeBaron family's vast La Mojina Ranch, and where the coordinated series of attacks was planned.

Michael S. Vigil scoffed at this scenario, saying, "Caro Quintero is not in command of anything," calling him a "phantom old man who hasn't been a Capo since the 1980s." He is a "marijuana has-been who even the Juárez Cartel probably doesn't want," Vigil said, pointing out that marijuana is no longer a big cash crop, and the evolution of the drug cartels has passed him by. "Caro Quintero is on the run, and the last thing he wants is to be caught and returned to the US to face charges because he would never get out."

* * *

The murders devastated La Mora and LeBaron but also appeared to create new opportunities. In November 2019, in the days following the massacre, the LeBarons who owned La Mojina Ranch began building a network of utility poles to bring electricity to pumps for the nine drilled wells that the National Water Commission had declared illegal.

The *Barzonistas* were incensed over what they saw as an audacious water grab, but they decided not to mobilize, out of "respect for the family's grief." But as the LeBarons continued the work of connecting the wells, their neighbors lost patience. Five months after the attacks, on April 19, 2020, some of those neighbors organized a protest at the ranch to stop the new power lines "and were received by bullets by the LeBarons" that injured two people, according to the newsmagazine *Proceso*. "It wouldn't take much to convince the neighboring farms to go after the LeBarons after all the years of feeling abused and violated," said a family member who had witnessed the decades of conflict.

In response to the shooting, some of the *Barzonistas* decided to arm them-selves against "these predators" who were increasing the sizes of their nut farms and violating environmental laws. "The family has used their status as victims to build a transmission line on the La Mojina property in order to elec-trify more wells that are illegal," the members of the *Ejido Constitucion* claimed, demanding intervention by the federal government. Chihuahua State Police and the National Guard arrived to help establish and maintain peace.

Still, the *Barzonistas* vowed to "continue in permanent resistance." On April 21, they blocked a stretch of highway near La Mojina Ranch to broad-cast their demands. At the same time, the LeBarons themselves reached out to the Mexican Government, asking it to stop the conflict and inviting federal authorities to the ranch to inspect the property.

On May 28, 2020, a federal delegate in the state of Chihuahua spent five hours touring the ranch, hosted by Joel LeBaron Soto and more than fifty family members. "We don't have a state authority that listens to us. . . . We need impartiality, the thing is so simple," Joel Jr. told the representative. Calling Chihuahua Governor Javier Corral "an inept person," he demanded that the LeBarons' case be removed from what he dubbed the "corrupt state" of Chihuahua and adjudicated in the courts of Mexico City. "The state gov-ernment is our declared enemy and we do not trust it."

Several of Joel Jr.'s sons told the federal delegate that it had taken them ten years of working in the US to be able to afford a piece of the La Mojina Ranch and to reap the benefits of the family heritage, only to watch the *Barzonistas* destroy things "every time they feel like it." Accompanied by his personal bodyguard, a former member of the Mexican Federal Police, Joel Jr. described how the family was shot at during the most recent confronta-tion with the farmers. Family members spoke of how they are "the objects of hatred," claiming that the farmers tell them to go back to where they came from—that is, the United States. As Julian said, "But we are born here in Mexico. We are more Mexican than Governor Javier Corral because he was born in El Paso, Texas."

For his part, Governor Corral, whom the LeBarons denounced as both incompetent and corrupt, was busily leading an anticorruption campaign, seizing for the state of Chihuahua hundreds of millions of pesos worth of property that had been appropriated by former Governor César Duarte. Corral's "Operation Justice" had set out not only to recover diverted public resources that had been stolen by the previous administration, but also to bring to justice those who had looted the government treasury for personal purposes. Duarte, by this point, had been arrested in the US and was sitting in jail in Miami, fighting extradition to Chihuahua. Corral's administration recouped mega-ranches comprising thousands of acres, as well as thousands of Angus, Brangus, and Charolais cattle, horses of various breeds, hydroponic agricultural properties, urban estates, condominium penthouses, and multiple vehicles—all to be returned to "the people of Chihuahua." The Office of the Anticorruption Prosecutor filed eighty-six criminal complaints against public officials as well as private individuals, and Corral announced that, when the case was resolved, nearly 1.8 billion pesos would be returned to Chihuahua's "neediest population."

Around the same time, Chihuahua's attorney general reopened a five-year-old cold case, announcing a 150,000-peso reward for information about seven Mexican construction workers who disappeared in 2015 from Colonia LeBaron. Ranging in age from seventeen to fifty-seven, the men were installing an encrypted communications system as subcontractors for the US Government–funded Merida Initiative—a US–Mexico intelligence and security partnership formed to combat drug trafficking, transnational organized crime, and money laundering. The technicians began working on the LeBaron property on August 22, 2015, and, over the next week, they were in constant communication with relatives, to whom they reported receiving death threats. On August 29, 2015, they were notified by phone that they could collect their payment at a store in Colonia LeBaron and were last seen depositing their paychecks in a bank in nearby Buenaventura. Dubbed the "Galeana 7," together they left behind more than ten children. "There is a lot of money involved" in the case, a mother of one of the disappeared told *Proceso*, and at least three of the workers were identified as members of the Juárez Cartel, according to the attorney general.

* * *

On the first anniversary of his family's massacre, November 4, 2020, Adrian LeBaron gave an extensive interview to the conservative British tabloid the

Daily Mail. Still an outspoken critic of the Mexican Government's handling of the case, Adrian said he had been promised by President López Obrador that there would be a significant announcement in the coming weeks. Adrian claimed that twelve suspects had been arrested for links to organized crime, but that only one was actually charged in connection with the family murders.

"In Mexico, if you don't do a follow-up on an investigation, it dies," Adrian said. For that reason, he declared his purpose in life was to find justice for his daughter, his grandchildren, and the other victims who lost their lives on that fateful fall morning. "Do you know why they didn't do an autopsy on my daughter, grandchildren and family?" Adrian would ask on Twitter, challenging the government's claim that law enforcement did not have sufficient gasoline to reach the scenes of the attack before the family removed the corpses for burial. "We took them away so that the coyotes did not eat the remains, the rest were ashes, mixed with tears and pain," Adrian revealed. Without dead bodies or DNA as evidence, he implied, officials claimed they were unable to bring murder charges.

Adrian told the *Daily Mail* that he and Shalom were now raising three of his ninety-nine grandchildren—Tristan, age nine, Amaryllis, age six, and Zack, age four—after their father, Howard Miller, had left them behind when he returned to North Dakota, where he was engaged to remarry fourteen months after the murders. Rhonita's widower "now lives abroad and does not want to return to Mexico," law-enforcement officials told the Mexican media. "He is going there to work," Adrian told Reuters. "Don't confuse someone seeking their livelihood with fleeing. His heart, his soul remains in La Mora." Adrian said the toughest thing for him and Shalom "is they are still jumping in bed at night and the oldest one has nightmares and it's bad. He always crawls into the bed, especially with the Grandma. So, it hasn't been easy there. They miss their mother." Kenneth and Loretta Miller told a television documentarian that they, too, were involved in rearing the Miller kids.

Two weeks after the first-year anniversary, the López Obrador administration announced that it had arrested more than thirty people on numerous charges relating to the massacre—significantly more than Adrian had earlier reported—including a man they claimed was the "mastermind." That man was not Rafael Caro Quintero, but Roberto Gonzalez Montes, a former cop-turned-drug-trafficker who goes by *"El Mudo,"* for "The Mute," or "El 32," and who is the alleged leader of *La Línea*'s western Chihuahua cell. Two other men were arrested along with Gonzalez Montes near the town of Nuevo Casas Grandes, where Julian lived. Julian described him as the "top cartel dog, the top enforcer for the Juárez Cartel." The LeBaron family is now "one more step towards knowing the truth about those who killed my children," Adrian had posted on Twitter after Gonzalez Montes's arrest. He publicly praised the Mexican Government for apprehending him but disputed his cousin Julian's claim that Gonzalez Montes was the top dog.

Adrian continued to press for the arrest of Caro Quintero as the true culprit, even though no one in law enforcement had confirmed Caro Quintero's involvement. "I want to see his [Gonzalez Montes's] face and ask him to spill the beans, what happened? So that our soul can be calm," Adrian told a Mexican newspaper. "We do not know what happened, we do not know the truth. . . . That is one of the greatest objectives, to know, who ordered this massacre to be carried out? A bigger boss? Or maybe he is going to say that the devil himself was the one who sent it." Adrian told the *Diario de Chihuahua*, a regional newspaper, that a Mexican judge overseeing the charges against the assassins confided in him that Caro Quintero had had a falling out with the *Chapitos* and had defected from his old Sinaloa Cartel and joined forces with *La Línea* to plan the attacks.

The Mexican Government had eventually brought in the FBI to help with ballistics analyses of the attacks, since nearly all of the ammunition had been manufactured in the US by Remington Arms. The agents were ordered to follow strict protocols that precluded them from identifying themselves as US law enforcement, being armed, or consuming any local food during their probe. So, over a period of several days, they flew by helicopter from the US to La Mora, "taking bags of food and water with them," according to one account. They gathered evidence and interviewed witnesses, but, more than a year after the massacre, the crime scene was of limited use. As of this writing, the FBI's results have not been released to the public.

Then, in January 2021, Mexican authorities announced that the number of suspects identified in connection with the killings had increased to forty, and that seventeen of those people had been arrested specifically for allegedly participating in the attacks. Among them was a LeBaron acquaintance, one Fidencio G., alias "Jano," who, according to the government, had guided the hit men on November 4. López Obrador told Adrian and other family members that Jano had confessed to having given the order to burn Rhonita's vehicle, and having filmed the cell-phone video that had gone viral just days after the attack. The thirty-five-year-old was from the village of Pancho Villa in the municipality of Janos, Chihuahua, and, according to Adrian, knew Rhonita personally. Adrian said he was shown the phone video five times, including once in the presence of the president. There were a dozen family members from La Mora and LeBaron in the prosecutor's office, Adrian recalled, and they showed the video "to us in slow motion, and they explained it to us."

As Adrian described Jano in the video, "you can see" the gunmen started to shoot only when they were close to Rhonita's truck. "A bullet is heard and Jano yells: 'Burn her.'" Without Jano, there would be no case, Adrian said. "Jano is the first bastard who gave himself up. Jano is the one who knew the Langford family the most." Jano told Mexican authorities that many of the hit men were not from the area or even from the region. They were, as he described them, one hundred "well-prepared people, apparently brought from other places," including some who spoke Chinese. Jano confessed that he took them through the back roads that wound through the valleys, mesas, and foothills of the Sierra Madre. After the massacre, fighting broke out among the hit men, leading to more deaths, Jano told investigators, though police reported no additional victims.

Meanwhile, President López Obrador lauded the exhaustive investigation directed by the Office of the Attorney General (FGR), which AMLO's office claimed included 582 interviews with witnesses and collection of a wide range of evidence. On December 17, 2020, the Mexican president had traveled to Bavispe, Sonora, to unveil a monument to those murdered. "This memorial will be a permanent tribute to the victims," López Obrador said at the ceremony. The monument, installed in La Mora, bore the images of the three women and six children, showing them embracing affectionately, and the tree of life, which has symbolic importance in *The Book of Mormon*, representing "the love of God, which sheddeth itself abroad in the hearts of the children of men." Atop the monolith was a statue of the Angel Moroni. Many Mexicans felt that the religious symbolism on a secular government installation seemed out of place. One plaque at the bottom of the monument listed the names of the dead and called them "victims of cartel violence." It went on: "May your spilled blood cry out to God for justice. May the innocence of each soul silenced be remembered. May the anguish of the children that witnessed the killing of their mother and siblings be remembered."

The ceremony on that cold December day highlighted the post-massacre chasm between the families of La Mora and Colonia LeBaron. The LeBaron name appeared nowhere on the monument. No LeBarons were invited to speak.

* * *

Early 2021 brought not only the additional arrests by the Mexican Government but also renewed violence within the LeBaron world. This time, the violence occurred nearly a thousand miles from Colonia LeBaron, on the Pacific Coast, where the family's bloody religious war had begun nearly fifty years earlier with the murder of Joel the Prophet.

Located within the coastal San Quintín municipality, Los Molinos, the eighty-five-hundred-acre colony purchased by Joel LeBaron's Church of the Firstborn in 1965, was again a battleground, with the descendants and followers of Joel, Ervil, and Verlan LeBaron reviving old conflicts over control of the land and water. In 1974, Los Molinos had been the scene of a paramilitary-style assault against the "Joelites" that was orchestrated by the "Ervilistas," leaving two dead and thirteen wounded. Located 180 miles south of the California border at Tijuana, the property's beachfront was the site of Ervil's grandiose plans for a resort and marina, and the place where Ervil planned to dock boats used to dump the corpses of his blood-atoned victims who deserved what he referred to as cement overcoats.

In the years before his death, Joel the Prophet had been petitioning the Mexican Government for the creation of an *ejido* that would protect Los Molinos in perpetuity as a community of small farms for church members and neighboring Mexicans—those "Lamanites" Joel had converted to his version of the faith. Yet, in the meantime, Joel unwisely chose his brother Ervil to carry out his wishes, while awaiting the government's approval of the *ejido*.

Rather than purchasing the land in the name of the church, Ervil had the titles placed in his own name. Then he set about trying to seduce American investors for his vision of a high-end hotel and casino. His plan did not include turning any land over to Lamanites. "It was emblematic of Ervil's racism and belief in white supremacy," said one of his relatives who was living in Los Molinos at the time. "He believed that the lighter the skin, the bluer the eyes, the purer the person." Doctrine called for the Mormons to "sweeten the delightsome Lamanites as the rose," said the relative. "We were to elevate the indigenous people of Mexico. Instead, Ervil was doing dirty deals and screwing them."

On August 18, 1972, Ervil's dreams of becoming rich from the development of the village were dashed when he lost the titles to the land. On that day, the Mexican Government announced—after Joel's persistent requests over a period of several years—that Los Molinos would become a communally owned *ejido* that would be governed by the Church of the Firstborn and that could not be sold for private interests. Rechristened *Ejido Zarahemla*, it was named for an ancient city in *The Book of Mormon* and would be ruled by members of Joel's church. The designation triggered Ervil's rage, and, two days later, at his behest, two devotees fatally shot Joel, setting off the string of an estimated fifty blood-atonement murders carried out by Ervil's children, wives, and several other disciples at Ervil's direction.

Adrian LeBaron, Joel's third-born son with his first wife, Magdalena Soto, had deep roots in *Ejido Zarahemla*. Following his father's assassination in Ensenada, 114 miles north of *Zarahemla*, when Adrian was eleven years old, he moved from Colonia LeBaron to spend his teen years in the community, where he first married and where some of his fifty-nine children were born. His fellow *ejidatarios* included his aunts and uncles, brothers and sisters, many cousins, and devout Joelites such as DeWayne Hafen. By 2021, San Quintín had become a popular tourist destination and the world's largest producer of tomatoes. Once again, though, visions of resorts and vacation homes led certain factions within the LeBaron family to bristle at the *ejido* constrictions limiting commercial development.

The trouble in early 2021 had its roots in events back in 2014. Hafen, who was one of Joel Sr.'s earliest converts, and who had been ordained in the patriarchal priesthood of Joel's church, had been a member of the *ejido* since its creation in 1972. In 2014, Hafen's son Carlos, a politician fresh off a failed bid for the municipal presidency of Ensenada, capital of Baja California, returned to his father's farm in the *ejido* to claim ownership. Carlos had been born and raised in *Ejido Zarahemla*, and he appealed to the *ejido* members—a community of approximately seventy Saints, descendants of Joel the Prophet—to lend him an additional fifty acres for his strawberry farm. Given his parentage, Carlos's request was received favorably, and he began cultivating the inland fields granted to him. By 2021, though, he had aggravated the other *ejidatarios* by spreading beyond his allotment, inching toward the nine miles of seafront property owned by the *ejido* and drilling seven wells listed in his name.

Carlos Hafen "wants to appropriate land that belongs to more than 200 families," Julian LeBaron told a reporter in January 2021. That month, Adrian LeBaron, accompanied by one of his four wives and thirty other relatives, demonstrated before a Baja court, demanding Hafen's eviction. "Carlos Hafen is the son of us, the son of the people, he is one of us," Adrian told the press, even while dismissing Hafen's claim to the land, implying that Hafen was mentally unstable, and stating that the LeBarons had owned the property since 1965.

Adrian accused Hafen of encroaching toward the Pacific Ocean in order to build a seaside resort. "It is very beautiful," Adrian said. "You go up the hill and there is the beach. The place is powerful." Adrian said that hundreds of Hafen's henchmen, armed with machetes and other weapons, had recently tried to take the *ejido* by force, burning six houses that belonged to the LeBarons and their neighbors. "They came to our lands, lands that belong to us, saying that Carlos is the owner," Chelsea Zarate, one of the *ejidatarios*, said in a forty-four-minute video she posted on Facebook showing approximately forty people with pickaxes.

The fertile land and seven wells of fresh water have made it "an Eden in contention," as *Milenio* described it in January 2021. "They want all this water," said Fidel Bautista, one of Hafen's field laborers, referring to the LeBarons. Bautista told a reporter that for twelve years he had been working the land for the Hafens, harvesting brussels sprouts, tomatoes, tomatillos, strawberries, and watermelons. He said that his twenty-year-old son

Emmanuel was driving a tractor in one of the fields when twenty vehicles driven by LeBaron *ejidatarios* surrounded him. He reported that one of the assailants was carrying a firearm, and another attacked him, hitting him on the head with a metal tube.

Calling Hafen a criminal and a hit man, Adrian accused the National Guard of failing to provide the LeBarons with security. He then claimed that Hafen had threatened his life, and he called on President López Obrador to rectify the situation. "It is illegal, and we are not going to leave. We will put up barricades, and if they insist, we will take it to the international level," Adrian warned. He referred to *Ejido Zarahemla* as sacred property, founded by his father, Joel the Prophet, who had been divinely guided to this Promised Land.

"This story has been written many times," Adrian said of the latest agrarian conflict and invasion of LeBaron property.

"We are being persecuted."

EPILOGUE

Sisterhood

———————— ✳ ————————

"Until now I only have the monument in memory of my daughter," Adrian LeBaron posted on Twitter on May 25, 2021. Lamenting that he had seen nothing but "crumbs of justice," Adrian then tweeted that he was celebrating his sixtieth birthday, along with the recent birth of his one hundred fifth grandchild. Since the November 2019 massacre of Rhonita and four of his grandchildren, the little-known polygamist had become a minor celebrity, his Twitter followers swelling to forty-five thousand and surpassing the count of his famous activist cousin, Julian.

A week earlier, Adrian's lawyer, Abel Murrieta, had been murdered in broad daylight in Sonora. A candidate for mayor in the city of Cajeme, the fifty-eight-year-old politician was distributing campaign flyers at a rally in Ciudad Obregón on May 13 when gunmen surrounded him and shot him at least ten times, including twice in the head. The former attorney general in Sonora, Murrieta had been appointed as the legal representative of the LeBaron, Langford, Miller, and Johnson families. "They killed my lawyer, the one who has helped me link the murderers of my daughter. . . . Now I am in mourning," Adrian wrote on his Twitter account. The LeBarons quickly connected his assassination to the attacks, telling the press that Murrieta knew more about the case than anyone. "We are all crying here," Adrian said, revealing that he and Murrieta had been scheduled to meet on May 14 in Tijuana to discuss new evidence in the case, and adding, "What he had to tell me he couldn't do over the phone."

On June 6, 2021—the day of Mexico's midterm elections, which was, as predicted, a referendum on López Obrador's presidency—Adrian tweeted his unchanged thoughts on the president's strategy toward the drug cartels. "I don't want hugs for the hit men who shot my daughter and grandchildren. I don't want bullets either. I demand justice for my family." Not surprisingly, Adrian blamed *La Línea* for Murrieta's murder and fingered former drug kingpin Rafael Caro Quintero as the man behind it.

Shortly before Murrieta's death, he and Adrian had met with authorities from the Office of the Special Prosecutor for Organized Crime Investigation (SEIDO) to review the progress of the 2019 case. While at least one hundred people have been identified as participants in the savage attacks, only five have been arrested for the murders—including Roberto Gonzalez Montes and two of his bodyguards. Those were the result of FBI efforts, not Mexican law enforcement, according to Adrian, who said he was working closely with the FBI. SEIDO officials had promised to keep him apprised of the progress of the investigations, but the FBI was far ahead of them, he said. Adrian added that he was told Caro Quintero and others will not be prosecuted because they haven't found "enough evidence in that spider's web."

Neither the LeBaron family nor American law enforcement believes the case has been resolved, nor that whoever ordered the hit will ever be held accountable. "López Obrador doesn't want a confrontation with the cartels, and he has no intention of cleaning out corruption," said Michael S. Vigil. "When the Mexican government is under pressure, they make arrests and that's that. They create an illusion that the case is solved so the public will stop forcing the issue. Wait and see if anyone is tried, convicted, and imprisoned. The governors and police in Chihuahua and Sonora are corrupt from top to bottom, and that's not going to end with these arrests."

* * *

If the patriarchs of Colonia LeBaron felt that justice had eluded them, their impotence only threw into relief the potency of the colony's women. The men traveled between Chihuahua and Sonora, San Quintín and Tijuana, Mexico City and Washington, DC, meeting with high-level government officials on both sides of the border, cultivating their own political and business careers even as they pursued justice. Buffeted by tragedy and toil, their wives, mothers, and daughters, as always, "held down the fort." It was this "sisterhood," as more than one told me, that maintained the daily routines, providing the sense of security to each other and their hundreds of children. "It is the strength of the women that keeps the colony together," said one of the LeBaron widows, "not the men with their militias and posses and sabre rattling and protest marches." Indeed, like El Chapo's Sinaloa Cartel, Colonia LeBaron seemed to be slowly evolving toward matriarchy. "The men have always been absent," a polygamist's granddaughter explained to me. "But now the women aren't waiting helplessly for them to return. They are running businesses and forging alliances of their own."

Much has changed over the decades, and "the standards and ways of being have evolved differently for different families," said the elderly widow of a polygamist. "The strictness and adherence to doctrine is no longer uniform." New generations of women have risen within the community to sustain the traditions of their fundamentalist forebears. "We believe that God is the same today as he was yesterday and will be forever," said another widow. "So if it [polygamy] was right back then, why wouldn't it be right now?"

Listening to the women of Colonia LeBaron, I could not help but think of my own great-great-grandmother, Jean Rio Baker, and my great-grandmother, Nicolena Bertelsen Baker, and their roles within a polygamous culture. Nearly two centuries ago, one of them came to Zion by sailing ship and wagon train, while the other trudged along with a handcart group. At the end of their long and difficult lives, each was disillusioned with her church. But somehow, neither lost her faith in God.

Acknowledgments

In November 2019, from the moment I first learned on CNN about the massacre of Rhonita, Christina, Dawna, and their children, I knew it would be the subject of my next book. As a longtime investigative journalist and author, I have written extensively about organized crime, murdered women, drug cartels, Western history, polygamy, and Mormons. The brazen daylight attack on the controversial LeBaron clan instantly grabbed my attention as a reporter. But as a descendant of Mormon pioneers and polygamists, I had a personal impulse to unravel it.

I instinctively sensed that the story would illustrate the many conflicts raging in the borderlands of the American West, where I was born and raised, and where I live: drug addiction, cartel violence, exploited women, and water wars. Set against the backdrop of a long and controversial history of polygamy and religious extremism, the massacre was certain also to expose the contemporary world of Mormonism in Mexico.

In addition to my innate and subjective interest in Mormon fundamentalism, my 1970s apprenticeship with Washington, DC, columnist Jack Anderson gave me a rarefied glimpse into Colonia LeBaron. Shortly before I began working as a reporter for Anderson, the nationally renowned Mormon muckraker had broken sensational, exclusive stories about Joel LeBaron's murder by Ervil LeBaron's homicidal acolytes. Anderson had given Ervil the moniker of "the Mormon Manson" and had covered what he called "polygamist cults" since the 1940s. Starting as a cub reporter in Salt Lake City,

Anderson got the "first big scoop" of his investigative career by infiltrating Utah's polygamy underground.

Today, Mexico is one of the deadliest countries for journalists. I owe a debt of gratitude to the many reporters and writers who put their lives at risk every day, covering unfathomable bloodshed and corruption.

This book is based on more than a dozen interviews with primary sources, most of whom preferred not to be acknowledged. Among them are women from Colonia LeBaron and La Mora, as well as both women and men who have left their homes in Chihuahua and Sonora for permanent residence in the US. The request for anonymity is understandable, given the past and present violence their families have faced. I am overwhelmed by the generosity they have shown in telling their stories despite fear of retribution, both physical and emotional. Secrecy has been the foundation of the polygamous experience on both sides of the border for more than a century. The practice remains illegal in Mexico and the United States, and the silence and concealment necessary for survival has been passed down through numerous generations. That so many people trusted me to protect them, as I shared their most private truths with the world, is humbling. While their stories were different, their motivation was the same: To bring light to a dark place, with the hope of some kind of salvation.

I was extraordinarily fortunate to gain the confidence of experienced, knowledgeable, and dedicated law-enforcement agents who, like journalists in Mexico, are working in a war zone. I especially want to thank retired DEA agent Michael S. Vigil, who has an encyclopedic and generational understanding of the Mexican drug trade, and who was unstinting in his response to my never-ending questions.

Once again, I am profoundly grateful to my dear friend Don Lamm, without whom this book would not exist. He recognized the unique pairing of subject and author, worked his literary brilliance in shaping the story, and guided it deftly to the impeccable Liveright. There is no fiercer author's advocate than Gloria Loomis, my agent and friend of nearly thirty years. I owe her a debt of gratitude for keeping my career afloat, mostly while I was a single mom struggling to raise three sons as a full-time freelance writer. Gloria's legendary Watkins/Loomis Agency, with Julia Masnik on board, is a writer's dream team. Dan Gerstle is the editor I've been waiting for all these years. With his intellect and vision, he put me through my paces. Dan was attentive to every detail, nuance, and tone, helping to illuminate the book we both knew was in there. The Norton team of professionals was impressive at every turn.

As always, none of this would exist without my family. My mother, Sara Denton, gave me my first Mead Composition notebook when I was eight years old. She glued wallpaper to the cover to make it look like a real book jacket and told me it would be the first of many books I would write, which set me off and running. This is the book I most wish my father, Ralph Denton, had lived to see. He first showed me the site of the Mountain Meadows Massacre when I was a child, telling me how the sins of the fathers who took part were visited upon their children for generations to come. More than a century after his Danish grandmother pushed a handcart to "Zion," he was haunted by the ignominy of her final resting place. In a section of a Richfield, Utah, cemetery—apart from the obelisks marking the graves of prominent polygamists and their first wives—was what looked like a potter's field. There, among crumbling markers surrounded by weeds, was a plain, barely legible headstone that said: Nicolena Bertelsen Baker, 1845–1905. My sons, Ralph, Grant, and Carson Samuel, have been my inspiration every step of the way. Philosophers all, they approach life with curiosity, humor, courage, and kindness—and always with a sense of adventure that provides me with endless vicarious entertainment.

Saving the best for last, deepest love and appreciation go to my husband, John L. Smith. Thank you for holding up the sky for me. Every single day.

SALLY DENTON
JULY 18, 2021

Notes

Prologue: She Was the Whitest

1   **On the morning of their murders:** The three mothers were uneasy about the journey, according to several accounts of the morning of November 4, 2019. Quotations in this paragraph from Ana Gabriela Rojas, "In the Line of Fire," BBC *World News*, March 23, 2020, https://www.facebook.com/amber.compton.589/videos/4138812756132719/UzpfSTU0MTI4ODYzMzoxMDE1NzEzMjc5NzggzMzYzNA/?fref=search&eid=ARA3kmVLcJfU9C2IIWp-e1S6pcLvtyfo67AcEuXo5PVc0bRabE1CctU2lq3PFpKmPM7kj1Bb10fXiysl.

1   **"Sometimes they get the warning":** *Infobae*, "'They Knew, Before They Shot, That They Were Women': The Story Behind the LeBaron Massacre on the Border Between Sonora and Chihuahua," Nov. 6, 2019.

2   **"typical American mom":** Doug Kari, "How an American Mom Died at the Hands of a Mexican Cartel," *Las Vegas Review-Journal*, Dec. 20, 2019.

2   **"spunky lass":** Author's interview with Rhonita LeBaron Miller's aunt.

3   **"Though she loved":** Azam Ahmed, "After Mormon Family's Terror in Mexico, a Message Emerges: No One Is Safe," *New York Times*, Nov. 7, 2019.

3   **"fireball":** Quotations in this paragraph from BBC News *Mundo*.

3   **"very disciplined":** Quotations in this paragraph from Ioan Grillo, "9 American Mormons Died in a Brutal Ambush in Mexico. This Is the Untold Story of the Hunt for Justice by Those Left Behind," Insider.com, May 7, 2020.

3   **"Dawna could take mundane":** Nate Carlisle, "I Do Not Feel Safe Here," *Salt Lake Tribune*, Nov. 7, 2019.

3   **"model people":** Quotations in this paragraph from Anderson Cooper, "Sister-in-law of Mexico Victim Describes Scene of Massacre," CNN, *Full Circle*, Nov. 6, 2019.

4   **"We were at my house":** Quotations in this paragraph from BBC News *Mundo*.

4   **"We'd been a little more nervous":** Quotations in this paragraph from Kari, *Las Vegas Review-Journal*.

4   **"I have a bad feeling about this"**: Kevin Sieff, "How Mexico's Cartel Wars Shattered American Mormons' Wary Peace," *Washington Post*, Nov. 7, 2019.

4   **they had all talked about security concerns**: *Lara Logan Investigates*, Fox News, Jan. 31, 2021.

5   **"Do you think it's a sign?"**: Quotations in this paragraph from Kari, *Las Vegas Review-Journal*.

6   **"I couldn't tell"**: Ahmed, "After Mormon Family's Terror."

6   **"an arrangement more forced"**: Ahmed, "After Mormon Family's Terror."

6   **"50 or 60 of them, armed to the teeth"**: Mark Stevenson, "At Least 9 U.S. Citizens Killed in Cartel Attack in North Mexico," Associated Press, Nov. 5, 2019.

6   **"hard trucks, Tritons"**: Grillo, "9 American Mormons."

6   **"This is for the record"**: Kari, *Las Vegas Review-Journal*.

7   **"Howie's wife and four kids"**: Quotations in this paragraph from Simon Romero, Elizabeth Dias, Julie Turkewitz, and Mike Baker, " 'Innocence Is Shattered': A Storied Mormon Family Reels After Mexico Murders," *New York Times,* Nov. 7, 2019.

7   **"are hard to listen to"**: Dan Browning, "Williston Family Members Slain in Mexico Were Preparing for Wedding," *Star Tribune* [Minneapolis], Nov. 6, 2019.

7   **"They shot the shit"**: Quotations in this paragraph from David Agren, "How an Isolated Group of Mormons Got Caught Up in Mexico's Cartel Wars," *The Guardian,* Nov. 8, 2019.

7   **"It was awful"**: NBC News, "Family Member of Mexico Ambush Victims Reacts: 'How Is This Even Real?' " Nov. 7, 2019.

7   **"They just unleashed hell"**: Fox News, Nov. 6, 2019.

7   **"The location seemed chosen"**: Quotations in this paragraph from Ahmed, "After Mormon Family's Terror."

9   **"Get down right now!"**: Quotations in this paragraph from ABC *World News Tonight with David Muir*, "American Father Speaks Out for the 1st Time Since Deadly Mexican Ambush," Nov. 10 and 11, 2019.

10   **"We have to go back!"**: CNN *New Day*, Nov. 6, 2019.

11   **"The first [person] that came across the bodies"**: Matt Rivers, "Mexico Family Ambush: LeBaron Family Interview," ABC4Utah, Nov. 7, 2019.

11   **"She was shot with her hands"**: Ahmed, "After Mormon Family's Terror."

11   **"We never dreamed"**: Kari, *Las Vegas Review-Journal*.

11   **"She opened her eyes"**: Grillo, "9 American Mormons."

11   **"When we found out"**: Rojas, "In the Line of Fire."

11   **"so full of bullets"**: Anderson Cooper, CNN, *Full Circle*.

12   **"When they brought her to us"**: Quotations in this paragraph from Grillo, "9 American Mormons."

12   **"had clearly been targeted"**: Lauren Edmonds, "Mormon Father Whose

Daughter and Four Grandkids Were Massacred in Mexico Wants to Set Up 'Wild West-Style Militias' to Take On the Cartels Because He Doesn't Trust the Government," *Daily Mail*, Dec. 21, 2019.

12   **"They knew it was the women"**: Nate Carlisle, "Video of Killings of US Citizens in Mexico Shows Gunmen Poised to Torch SUV, Says Relative," *Salt Lake Tribune,* Nov. 22, 2019.

13   **"She would cry"**: Grillo, "9 American Mormons."

13   **"All the conclusions that we've reached"**: "Attackers Not Confused: They Knew They Were Killing Women, Children," *Mexico News Daily,* Nov. 6, 2019.

13   **"We know that if we want justice"**: Isabel Vincent, "Defiant Patriarch Wants to Start Militias to Fight Mexican Cartels after Mormon Family Massacre," *New York Post*, Dec. 21, 2019.

13   **"Burn it!"**: Carlisle, "Video of Killings."

13   **"Shoot him!"**: Howard Miller et al. vs. Juárez Cartel, La Línea, Vicente Carrillo Fuentes Organization and CFO, US District Court for the District of North Dakota, Case: 1:20:cv-00132-DMT-CRH, Filed July 23, 2020.

13   **"It was a massacre"**: Nancy Dillon, "Funerals Begin as Mormon Families Grapple with 'Unimaginable' Grief Following Mexico Cartel Massacre," *Daily News*, Nov. 7, 2019.

14   **"They shot us up"**: Lisbeth Diaz, "Killed American Family May Have Been 'Bait' in Mexican Cartel Fight: Relatives," Reuters, Nov. 6, 2019.

14   **"This was deliberate"**: Quotations in this paragraph from Kate Linthicum, "For Mexico Ambush Victims, There Was No Safety in Numbers," *Los Angeles Times,* Nov. 6, 2019.

14   **"She was the coolest"**: Liliana Padilla, "We Have No Other Place in the World Than Galeana and Bavispe," *Milenio*, Nov. 16, 2019.

14   **"The beautiful LeBaron girl"**: Kari, *Las Vegas Review-Journal.*

14   **"She just wanted"**: Quotations in this paragraph from Padilla, "We Have No Other Place."

15   **"They had stood up to the drug cartels"**: Quotations in this paragraph from Gaby Del Valle, "Everyone Has a Different Theory about Why the Mormon Family Was Massacred in Mexico," VICE News, Nov. 7, 2019.

15   **"We're living in a war zone"**: Quotations in this paragraph from William Booth, "Ambushed by a Drug War," *Washington Post,* July 23, 2009.

15   **"We've been here for more than fifty"**: Lauren Fruen, "Life in the LeBaron Mormon Stronghold," *Daily Mail*, Nov. 5, 2019.

15   **"There is one ominous signal"**: Quotations in this paragraph from Ricardo Castillo, "Who Slaughtered the Innocent Mormon Family?" *Pulse News Mexico,* Nov. 11, 2019.

16   **"a rhetorical device"**: Will Bagley, *Blood of the Prophets: Brigham Young and the Massacre at Mountain Meadows.* Norman: University of Oklahoma Press, 2002, 51.

17   **"It was the first thing"**: Author's interview with a Langford family member.
17   **"an outlaw by birth"**: Dorothy Allred Solomon, *Predators, Prey, and Other Kinfolk: Growing Up in Polygamy*. New York: W. W. Norton, 2003, 11.

Chapter One: "We're Not Radical Cultists"
19   **"even some agnostics"**: YouTube, "Langford Family Member Talks About What People Got Wrong About Her Family," Emily Langford interview.
19   **"We are heartbroken"**: Quotations in this paragraph from Sydnee Gonzalez, "Church Releases Statement Following Shooting in Mexico," *Daily Universe*, Nov. 5, 2019.
19   **"terrible and tragic"**: Quotations in this paragraph from church statement to CNN, https://www.cnn.com/us/live-news/mormon-attack-us-mexico-border/h_cc168168ad550cbe0beafbb1baa8cea0.
19   **"super cold, unfeeling"**: Quotations in this paragraph from YouTube, "Langford Family member."
19   **"We can never forget"**: Jeremy Turley, "Williston Vigil Remembers Family Killed in Mexico," Forum News Service, Nov. 8, 2019.
20   **"living by the river"**: *Lara Logan Investigates*.
20   **"smattering of marriages"**: Grillo, "9 American Mormons."
21   **"cordial relationship"**: Linthicum, "For Mexico Ambush Victims," *Los Angeles Times*.
22   **"protection payments"**: Carlisle, "Video of Killings."
22   **"They marked out the line"**: Will Grant, "How a US Mormon Family Ended Up Dead," BBC News, Nov. 8, 2019.
22   **"confirmation that this was orchestrated"**: Quotations in this paragraph from Anderson Cooper, CNN, *Full Circle*.
23   **"I don't want to say more"**: Quotations in this paragraph from *La Opcion de Chihuahua*, Interview with Joel LeBaron Soto, Nov. 7, 2019.
23   **"The government of Javier Corral"**: René Delgado, "LeBaron Points Out Police Chief for Massacre," *Reforma*, June 5, 2020.
23   **"clean out the monsters"**: Quotations in this paragraph from Twitter, @realDonaldTrump, Nov. 5, 2019.
23   **"Want to help?"**: León Krauze,"This Family Suffered a Brutal Attack in Mexico, Now It Has a Message for Washington," *Washington Post,* Dec. 12, 2019.
24   **"What worries me more than anything"**: Angel Daily, "Massacre to US Citizens Was Due to Water Disputes and Sex Cult with the LeBarons and Not Cartels," Medium.com. Nov. 7, 2019.
25   **"is where underlings"**: "Women Killed in Mexican Cartel Murders Had Alleged Ties to NXIVM Sex Cult," *Mazatlan Post*, Nov. 9, 2019.
25   **"brand of fringe delusion"**: Quotations in this paragraph from Ben Bradlee Jr. and Dale Van Atta, *Prophet of Blood: The Untold Story of Ervil LeBaron and the Lambs of God*. New York: G. P. Putnam's Sons, 1981, 350.

25 **"to escape irate creditors":** Quotations in this paragraph from James Coates, *In Mormon Circles: Gentiles, Jack Mormons, and Latter-Day Saints*. Reading, MA: Addison-Wesley, 1991, 7.

26 **"He began the book":** Fawn M. Brodie, *No Man Knows My History: The Life of Joseph Smith the Mormon Prophet*. New York: Alfred A. Knopf, 1990, 62.

26 **"BLASPHEMY!":** Brodie, 82.

27 **"In no other period":** Brodie, 101.

27 **"seized by swiftly spreading fear":** Brodie, 63.

27 **"The stupendous claim":** Quotations in this paragraph from Verlan M. LeBaron, *The LeBaron Story: The Saga of a Modern Cain and Abel*. Lubbock, TX: Keels & Co., 1981, 3–4.

28 **"needful for the support":** Brodie, 106.

28 **"And thus did they imitate":** Joseph Smith, quoted in Brodie, 88.

29 **"In the year 1829":** Quotations in this paragraph from Benjamin Franklin Johnson, *My Life's Review: Autobiography of Benjamin Franklin Johnson*. Independence, MO: Zion's Printing & Publishing, 1947.

29 **"convert the Lamanites":** Quotations in this paragraph from Coates, *In Mormon Circles*, 27–28.

29 **"treated as enemies":** Quotations in this paragraph from Brodie, 235.

30 **"fine chestnut stallion":** Quotations in this paragraph from Brodie, 255–56.

30 **By 1844, the religion numbered thirty thousand adherents, with ten thousand of those located in Nauvoo:** https://www.beautifulnauvoo.com/nauvoo-during-the-mormon-period-(1839-1846).html and https://earlyamericanists.com/2016/08/17/the-mormon-political-convention-1844/.

30 **"sovereign Mormon state":** Brodie, 356.

30 **"last stopover":** Coates, *In Mormon Circles*, 40.

31 **"embryo kingdom":** E. Dale LeBaron. *Benjamin Franklin Johnson: Friend to the Prophets*. Provo, UT: Grandin Book Company, 1997, 180ff.

31 **"princes":** Quotations in this paragraph from Brodie, 356.

31 **"in appearance":** Quotations in this paragraph from Johnson, *My Life's Review: Autobiography of Benjamin Franklin Johnson*. Independence, MO: Zion's Printing & Publishing, 1947.

31 **"Although the prophet's well-known zest":** Coates, 45.

32 **"It was a Sunday morning":** Brodie, 476.

32 **"After breakfast":** E. Dale LeBaron, 226.

32 **"the Lord revealed to him":** Brodie, 476.

32 **"He came now":** E. Dale LeBaron, 180ff.

32 **"No, but she is for you":** Jaimee Rose, "Cousin Up a Storm," *Washington Post*, Aug. 7, 2005.

32 **"gave me my first":** Quotations in this paragraph from E. Dale LeBaron, 180ff.

33 **"Even so close":** Hyrum L. Andrus and Helen Mae Andrus. *They Knew the Prophet*. Salt Lake City: Bookcraft, 1974, 91.

33   **"To men who loved"**: Brodie, 300.

34   **"the One Mighty and Strong"**: Quotations in this paragraph from Joseph
      Smith Jr., The Doctrine and Covenants of the Church of Jesus Christ of
      Latter-day Saints. Salt Lake City: Church of Jesus Christ of Latter-day Saints,
      1981, Section 85, 7.

34   **"Will you stand by me"**: Brodie, 378–79.

34   **"To attempt to delineate"**: Quotations in this paragraph from E. Dale
      LeBaron, 180ff.

34   **"arose and roared"**: John D. Lee (Samuel Nyal Henrie, ed.), *Writings of John
      D. Lee*. Tucson: Hats Off Books, 2001, 142.

35   **"One of the most remarkable"**: Quotations in this paragraph from Bagley, 18.

35   **"own little mill stream"**: M. R. Werner, *Brigham Young*. New York:
      Harcourt Brace, 1929, 13.

35   **"the bloodthirsty Christians"**: Bagley, 19.

35   **"thus making the entire"**: Lee, 147.

35   **"There is a tinge of Cromwell"**: T. B. H. Stenhouse, *The Rocky Mountain
      Saints: A Full and Complete History of the Mormons, From the First Vision of Joseph
      Smith to the Last Courtship of Brigham Young*. London: Ward, Lock, and Tyler,
      1871, 205.

36   **"vowed he would kill"**: Stanley P. Hirshson, quoted in Coates, 54.

36   **"Flee Babylon"**: Susan Black and Larry C. Porter, eds., *Lion of the Lord:
      Essays on the Life and Service of Brigham Young*. Salt Lake City: Deseret Book
      Company, 1995, ix.

36   **"the Holy City by the Dead Sea"**: Wallace Turner, *The Mormon
      Establishment: How Does This Uniquely American Religion Rule the Lives of Two and
      a Half Million Americans Today?* Boston: Houghton Mifflin, 1966, 1.

36   **"laying the foundation"**: Marc Reisner, *Cadillac Desert: The American West
      and Its Disappearing Water*. New York: Viking, 1986, 2.

37   **In 2020, the church became the richest in the world:** See
      https://www.tuko.co.ke/365971-15-richest-churches-world-2020
      .html?utm_source=Salt+Lake+Tribune&utm_campaign=ceab255ba1
      -mormonland070920&utm_medium=email&utm_term=0_dc2415ff28
      -ceab255ba1-44959501&mc_cid=ceab255ba1&mc_eid=028292255c.

37   **"nearly fifty years of cold war"**: Quotations in this paragraph from David
      L. Bigler, *Forgotten Kingdom: The Mormon Theocracy in the American West, 1847–
      1896*. Logan: Utah State University Press, 1998, 45–46.

38   **"deliberately snubbed"**: Quotations in this paragraph from Mark Twain,
      Roughing It. New York: Penguin, 1987, 425.

38   **"a prophet of God"**: E. Dale LeBaron, 180ff.

39   **"God never introduced"**: Brigham Young, quoted in Coates, 1.

39   **"Taylor is dead and in hell"**: Stanley P. Hirshson, *The Lion of the Lord*. New
      York: Alfred A. Knopf, 1969, 111.

39 **"laying to rest speculation"**: https://www.courier-journal.com/
story/news/history/river-city-retro/2014/07/08/zachary-taylor-death
-solved/12363933/.

40 **"great cause of disruption"**: Lieut. J. W. Gunnison, *The Mormons, or Latter-Day Saints, In the Valley of The Great Salt Lake: A History of Their Rise and Progress, Peculiar Doctrines, Present Condition, and Prospects, Derived from Personal Observation During a Residence Among Them*. Philadelphia: Lippincott, Grambo & Co., 1852, 157–59.

40 **"tempest"**: Gunnison, *The Mormons*, 29.

41 **"snubbed his nose"**: Author's correspondence with Benjamin E. Park, March 8, 2021.

41 **"a living monument"**: Scott Anderson, *The 4 O'Clock Murders: The True Story of a Mormon Family's Vengeance*. New York: Bantam Doubleday, 1993, 43.

41 the **"White Horse Prophecy"**: Sandra Tanner, "Joseph Smith's 'White Horse' Prophecy." Salt Lake City: Utah Lighthouse Ministry. Undated post on http://www.utlm.org/onlineresources/whitehorseprophecy.htm.

42 **"When I die, my mantle"**: Anderson, *The 4 O'Clock Murders*, 45.

42 **"the great things to transpire"**: Charlotte K. LeBaron, *Maud's Story: With Entire Sections in Her Own Words*. Bloomington, IN: Author House, 2014.

42 **"100-year vision"**: Quotations in this paragraph from Bradlee and Van Atta, 38.

Chapter Two: The Englishman and the Danish Girl

43 **"Come girls come"**: Mormon Folk Song, *Music of the Mormons*, 26.

43 **"Where was the excitement"**: Susan Ray Schmidt, *His Favorite Wife: Trapped in Polygamy, A True Story of Violent Fanaticism*. Twin Falls, ID: Kassidy Lane Publishing, 2006. Jacket copy.

44 **"miserable prescription"**: Irene Spencer, *Shattered Dreams: My Life as a Polygamist's Wife*. N.p.: Gold-Donn Opportunities Publishing, 2019, 347.

44 **"Irene was a precious"**: Author's interview with a LeBaron plural wife.

44 **"decided it was finally"**: Quotations in this paragraph from Spencer, *Shattered Dreams*, 347.

44 **"birthright and destiny"**: Quotations in this paragraph from Solomon, *Predators, Prey, and Other Kinfolk*, 54.

44 **"heavy duty brainwashing"**: Quotations in this paragraph from author's interview with a LeBaron plural wife.

44 **"At age nine"**: Quotations in this paragraph from Anna LeBaron, with Leslie Wilson, *The Polygamist's Daughter*. Carol Stream, IL: Tyndale House Publishers, 2017, ix–x.

45 **"believed that polygamy"**: Quotations in this paragraph from Ruth Wariner, *The Sound of Gravel*. New York: Flatiron Books, 2015, 11.

45   **"It brought out the poetesses"**: Quotations in this paragraph from author's interview with the daughter of a Colonia LeBaron polygamist.

45   **"We all lived in this euphoria"**: Quotations in this paragraph from Bradlee and Van Atta, 75–76.

46   **"We felt we were making"**: Quotations in this paragraph from Rena Chynoweth, *The Blood Covenant*. Fort Worth: Eakin Press, 1990, 25.

46   **"When God said"**: Mohamed Madi and Ana Gabriela Rojas, "Mexico Ambush: Mormon Families Waiting for Justice a Year On from Massacre," BBC News, Nov. 9, 2020.

46   **"sin and unworthiness"**: Taylor, 19. For John Taylor's biography, see https://history.churchofjesuschrist.org/chd/individual/john-taylor -1808?lang=eng.

47   **"the pure Queen's English"**: William George Baker told this to his daughter, Hazel Baker Denton. Author's collection.

48   **"preaching the glory"**: Brodie in Frederick Hawkins Piercy, *Route from Liverpool to Great Salt Lake Valley*, edited by Fawn Brodie. Cambridge: Belknap Press/Harvard University Press, 1962, xiv. Personal documents of Jean Rio Baker claim that the Baker family was baptized by John Taylor, while Jeffery Johnson, one of her descendants who is a Mormon history scholar, disputes this claim.

48   **"signs of the times"**: https://eom.byu.edu/index.php/Signs_of_the_Times.

49   **"I this day took leave"**: Quotations in this paragraph from Jean Rio Diary. See Denton, *Faith and Betrayal*, 43.

51   **"Read it every day"**: Quotations in this paragraph from Nicolena Bertelsen recollections, as told to her daughter, Hazel Baker Denton. Author's collection.

54   **"Her sweetheart lingered"**: Quotations in this paragraph from "The Morning and the Evening Star," Recollections of Louise Baker Pearce. Private family manuscript.

55   **"unusual fresh beauty"**: Quotations in this paragraph from personal family recollections. Author's collection.

55   **"who hungered and thirsted"**: Quotations in this paragraph from "Portrait of a Danish Family," by *Daughters of the Utah Pioneers*. Lessons for March and April 1981, 303.

56   **"in a precise line"**: Quotations in this paragraph from descendants' recollections. Author's collection.

56   **"The little happinesses"**: Recollection of Nicolena Bertelsen's daughter, Ruth Henrietta Baker Seegmiller, and 1951 Baker Family Reunion Record. Author's collection.

57   **"a little patch of worthless land"**: Hazel Baker Denton, 1951 Baker Family Reunion Record. Author's collection.

57   **"twin relics of barbarism"**: John A. Wills, "The Twin Relics of

Barbarism." *Historical Society of Southern California, Los Angeles*, vol. 1, no. 5, 1890, pp. 40–44, JSTOR. www.jstor.org/stable/41167826. Accessed March 13, 2021.

58   **"Mormon Reformation"**: Quotations in this paragraph from Josiah F. Gibbs, *The Mountain Meadows Massacre*. Salt Lake City: Salt Lake City Tribune Publishing Company, 1910, 8ff.

58   **"There are sins"**: Brigham Young, quoted in *Deseret News*, Oct. 1, 1856.

58   **"The brothers sneaked away"**: Quotations in this paragraph from author's interview with Baker descendant Barbara Baker.

58   **"They could not stand poverty"**: Quotations in this paragraph from Jean Rio Diary. Author's collection.

60   **"Tall and symmetrical"**: Quotations in this paragraph from Hal Schindler, "Brigham Young's Favorite Wife," *Salt Lake Tribune*, July 30, 1995.

Chapter Three: Mountain Meadows Dogs

62   **"While eating breakfast"**: Sarah Baker memoir, *Higbee History and Stories*, Gerald R. Sherratt Library, Southern Utah University, Cedar City. See also Bagley, *Blood of the Prophets,* 123.

64   **"held by all civilized nations"**: T. B. H. Stenhouse, *Rocky Mountain Saints,* 234.

64   **"said the Indians had gone hog wild"**: Sallie Baker, quoted in 1940. Found in *Higbee History and Stories*, Special Collections, Gerald R. Sherratt Library, Southern Utah University, Cedar City (including synopsis of interview with eighty-five-year-old massacre survivor Sallie Baker Mitchell in September 1940).

65   **"the only man in the country"**: Bagley, 100.

65   **"harvest field"**: Juanita Brooks, *The Mountain Meadows Massacre*. Norman: University of Oklahoma Press, 1962, 84.

65   **"Gather up the Indians"**: http://www.1857ironcountymilitia.com/index.php?title=A_Basic_Account.

65   **"stir up all the other Indians"**: William Wise, *Massacre at Mountain Meadows: An American Legend and a Monumental Crime*. New York: Thomas Y. Crowell, 1976, 211.

66   **"old enough to tell tales"**: https://www.mtn-meadows-assoc.com/bakermitchell1940transcription.htm.

66   **"The children cried nearly all night"**: Interview with Albert Hamblin in US House of Representatives, *Mountain Meadow Massacre, Special Report of the Mountain Meadow Massacre by J. H. Carleton, Brevet Major, United States Army, Captain, First Dragoons*, Doc. 605. 57th Cong., 1st sess., 1859.

66   **"Do you want to know?"**: Juanita Brooks, *The Mountain Meadows Massacre*, 86.

66   **"We ordered the people"**: John D. Lee, *Mormonism Unveiled or Life and Confession of John D. Lee*. Albuquerque: Fierra Blanca Publications, 2001, 251.

67   **"The whole United States":** Mark Twain, 428.
68   **"My father was killed by Indians":** Bagley, 154.
68   **"It was too heavy to move":** Bradlee and Van Atta, 34.
69   **"Make yourself scarce":** Juanita Brooks, *John Doyle Lee: Zealot, Pioneer Builder, Scapegoat.* Logan: Utah State University Press, 1992, 296.
69   **"the butcher in chief":** *Salt Lake Daily Tribune,* Nov. 14, 1874.
69   **"Trial of the Century":** *Salt Lake Daily Tribune,* July 19, 1875.
70   **"a preferred location":** Bagley, 121.
70   **"I have been sacrificed":** Quotations in this paragraph from *Salt Lake Daily Tribune,* whose correspondents at the scene reported Lee's execution. The stories are reprinted in Robert Kent Fielding, *The Unsolicited Chronicler: An Account of the Gunnison Massacre, Its Causes and Consequences.* Brookline, MA: Paradigm Publications, 1993, 261ff.
70   **"Those with me at that time":** *New York Herald,* March 21, 1876, reprinted in the *San Francisco Chronicle, Salt Lake Daily Tribune,* and *Pioche* [NV] *Record.*
70   **"If I am not guilty":** Bagley, 319.
72   **"greatly attracted":** Quotations in this paragraph from Bagley, 348–49.
72   **"withered and blasted":** Stenhouse, 447.
73   **"killing to save":** Bigler, *Forgotten Kingdom,* 131.
73   **US Army escorts began accompanying:** Polly Aird in *Nevada Historical Society Quarterly,* Fall 2001, 197.
73   **"I have every temporal comfort":** Jean Rio Diary. Author's collection.
73   **"I have lived in firm belief":** Jean Rio Last Will and Testament, June 6, 1882. Author's collection.
73   **"Plucked from the lap of luxury":** Quotations in this paragraph are William Baker's descendants' recollections. Author's collection.

Chapter Four: Zion in a Dry Place
75   **"sort of safety valve":** Thomas Cottam Romney, *The Mormon Colonies in Mexico.* Salt Lake City: University of Utah Press, 1938, 3.
75   **"in the event that persecution":** Quotations in this paragraph from Romney, 39ff.
76   **"I know that the church will kill me":** Bagley, *Blood of the Prophets,* 324–25.
76   **"W[hen] they enact tyrannical laws":** Jon Krakauer, *Under the Banner of Heaven: A Story of Violent Faith.* New York: Random House, 2004, 252.
77   **"No other name in Mormon history":** Verlan M. LeBaron, *The LeBaron Story,* 12.
77   **"I defy the United States":** Taylor, quoted in Krakauer, 252.
77   **"Lewd or unlawful":** Quotations in this paragraph from Verlan M. LeBaron, 13.
77   **"resulted in an agreement":** Quotations in this paragraph from *New York Times,* "The Mormons in Mexico," June 29, 1885.

78   **"all the plows, shovels"**: Quotations in this paragraph from Lynn Smith, "The Mormon Enclave in Mexico: Descendants of Pioneers Gather to Celebrate Centenary," *Los Angeles Times,* Aug. 18, 1985.

79   **"The federal government then dealt"**: Verlan M. LeBaron, 14.

79   **"It says something about bounty"**: Jaimee Rose.

79   **"The church was disincorporated"**: Verlan M. LeBaron, 14.

80   **"I went before the Lord"**: Quotations in this paragraph from Wilford Woodruff, quoted in Verlan M. LeBaron, 16–17.

81   **"that a man will be judged"**: Verlan M. LeBaron, 33–34.

81   **"the Mexico LeBarons"**: Verlan M. LeBaron, 3.

82   **"the biggest family in the Americas"**: Grillo. "9 American Mormons." There are forty-four-thousand descendants of Benjamin Franklin Johnson in the B. F. Johnson family database, according to Jaimee Rose, "Cousin Up a Storm," *Washington Post,* Aug. 7, 2005.

82   **"the legitimate one"**: Quotations in this paragraph from Jaimee Rose.

82   **"They have been taught"**: Verlan M. LeBaron, 25.

83   **"in the end of the Times of the Gentiles"**: Antonio Trevisan Teixeira, "Was Ross LeBaron a Mormon Fundamentalist?" *Ross LeBaron, the Holy Order and the Church of the Firstborn,* Holyorder.org.

83   **"direct descendants of Jesus"**: Scott Anderson, 439.

83   **"Husbands were expected"**: Recollections of Nicolena Bertelsen, as told to her daughter, Hazel Baker Denton. Author's collection.

84   **"Do not be uncaring"**: Quotations in this paragraph from 1890 letters to Nicolena Bertelsen from William George Baker. Author's collection.

85   **"who had known nothing"**: Romney, 147.

86   **"There appeared to be a concerted plan"**: Romney, 218.

86   **"fearsome desperado"**: Quotations in this paragraph from Lynn Smith, "The Mormon Enclave in Mexico."

87   **"the most well-to-do people"**: Romney, 182.

87   **"Long live the Liberals"**: Romney, 200.

87   **"is historically true that the immediate cause"**: Romney, 148.

87   **"Scarcely had the whistle of the last train"**: Romney, 221.

87   **"Suddenly, a firm hand"**: Quotations in this paragraph from Verlan M. LeBaron, 41.

88   **"one of the well-respected McDonalds"**: Bradlee and Van Atta, 36.

88   **"Plans were hurriedly made"**: Verlan M. LeBaron, 42.

88   **"carefully orchestrated"**: Scott Anderson, 50.

88   **"prospects for crops"**: Romney, 250.

88   **"awaiting the magic touch"**: Romney, 256–57.

89   **"against the doctrine"**: Scott Anderson, 55.

89   **"Dayer was regarded"**: Bradlee and Van Atta, 40.

89   **"It broke Dayer's heart"**: Author's interview with a LeBaron family member.

90   **"Father said that the church"**: Verlan M. LeBaron, 53.

90   **"The boys were as good young fellows"**: Scott Anderson, 58–59.

90   **"bastard child"**: Janet Bennion, *Desert Patriarchy: Mormon and Mennonite Communities in the Chihuahua Valley*. Tucson: University of Arizona Press, 2004, 123–24.

90   **"had implicit faith"**: Verlan M. LeBaron, 109.

90   **"The poverty and abuse"**: Author's interview with family member.

91   **"Instead of the land of milk and honey"**: Quotations in this paragraph from Solomon, *Predators, Prey, and Other Kinfolk*, 167.

91   **"rattle day snakes"**: Author's interview with a LeBaron family member.

91   **"felt spiritually superior"**: Irene Spencer, *Cult Insanity: A Memoir of Polygamy, Prophets, and Blood Atonement*. New York: Center Street, 2009, 9.

92   **"That's more than you can do"**: Spencer, 10.

92   **"the true representative"**: Bennion, 128.

92   **"Seeing men vying"**: Spencer, *Cult Insanity*, 8.

Chapter Five: "Am I About to Have a Cain in My Family?"

93   **"knew and interpreted"**: Author's interview with a Church of the Firstborn member.

94   **"nations of Babylon"**: Quotations in this paragraph from Janet Bennion, *Desert Patriarchy*, 127.

94   **"dunked in the water"**: Author's interview with a LeBaron family member.

94   **"They not only preached the scriptures"**: Author's confidential interview with a Tucker family member.

94   **"the highest honor"**: Bradlee and Van Atta, 64.

94   **"Such a thing had never happened"**: Bradlee and Van Atta, 68.

95   **"euphoric"**: Quotations in this paragraph from Alice Spencer, *Cult Insanity*, 77.

95   **"serious menace"**: Bradlee and Van Atta, 77.

95   **"They used the term 'Lamanites' "**: Author's interview with a confidential source.

95   **"white and delightsome people"**: *Book of Mormon*, 2 Nephi 30:6. The original phraseology of "white and delightsome people" was retained in *The Book of Mormon* until it was replaced with "pure," in the 1840 edition, apparently at the direction of Joseph Smith himself.

95   **"represented some of the best blood"**: Quotations in this paragraph from Romney, 265.

95   **"heathen and take on the 'curse' "**: Bradlee and Van Atta, 83.

95   **"beat both his Mexican wives"**: Leroy Hatch, quoted in Bradlee and Van Atta, 85.

95   **"a cultish nest"**: Richard Grant, *God's Middle Finger: Into the Lawless Heart of the Sierra Madre*. New York: Free Press, 2008, 55.

96   **"one ill-fated project"**: Bennion, 128.

96   **"could swing a grubbing hoe"**: Verlan M. LeBaron, 183.

96   **"Only a few days ago"**: Verlan M. LeBaron, 190.

96   **"Faded denim pants"**: Verlan M. LeBaron, 184.

97   **"*dollars* not pesos"**: Quotations in this paragraph from Verlan M. LeBaron, 195.

97   **"Ervil talked about bringing in tanks"**: Quotations in this paragraph from DeWayne Hafen interview, https://holyorder.org/2018/08/14/dewayne-hafen-interview-to-dale-von-atta-1978/.

97   **"sacred duty"**: Quotations in this paragraph from Verlan M. LeBaron, 186.

97   **"the Civil Law of God"**: Solomon, *Predators, Prey, and Other Kinfolk*, 237.

98   **"we just might have to kill"**: Quotations in this paragraph from DeWayne Hafen, 1978 interview with Dale Van Atta, 3, https://holyorderorg.files .wordpress.com/2018/08/dewaynehafen-mss-2258-box-2-interview-to-van -atta-in-los-molinos-1978.pdf.

98   **"how the corpses would be taken care of"**: Quotations in this paragraph from Bradlee and Van Atta, 130.

99   **"The Black Hand"**: Scott Anderson, 108.

99   **"I'll never forget"**: Quotations in this paragraph from Spencer, *Cult Insanity*, 81–82.

99   **"He was considered the goodwill ambassador"**: Quotations in this paragraph from author's interview with a Jensen family member.

100   **"speaking to me now"**: Spencer, *Cult Insanity,* 199.

100   **"Each time we got a new threat"**: Ruth Wariner, *The Sound of Gravel*, 16–17.

100   **"Dear Son Ervil"**: Verlan M. LeBaron, 205.

100   **"Maud had frequently"**: Author's interview with a LeBaron family member.

100   **"Your father has warned you"**: Quotations in this paragraph from Verlan M. LeBaron, 208–9.

100   **"He was paranoid as hell"**: Quotations in this paragraph from Bradlee and Van Atta, 137–38.

101   **"Why don't you come into the house"**: Bradlee and Van Atta, 140.

101   **"Everyone knew it had been done"**: Verlan M. LeBaron, 212.

101   **"Some people don't take me seriously"**: Scott Anderson, 155.

101   **"How solemn he was"**: Verlan M. LeBaron, 219.

101   **"He stands with Abraham"**: Bradlee and Van Atta, 143.

102   **"He is a prince, not a prophet"**: Bradlee and Van Atta, 144.

102   **"Lord's hand came down"**: Author's interview with a relative of Ervil LeBaron.

102   **"Having successfully blood atoned Joel"**: Spencer, *Cult Insanity*, 227.

102   **"Everyone in the colony"**: Author's interview with a relative of Ervil LeBaron.

103   **"Since Joel's death"**: Verlan M. LeBaron, vii.

103   **"minute you step into this"**: Bradlee and Van Atta, 145.

103   **"far-sighted police officers"**: Verlan M. LeBaron, 265.

104   **"the wicked Babylon"**: Scott Anderson, 453.

104   **"rise up and militantly throw off"**: Quotations in this paragraph from Verlan M. LeBaron, 271.

104   **"seemed to demand more"**: Jack Anderson, with Daryl Gibson, *Peace, War, and Politics: An Eyewitness Account*. New York: Forge Books, 1999, 31.

104   **"We are living in the last dispensation"**: Solomon, *Predators, Prey, and Other Kinfolk,* 277.

105   **"a law unto themselves"**: Solomon, 168.

105   **"Satan is doing his utmost"**: Solomon, 277.

105   **"Apparently threats on a polygamist"**: Solomon, 280.

105   **"There are no drugs or drinking"**: Lou Cannon, "Violent Death Shadows Polygamist Sect," *Washington Post*, Aug. 8, 1977.

105   **"a new and bloodier brand"**: Quotations in this paragraph from "The Nation: A Deadly Messenger of God," *Time,* Aug. 29, 1977.

106   **"Butch Cassidy loved"**: Bradlee and Van Atta, 322.

106   **"mind that was in turn"**: Jack Anderson, 31.

106   **"death team"**: Quotations in this paragraph from Spencer, *Cult Insanity*, 289.

106   **"made it his business"**: Spencer, 324.

106   **"worldwide patriarch"**: Spencer, 327.

107   **"Brother, it looks like"**: Shane Smith, "The Mexican Mormon War, VICE News, Sept. 26, 2012.

107   **"with a sort of misty-eyed reverence"**: Verlan M. LeBaron, 297.

107   **"Might Joel's people?"**: Verlan M. LeBaron, 301. Various accounts place the time of Verlan's death as between one and two days after Ervil's death.

107   **"the succession that began"**: Chynoweth, *The Blood Covenant*, 340.

107   **"When you have already decided"**: Solomon, *Predators, Prey, and Other Kinfolk,* 280.

108   **"a Mormon fundamentalist version"**: Scott Anderson, 328.

108   **"It was with the profits"**: https://archives.fbi.gov/archives/houston/press-releases/2011/jacqueline-lebaron-sentenced-to-prison.

108   **"a bad scene"**: Quotations in this paragraph from Chynoweth, 346.

109   **"Because our legal business"**: Heber LeBaron confession, http://www.people.vcu.edu/~dbromley/undergraduate/spiritualCommunity/ChurchOfTheLambOfGodReadingsLink.html.

109   **"They had their hair cut short"**: Scott Anderson, 329.

109   Linda gave **"the impression"**: Scott Anderson, 331.

110   **"While planning the murders"**: "Jacqueline LeBaron Sentenced to Prison," FBI, Sept. 8, 2011, https://archives.fbi.gov/archives/houston/pressreleases/2011/jacqueline-lebaron-sentenced-to-prison.

110   **"blood atoned by her own son"**: Spencer, *Cult Insanity*, 328.

110   **"Tarsa was like a little Ervil"**: Scott Anderson, 336.

110   **"You can deal with a criminal who kills for greed"**: Garry Abrams, "A Family's Legacy of Death: Ervil LeBaron Said God Told Him to Kill Anyone Who Strayed from His Polygamist Cult. A Tenacious Salt Lake Investigator Tracked the LeBarons for 15 Years. Now, an Anonymous Tip May Have Helped Him Close a Case That Claimed as Many as 30 Lives," *Los Angeles Times*, Sept. 20, 1992.

110   **"Everyone is an infidel"**: Author's interview with a LeBaron family member.

111   **"We were taught that we were being persecuted"**: Anna LeBaron, 11.

111   **"this melodrama of the Modern West"**: Abrams, "A Family's Legacy of Death."

111   **"born to the most notorious"**: Quotations in this paragraph from *My Name is William Heber LeBaron, Federal Prisoner Number 22254-077,* http://www.people.vcu.edu/~dbromley/undergraduate/spiritualCommunity/ChurchOfTheLambOfGodReadingsLink.html.

113   *consigliore* **for the LeBaron crime family**: https://www.foxnews.com/story/most-wanted-murder-suspect-jacqueline-tarsa-lebaron.

113   **"a blue blouse"**: Quotations in this paragraph from Mike Tolson, "Cult Leader's Daughter Faces Trial in 4 Deaths Father Ordered," *Houston Chronicle,* May 14, 2010.

114   **"Hallelujah"**: Ben Winslow, "FBI Arrests Fugitive Mormon Fundamentalist Wanted for Murders Ordered by Her Violent Cult Leader Father," Fox News, May 13, 2010.

114   **"She should have gotten the death penalty"**: Author's interview with Michael S. Vigil.

114   **"It's probably over"**: John Hollenhorst, "Retired Prosecutor Speaks Candidly About High-Profile Cases," *Deseret News,* Feb. 3, 2014.

114   **"It's a fact that the LeBarons"**: Bradlee and Van Atta, 51.

115   **"We became nomads"**: Quotations in this paragraph from author's interview with a LeBaron family member.

115   **"I think we are a most unusual family"**: Lou Cannon, "Violent Death Shadows Polygamist Sect."

Chapter Six: Saint Benji and the Vanguard

116   **"basic camps"**: Quotations in this paragraph from Janet Bennion, *Desert Patriarchy,* 59.

117   **"the world's largest drug lord"**: Author's interview with Michael S. Vigil. For more on El Chapo's capture, see: "Infamous Drug Lord 'El Chapo' Is Captured by Mexican Authorities. History Channel, https://www.history.com/this-day-in-history/el-chapo-drug-lord-captured-by-authorities-in-mexico.

119 **"Once he took down"**: Author's interview with Michael S. Vigil.
119 **"Two hundred miles south of Juárez"**: Shane Smith, "The Mexican Mormon War."
120 **"elite"**: Quotations in this paragraph from Bennion, 5.
120 **"marry all the young"**: Bennion, 7. LeBaron Pecans marketing material: https://www.lebaronpecans.com/about.
122 **"A beautiful thing"**: Madi and Rojas, "Mexico Ambush."
122 **"The next day, 150 men"**: Quotations in this paragraph from Booth, "Ambushed by a Drug War."
123 **"sever the head"**: Shane Smith, "The Mexican Mormon War."
123 **"latched onto self-help groups"**: Author's interview with a LeBaron family member.
124 **"one of the top three problem solvers"**: Michael Freedman, "The World's Strangest Executive Coach: Keith Raniere's Rich and Famous Clients Pay Thousands of Dollars, Bow and Call Him 'Vanguard,'" *Forbes*, Oct. 2003.
124 **"Raniere and the NXIVM community"**: Quotations in this paragraph from the Government's Sentencing Memorandum as to Defendant Keith Raniere, Eastern District of New York, Sept. 18, 2020, https://wnyt.com/wnytimages/Keith-Raniere-sentencing-memorandum.pdf.
125 **"His teachings are mysterious"**: Quotations in this paragraph from Freedman, "The World's Strangest Executive Coach."
125 **"If we pay"**: Quotations in this paragraph from *Encender el Corazon* trailer.
125 **"The first was denial"**: Quotations in this paragraph from Keith Raniere's defense attorneys' Sentencing Memorandum, filed in the Eastern District of New York, Sept. 18, 2020.
126 **"What we are saying"**: *Encender el Corazon* trailer.
127 **"liberated without payment"**: Lolita Bosch, *45 Voices Against Barbarity*. Ocean, http://www.oceano.mx/ficha-libro.aspx?id=12833. For details about ransom payments the LeBaron family made, see KVIA ABC-7, "Mexican Soldiers Arrest Suspect in Deadly LeBaron Kidnappings," April 25, 2010; Berenice Gaytán, "Oral Proceedings Against 'Hawk' Begin in Plagiarism of LeBaron," *El Diario*, Jan. 17, 2013.
127 **"The Mexican people were amazed"**: Quotations in this paragraph from Keith Raniere's defense attorneys' Sentencing Memorandum, filed in the Eastern District of New York, Sept. 18, 2020.
127 **"Keith, along with his team of people"**: Wayne LeBaron letter to the sentencing judge in Raniere's criminal case: Sentencing Memorandum.
127 **"People began to call us"**: Quotations in this paragraph from Elisabeth Malkin, "Side Effect of Mexico's Drug War: Fear and Death in a Mormon Town in Mexico," *New York Times*, July 26, 2009.
128 **"We had to go to the government"**: Shane Smith, "The Mexican Mormon War."

128 **"became a hero"**: Dudley Althaus, "Defying Mexican Gangs Costs Mormons Their Lives," *Houston Chronicle*, July 10, 2009.

128 **"You are me"**: Salinas website for Inlak-ech, https://medium.com/@esalinas1819/emiliano-salinas-mission-for-a-non-violent-mexico-e95a5760aac4.

128 **"like a practical MBA"**: Freedman, "The World's Strangest Executive Coach."

128 **"doing what they can"**: Mark Vicente promotional material for *Encender el Corazon*.

129 **"was to awaken the country"**: León Krauze, "What the Hell Did I Do? The Story of the ESP Movie in Mexico," *Letras Libres*, Oct. 23, 2017.

129 **"Everyone tells me not to show my face"**: Quotations in this paragraph from *Encender el Corazon* trailer.

129 **"Undoubtedly, the violent cartel members:** Quotations in this paragraph from Keith Raniere's defense attorneys' Sentencing Memorandum, filed in the Eastern District of New York, Sept. 18, 2020.

129 **"The pressure we put on the government"**: Quotations in this paragraph from *Encender el Corazon* trailer.

130 **"A linebacker-sized martial arts devotee"**: Althaus, "Defying Mexican Gangs."

130 **"Amid the blood and mesquite"**: Booth, "Ambushed by a Drug War."

130 **"They taped a big sign"**: Shane Smith, "The Mexican Mormon War."

131 **"personal"**: Quotations in this paragraph from Arturo Ilizaliturri, "Colonia LeBaron: 10 Years of Harassment," Newsbeezer.com, Nov. 6, 2019, https://newsbeezer.com/mexicoeng/colonia-lebaron-10-years-of-harassment/.

131 **"an exhausted remnant"**: Quotations in this paragraph from Booth, "Ambushed by a Drug War."

131 **"multiple mentions of tears and blood"**: Quotations in this paragraph from Rebecca Janzen, *Liminal Sovereignty: Mennonites and Mormons in Mexican Culture*. Albany: SUNY Press, 2018, 121.

131 **"Mormons' blood smolders"**: Javier Ortega Urquidi, *Los Gueros del Norte*. Fort Lauderdale, FL: Editorial Woodbine Books, 2010, 173.

132 **"was so outspoken"**: Quotations in this paragraph from Brooke Adams and Maria Villasenor, "Two with Polygamous Roots Gunned Down in Mexico," *Salt Lake Tribune*, July 8, 2009.

132 **"It's hard for me to understand"**: *Encender el Corazon* trailer.

133 **"The men who murdered them"**: Althaus, "Defying Mexican Gangs."

133 **"They had a cause"**: Malkin, "Side Effect of Mexico's Drug War."

133 **"We aren't leaving"**: Quotations in this paragraph from *Encender el Corazon* trailer.

133 **"Ask yourself"**: Booth, "Ambushed by a Drug War."

Chapter Seven: NXIVM: Ignite the Heart

134 **"Mom, I have a feeling":** Quotations in this paragraph from *Encender el Corazon* trailer.

134 **"activist mantle":** Quotations in this paragraph from León Krauze, "The Brutal Murder of the Mormon Family in Mexico Was Almost Inevitable," *Slate*, Nov. 6, 2019.

135 **"moving and devastating":** Krauze, "What the Hell Did I Do?"

135 **"to question certain fundamental assumptions":** www.MarkVicente.com.

135 **"The main thing is, we want to be respected":** Shane Smith, "The Mexican Mormon War."

135 **"burly and baby-faced politician":** Quotations in this paragraph from John Burnett, "Law-Abiding Mexicans Taking Up Illegal Guns," NPR, Jan. 28, 2012.

136 **"really no law":** Quotations in this paragraph from Shane Smith.

136 **"It's very easy":** Quotations in this paragraph from John Burnett.

137 **"My heart just dropped":** Quotations in this paragraph from Ioan Grillo, "9 American Mormons."

137 **"everyone became a watchman":** Shane Smith.

138 **"in the clearest possible terms":** Quotations in this paragraph from Will Grant, "How a US Mormon Family Ended Up Dead."

138 **"My brother and best friend":** *Encender el Corazon* trailer.

138 **"I've had people killed for my beliefs":** Sarah Berman, *Don't Call It a Cult: The Shocking Story of Keith Raniere and the Women of NXIVM*. Lebanon, NH: Steerforth Press, 2021, 164.

139 **"built more than 200 houses":** Vanessa Job, "Who Is Julian LeBaron?" *Milenio*, Nov. 11, 2019.

139 **"emphasis on 'readiness' ":** Quotations in this paragraph from Jessica Loudis, "Fall of the House of NXIVM," *London Review of Books*, June 25, 2019.

139 **"playing and positioning":** Catherine Oxenberg, *Captive: A Mother's Crusade to Save Her Daughter from the Terrifying Cult NXIVM*. New York: Gallery Books, 2018, 262.

139 **Clare and Sara Bronfman invested:** Will Yakowicz, "Dark Capital. From Heiress to Felon: How Clare Bronfman Wound Up in 'Cult-Like' Group NXIVM," *Forbes*, May 31, 2019.

140 **"Petition to the Mexican People":** Julian LeBaron, "Julian LeBaron: A Petition to the Mexican People," *Dallas Morning News*, April 16, 2010.

140 **"Two hundred years ago":** *Encender el Corazon* trailer.

140 **"Person of the Year 2011":** Quotations in this paragraph from Tim Padgett, "Why I Protest: Javier Sicilia of Mexico," *Time*, Dec. 14, 2011.

140 **"He traveled and met Sicilia:** Quotations in this paragraph from León Krauze, "What Did NXIVM Want in Mexico?" *Slate*, May 23, 2019.

141 **"A Civil Response to Violence":** https://www.youtube.com/watch?v=kktr4ssaC_Y&ab_channel=TED-Ed.

141 **"Julian and Emiliano share the conviction"**: Julio Hernández López, "The Young Guru Salinas, Emiliano with Sicilia, LeBaron, ESO's Ally," *La Jornada,* April 23, 2012.

141 **"What we are doing with Julian LeBaron"**: Rocio Muñoz Ledo and Juan Omar Fierro, "Emiliano Salinas's Movement Raised 9.5 Million Pesos to Promote the NXIVM Leader," *Aristegui Noticias,* July 16, 2018.

142 **"abandoned the path"**: Quotations in this paragraph from "Julian LeBaron Announces His Separation from the Movement for Peace," *Proceso,* Feb. 24, 2012.

142 **"bi-national grassroots campaign"**: http://www.angelicafoundation.org/activism.html.

142 **"the political class"**: Vanessa Job, "Who Is Julian LeBaron?"

142 **His activism remained:** *Ignite the Heart* trailers and promos, https://www.facebook.com/watch/encenderelcorazon/.

142 **"Maybe one of the reasons"**: Shane Smith, "The Mexican Mormon War."

144 **"some people see a darker"**: Freedman, "The World's Strangest Executive Coach."

145 **"radical ideas about polygamy, incest"**: Quotations in this paragraph from Scott Johnson and Rebecca Sun, "Her Darkest Role: Actress Allison Mack's Descent from 'Smallville' to Sex Cult," *Hollywood Reporter,* May 16, 2018.

145 **"young virgin successor"**: Nicole Hong and Sean Piccoli, "Keith Raniere, Leader of NXIVM Sex Cult, Is Sentenced to 120 Years in Prison," *New York Times,* Nov. 27, 2020.

145 **"billed as a spiritual experience"**: James M. Odato and Jennifer Gish, "In Raniere's Shadow," *Times Union* [Albany, NY], Feb. 28, 2012.

145 **"My family . . . might best be compared"**: Solomon. *Predators, Prey, and Other Kinfolk,* 12.

145 **"all about future glory"**: Spencer, *Shattered Dreams,* 7.

146 **"No mother"**: Quotations in this paragraph from Spencer, *Cult Insanity,* 140.

146 **"spread her protecting wings"**: Verlan M. LeBaron, 97.

146 **"There is more heated competition"**: Bradlee and Van Atta, 31. Books written about polygamy and Colonia LeBaron include: *Predators, Prey, and Other Kinfolk: Growing Up in Polygamy (Daughter of the Saints),* by Rulon Allred's daughter Dorothy Allred Solomon; *The Sound of Gravel,* by Joel LeBaron Sr.'s daughter Ruth Wariner; *The Polygamist's Daughter,* by Ervil LeBaron's daughter Anna LeBaron (with Leslie Wilson); *Cult Insanity: A Memoir of Polygamy, Prophets, and Blood Atonement* and *Shattered Dreams: My Life as a Polygamist's Wife,* by Verlan LeBaron's second wife, Irene Spencer; *His Favorite Wife: Trapped in Polygamy,* by Verlan LeBaron's sixth wife, Susan Ray Schmidt; and *The Blood Covenant: The True Story of the Ervil LeBaron Family and Its Rampage of Terror and Murder,* by Rena Chynoweth ("The Ex-Mrs. Ervil LeBaron," with Dean M. Shapiro).

147 **"welfare racket"**: Quotations in this paragraph from author's interview with a Miller family member.

147 **"patriarchy spun off"**: Quotations in this paragraph from Andrea Moore-Emmett, *God's Brothel*. San Francisco: Pince-Nez Press, 2014, 17.

147 **"This began in recent years"**: Quotations in this paragraph from author's interview with a LeBaron family member.

148 **"date night shopping"**: Author's interview with a LeBaron family member.

148 **Raniere studied the LeBarons' polygamous lifestyle closely**: Details of Raniere's creation of DOS as a parallel to Colonia LeBaron are based on author's confidential interviews with women from Colonia LeBaron.

148 **"like the Freemasons"**: Sarah Berman, "Don't Call It a Cult," 14.

148 **"force for good"**: Barry Meier, "Inside a Secretive Group Where Women Are Branded," *New York Times*, Oct. 17, 2017.

148 **Raniere recruited eleven girls from Colonia LeBaron**: For details of Rainbow Cultural Gardens, LeBaron teens, see testimony in Raniere criminal trial and sentencing. The Rainbow Cultural Gardens program was a failure, and after sex-trafficking charges were filed against Raniere in 2018, the schools were accused of experimenting on children who were unable to learn to speak any language and ultimately communicated only in gibberish.

149 **"the mothership"**: Sarah Berman, 34.

149 **"breeding a new, more evolved generation"**: Berman, 156.

149 **"first line" slave**: Testimony of Mark Vicente in Keith Raniere's criminal trial.

149 **"exposed to Raniere's pedophilic"**: Quotations in this paragraph from Robert Gavin, "Mexican Slaughter Victims Were from NXIVM Recruiting Ground," *Times Union* [Albany, NY], Nov. 8, 2019.

150 **"This felt like the right thing to do"**: Quotations in this paragraph from Mark Vicente post on Facebook, November 2019.

151 **"humanization and consciousness"**: *Encender el Corazon,* IMDb, https://www.imdb.com/title/tt1843953/fullcredits.

151 **"His words have echoed"**: Mark Vicente at the film premiere.

151 **"Raniere is presented"**: León Krauze, "What the Hell Did I Do?"

151 **"The film takes you on a journey"**: Mark Vicente at the film premiere.

151 **"The film's oversimplified and risky"**: Quotations in this paragraph from Krauze, "What the Hell Did I Do?"

152 **"film was being used"**: *Encender el Corazon,* IMDb.

152 **"This film, although it showed"**: Quotations in this paragraph from Krauze, "What the Hell Did I Do?"

152 **"One would think that given"**: Quotations in this paragraph from León Krauze, "What Did NXIVM Want in Mexico?" *Slate*, May 23, 2019.

152 **"My name does not appear"**: Posted on Emilio Salinas's website on October 18, 2017: "On October 18, *The New York Times* published a story that links,

without foundation, Executive Success Programs (ESP), a company that I lead in its Mexico chapter, with allegedly recent events in the United States. Although my name does not appear in the aforementioned article, nor is there a link with what I do in Mexico, there were some who, in social networks and taking advantage of the resonance in my country of my paternal surname, tried to link me personally and directly, thereby confusing public opinion with it." The website was later suspended: http://www.emilianosalinas.mx/cgi-sys/suspendedpage.cgi.

152 **"to be used as a recruiting tool"**: Krauze, "What Did NXIVM Want in Mexico?"

152 **"good way to promote citizen participation"**: Krauze, "What the Hell Did I Do?"

153 **"And though we may never"**: Quotations in this paragraph from the Government's Sentencing Memorandum as to Defendant Keith Raniere.

Chapter Eight: "Water Flows Uphill to Money"

154 **"Water flows uphill"**: Although occasionally apocryphally attributed to Mark Twain, the admonition "Water flows uphill to money" was popularized by Marc Reiser in *Cadillac Desert*, his prescient study of water policy and land development in the American West.

154 **"whom they saw as productive members"**: Rebecca Janzen, "Mormons in Mexico: A Brief History of Polygamy, Cartel Violence, and Faith," *The Conversation*, Nov. 6, 2019.

155 **"stewards over these"**: https://ldsearthstewardship.org/learn/resource-library/content/60-purity-of-water-air-and-land.

155 **"American invaders"**: Janzen, "Mormons in Mexico."

155 **"a close collaborator"**: Quotations in this and the next two paragraphs from Patricia Mayorga, "They Block the Way to Demand a Substantive Solution to the Barzon-LeBaron Conflict," *Proceso*, April 21, 2020.

156 **"a plural and inclusive"**: Angel Daily.

157 **"shouting racist and xenophobic remarks"**: *Jack's Newswatch*, "It's All About the Water," Nov. 11, 2019.

157 **"We're tired of this situation"**: *teleSurHD*, "Water Wars: Ranchers Clash Over Scarce Resources in Mexico," May 2, 2018.

157 **"by obtaining permits"**: https://mexiconewsdaily.com/news/dispute-over-water-fuelled-attack-on-lebaron-family/.

158 **"If the LeBarons connect"**: Mayorga, "They Block the Way."

158 **"were hated thrice over"**: Frank McLynn, *Villa and Zapata: A History of the Mexican Revolution*. New York: Carroll & Graf, 2001, 66.

158 **"protects"**: Rubén Villapando, "Corral Protects Aquifer Looters, Say Barzonistas," *La Jornada*, May 22, 2018.

158 **"El Barzón and the government"**: *teleSurHD*.

158 **"395 concessions to family members"**: Quotations in this paragraph from Jesús Estrada, "Authorities Overlap Illegal Depredation of Aquifers in Chihuahua," *La Jornada*, May 9, 2018.

158 **"having granted false permits"**: David Piñon, "LeBaron-Barzón, 6 Decades of Conflict Over Aquifer Dispute," *El Sol de Mexico*, Dec. 30, 2020.

159 **"put a price on the head"**: Quotations in this paragraph from Jeremy Kryt, "A New Twist in the Horrific Massacre of American Moms and Kids in Mexico," *Daily Beast*, Nov. 11, 2019.

159 **"very aggressive"**: Patricia Mayorga, "Barzonistas Denounce That LeBaron Family Put a Price on Their Heads," *Proceso,* May 21, 2018.

159 **"protecting water rights"**: Kryt. See also Ivette Lira, "Father and Son Were Killed for Taking Care of the Water in Chihuahua," *Ocmal*, June 15, 2018.

159 **"participated in the demand"**: Lira.

161 **"a mountain of evidence"**: Alan Feuer, "El Chapo Found Guilty on All Counts; Faces Life in Prison," *New York Times*, Feb. 12, 2019.

161 **"circuslike extravaganza"**: Quotations in this paragraph from Alan Feuer, "The Prosecution Rests Its Case, and El Chapo Decides Not to Testify," *New York Times*, Jan. 28, 2019.

161 **"I've never faced a case"**: Feuer, "El Chapo Found Guilty."

162 **"all while working hand in glove"**: Ryan Devereaux, "Prosecution of Top Mexican Security Official Exposes the Façade of the Drug War," *The Intercept*, Jan. 26, 2020.

163 **"as a self-help guru"**: Justice Department statement: https://www.justice .gov/usao-edny/pr/jury-finds-nxivm-leader-keith-raniere-guilty-all-counts.

163 **"He is not sorry"**: Carla Correa, "A Timeline of the Nxivm Sex Cult Case," *New York Times*, Nov. 27, 2020.

163 **"He remains proud"**: Raniere Defense Sentencing Memorandum.

164 **"drying up the desert"**: Patricia Mayorga, "Water Fight Confronts *Ejidatarios* with the LeBaron Family in Chihuahua," *Proceso*, April 30, 2018.

164 **"unleashed a smear campaign"**: Mayorga, "Barzonistas Denounce."

164 **"I can't tell you what Alex"**: *Akronoticias.com*, "LeBarons Request Intervention of the Federal Government in the Conflict Between Barzonistas and La Mojina Ranch," May 29, 2020.

164 **"panoramic view lots"**: https://www.facebook.com/The-Springs-Golf -Club-922960524449560/photos/929532327125713.

165 **"municipal public swimming pool"**: https://www.compartetusideas.mx/ wordpress/2016/08/07/se-construiran-albercas-publicas-municipales-en-galeana/.

165 **"There is no church organization"**: Quotations in this paragraph from author's interview with a LeBaron family member.

165 **"The men pretend"**: Author's interview with a LeBaron family member.

165 **"The colony is a magnet"**: Quotations in this paragraph from author's interview with a LeBaron family member.

Chapter Nine: "Innocence Is Shattered"

166 **"terrorists and evil mobsters":** Tadd Walch, "She Planned for Marriage on Monday. Instead She Buried Her Family in Mexico," *Deseret News*, Nov. 7, 2019.

166 **"We have beautiful homes":** Quotations in this paragraph from Anderson Cooper, CNN, *Full Circle*.

167 **"a light that shined":** Quotations in this paragraph from Tadd Walch.

167 **"I'm taking this step":** Nancy Dillon and Larry McShane, "Mormons Mourn Last of Nine Massacre Victims in Mexico, Head for Safer Pastures in US Under Renewed Spotlight," *Daily News,* Nov. 9, 2019.

167 **"their brothers and sisters":** *Lara Logan Investigates.*

168 **"Mom told us all to duck":** Quotations in this paragraph from *Lara Logan Investigates.*

168 **"they were attacked separately":** Alex LeBaron on CNN, Nov. 5, 2019.

168 **"We need to know":** *Infobae*, "They Knew Before They Shot."

168 **"They nodded to the sicarios":** Quotations in this paragraph from Kevin Sieff, "How Mexico's Cartel Wars Shattered American Mormons' 'Wary Peace.'"

168 **"The Chihuahua side":** David Agren, "How an Isolated Group of Mormons."

168 **"We thought the same thing":** Quotations in this paragraph from Sieff.

169 **"as simply an accepted part":** Jose Luis Gonzalez, "Faith in Mexico Shaken for 'True Believer' Mormon Communities," Reuters, Nov. 6, 2019.

169 **"gentlemen's agreement":** Author's interview with a Miller family member.

169 **"We won't bother you":** Sieff.

169 **"LeBaron is a generic term":** Quotations in this paragraph from Melissa Del Pozo, "Organized Crime Bloodied the Mormon Paradise," *Proceso*, Nov. 13, 2019.

170 **"Howard didn't speak":** Quotations in this paragraph from Pablo Ferri, "The LeBaron Family's Journey to Horror," *El País*, Nov. 7, 2019.

170 **"Are we sure no one got out of the car":** Quotations in this paragraph from *Lara Logan Investigates.*

170 **"I was at home in Xalisco":** Quotations in this paragraph from César Rodríguez, "'I Tried to Take Photos That Meant Something.' After the Cartel Ambush in Mexico," *Time,* Nov. 9, 2019.

171 **"Lashes of rage":** Ferri.

171 **"The day La Mora":** Kendal Blust and Murphy Woodhouse, "After La Mora Bids Loved Ones Farewell, Grieving Community's Future Unclear," KJZZ Radio, Nov. 14, 2019.

171 **"I don't want to think about it":** Rodríguez.

171 **"We're just trying to gather":** Nancy Dillon, "Funerals Begin as Mormon Families Grapple."

172 **"Innocence is shattered"**: Romero, Dias, Turkewitz, and Baker, *New York Times*.

172 **"The eyes of the world"**: Peter Orsi, "Mexico Farm Town Buries 3 of 9 Americans Slain," Associated Press, Nov. 7, 2019.

172 **"God will take care of the wicked"**: Grillo, "9 American Mormons."

172 **"She was a devoted wife and devoted mother:** Quotations in this paragraph from Azam Ahmed, "After Mormon Family's Terror."

172 **"I just felt a helplessness"**: Sieff.

172 **"La Mora had been tarnished"**: Quotations in this paragraph from Ahmed, "After Mormon Family's Terror."

172 **"five-hour, bone jarring drive"**: Peter Orsi, "Last Victim of Mexico Ambush Killings to Be Laid to Rest," Associated Press, Nov. 9, 2019.

173 **"I don't know if I'll ever come back"**: Ahmed, "After Mormon Family's Terror."

174 **"LeBaron showed its roots"**: Lisbeth Diaz, "After Burying Last Victims, Some in Mexico's Breakaway Mormon Community Head North," Reuters, Nov. 9, 2019.

174 **"mama hen"**: Quotations in this paragraph from Orsi, "Last Victim."

175 **"Justice for La Mora"**: https://www.facebook.com/amber .compton.589/videos/4138812756132719/UzpfSTU0MTI4ODYz MzoxMDE1NzEzMjc5NzgzMzYzNA/?fref=search&__tn__=,d,P -R&eid=ARA3kmVLcJfU9C2IIWp-e1S6pcLvtyfo67AcEuXo5PVc0bRabE 1CctU2lq3PFpKmPM7kj1Bb10fXiysl.

175 **"with her back"**: Kendraleemiller92 post on Instagram, Nov. 2019, https:// www.picuki.com/media/2176729256753670707.

175 **"One name is being used"**: Langford Family member: YouTube: "Langford Family Member Talks About What People Got Wrong About Her Family." Emily Langford interview.

175 **"Everyone is not a LeBaron"**: Karen Woolley on Adriana Jones's Facebook page.

175 **"good people"**: Quotations in this paragraph from Langford family member post on Facebook, Nov. 19, 2019.

175 **"The question we all have here"**: Sieff.

175 **"You will not find a more"**: Quotations in this paragraph from *Lara Logan Investigates*.

176 **"millions of US dollars"**: Nate Carlisle, "Families Plan to Move Out of Mormon Community in Mexico, But for Some It Won't Be Easy to Leave," *Salt Lake Tribune*, Nov. 9, 2019.

176 **"I owe it to Rhonita and my grandchildren"**: Lauren Edmonds, *Daily Mail*.

176 **"If I leave this town"**: Blust and Woodhouse.

176 **"I've always felt safe"**: Jose Luis Gonzalez.

176 **"What my family has all said"**: Quotations in this paragraph from Tadd Walch.

177 **"They're scared for their lives"**: Quotations in this paragraph from Nancy Dillon and Larry McShane, "Mormons Mourn Last of Nine."

177 **"absolute peace and prosperity"**: Jose Luis Gonzalez.

177 **"ghost town"**: Quotations in this paragraph from Lisbeth Diaz, "After Burying Last Victims."

178 **"Why should our family"**: Ahmed, "After Mormon Family's Terror."

178 **"They are American citizens"**: Quotations in this paragraph from Diaz, "After Burying Last Victims."

179 **"Fire on Fire"**: http://www.elchalanradiospot.com/Lebaron-Singoff-The-Kick-Off.html.

179 **"A wonderful family"**: Quotations in this paragraph from Donald Trump on Twitter, Nov. 4, 2019.

179 **"his willingness to support us"**: President López Obrador on Twitter, Nov. 5, 2019.

179 **"ensure justice"**: Lorena Rios, "Mexican President Declines Trump's Help After Mormon Family Killed in Attack," Bloomberg, Nov. 5, 2019, https://www.cnn.com/us/live-news/mormon-attack-us-mexico-border/h_cc168168ad550cbe0beafbb1baa8cea0.

180 **"the cunning murders"**: Quotations in this paragraph from Del Pozo.

180 **"I'm not saying I want"**: Sieff.

180 **"might invade Mexico"**: Christina Zhao, "Republican Senator Says U.S. 'May Have to Take Matters into Our Own Hands' Regarding Mexico Drug Cartel Violence," *Newsweek*, Nov. 6, 2019.

180 **"We are just pissed off"**: Quotations in this paragraph from Grillo, "9 American Mormons."

181 **"but they [the cartels]"**: Quotations in this paragraph from Alex Ward in Vox.com, quoted in *The Week*, Dec. 13, 2019.

181 **"Many feel that might lead"**: Rojas.

181 **"fell like a bomb"**: Quotations in this paragraph from Sugeyry Romina Gándara, "Alex LeBaron, former PRI Deputy in the César Duarte Era, Raises Dust for Asking Trump for Help," Sinembargo.mx, Nov. 27, 2019.

181 **"I would have stood up"**: Quotations in this paragraph from Krauze, "This Family Suffered."

181 **"truth, justice, and peace"**: Quotations in this paragraph from Grillo. "9 American Mormons."

181 **"I just couldn't take"**: David Agren, "The Mormons Standing up to Mexico's Drug Cartels: 'We Have to Overcome Our Fears,'" *The Guardian*, Jan. 23, 2020.

182 **"We can blame"**: Quotations in this paragraph from Grillo, "9 American Mormons."

182 **"amnesia":** Quotations in this paragraph from Sandy Fitzgerald, "Mexican President Refuses Meeting with Peace March Organizers," Newsmax, Jan. 27, 2020.

182 **"Enough hypocrisy":** Dave Graham, "Mexican Leader Blasts Critics After Supporters Hector Grieving Family," Reuters, Jan. 27, 2020.

183 **"There are a lot of powerful":** Author's interview with confidential source.

183 **"We have dual citizenship":** "Get Out of the Country," *The Guardian,* Jan. 27, 2020.

183 **"Because of everything":** Grillo, "9 American Mormons."

183 **"have had a federal police escort":** *Yucatan Times* Staff, "The LeBaron Family in Mexico . . . a History of Conflict," Nov. 5, 2019.

183 **"Wild West–style volunteer militias":** Lauren Edmonds.

183 **"Why are they raising an army?":** Author's interview with a LeBaron family member.

183 **"Creating a militia is tightening the noose":** Author's interview with Michael S. Vigil. Adrian's call to arms would be "a terrible mistake," according to John L. Smith, the author's husband, and author of the 2021 book *Saints, Sinners, and Sovereign Citizens,* about the ongoing battle to control federal lands in the West. "It's true that America's far-right militia movement is heavily armed and increasingly prone to violence," according to Smith. "Although the Bundys benefitted from the intimidating presence of armed Oath Keepers and III Percenters militias during a 2014 standoff with US federal land officials at their ranch near Bunkerville, the beer-can commandos would be no match for a truckload of experienced *sicarios* in Mexico."

184 **"traffickers want to get rid":** Isabel Vincent, "Defiant Patriarch."

184 **"They killed the wrong daughter":** Krauze, "This Family Suffered." Massacre social-media sites: massacre: https://www.instagram.com/lamorafamilymassacre/?hl=en; https://www.gofundme.com/f/langford-and-miller-family-tragedy; https://www.facebook.com/lamorafamilymassacre/; @lamorafamilymassacre: https://www.youtube.com/watch?v=dAP6x4AMns0&feature=share&fbclid=IwAR3XHsyuXfjzA1FfsM22uBbb-MxBUrO-uYtcj-kD82QfqoyTesH___tNk0_I;_https://www.facebook.com/photo.php?fbid=10162343897900316&set=a.10150235701950316&type=3&theater, http://www.elchalanradiospot.com/Lebaron-Singoff-The-Kick-Off.html.

Chapter Ten: "An Eden in Contention"
185 **"All events in Mexico":** Richard Grant, *God's Middle Finger,* 34.

185 **"The press ran with the story":** Jeremy Kryt, "A New Twist in the Horrific Massacre."

186 **"The only thing she was an activist for":** Gaby Del Valle, "Everyone Has a Different Theory."

186 **"My sister thought it was worth fighting for Mexico"**: Quotations in this paragraph from Adriana Jones petition.

186 **"The Barzon connection"**: Quotations in this paragraph from Kryt.

186 **"Now I am immersed in speculation"**: Gardenia Mendoza, "Peasant Organization, Suspected of the Massacre of the LeBaron Family of Mormons in Mexico," *LaOpinión*, Nov. 7, 2019.

187 **"Kids? Little babies?"**: Kryt.

187 **"far more intelligent, savage"**: Author interview with Michael S. Vigil.

187 **"deadlier than a rattlesnake"**: Tariq Tahir, "Cartel Kingpin El Mencho Who Is Even More Savage than El Chapo May NEVER Be Captured, Says Legendary Narco Cop," *Irish Sun*, Feb. 19, 2021.

188 **"Unfamiliar men"**: Quotations in this paragraph from Kevin Sieff, "How Mexico's Cartel Wars Shattered."

188 **"Our family has an interesting mix"**: Author's interview with a LeBaron family member.

188 **"to carry out the deadly assault"**: Adry Torres, "Mormon Father Relives the Morning His Daughter and Four of His Grandchildren Were Brutally Executed Along with Four Others in Mexico—and Says the Family Is Still Awaiting Justice," DailyMail.com, Nov. 4, 2020.

188 **"nothing more than a horse with one leg"**: Quotations in this paragraph from author's interview with Michael S. Vigil.

190 **"most powerful capo"**: Quotations in this paragraph from Kryt.

190 **"Why were there so many"**: Quotations in this paragraph from author's interview with confidential source.

190 **"a vendetta"**: Quotations in this paragraph from author's interview with Michael S. Vigil.

191 **"They knew exactly"**: Author's interview with confidential source.

192 **"vocal, public critics"**: Quotations in this paragraph from Howard Miller et al. vs. Juárez Cartel, La Línea, Vicente Carrillo Fuentes Organization and CFO, US District Court for the District of North Dakota, Case: 1:20:cv-00132-DMT-CRH, Filed July 23, 2020.

193 **"Caro Quintero is not in command of anything"**: Quotations in this paragraph from author's interview with Michael S. Vigil.

193 **"respect for the family's grief"**: Quotations in this paragraph from Mayorga, "They Block the Way."

193 **"It wouldn't take much"**: Author's interview with a LeBaron family member.

194 **"these predators"**: Quotations in this paragraph from Mayorga, "They Block the Way."

194 **"We don't have a state authority"**: Quotations in this paragraph from *Akronoticias.com*, "Chihuahua News," May 2, 2020.

195 **"neediest population"**: *Akronoticias.com*, "Chihuahua Removes Mega Ranch from Former Governor to Hand It Over to the People," Feb. 3, 2021.

195   **"There is a lot of money"**: Patricia Mayorga, " 'Even If the Earth Shakes, I Will Continue Looking for My Son': Mother of Disappeared in Chihuahua," *Proceso*, Dec. 4, 2015.

196   **"In Mexico, if you don't do a follow-up"**: Adry Torres, "Mormon Father Relives the Morning."

196   **"Do you know why they didn't"**: Adrian LeBaron, Twitter, https://twitter.com/AdrianLebaron/status/1357329485398499336.

196   **"now lives abroad"**: "LeBaron Family Accused Rosario Piedra of Derision and Revictimization After CNDH Rejection," *Infobae*, July 1, 2021, https://www.infobae.com/america/mexico/2021/07/02/familia-lebaron-acuso-a-rosario-piedra-de-escarnio-y-revictimizacion-tras-rechazo-de-cndh/.

196   **"He is going there to work"**: Lisbeth Diaz, "After Burying Last Victims."

196   **"they are still jumping"**: Torres, "Mormon Father Relives the Morning."

197   **"top cartel dog"**: David Agren, "Mexican Cartel Boss Arrested Over Mormon Massacre in Which Nine Died," *The Guardian*, Nov. 24, 2020.

197   **"one more step"**: Adrian LeBaron post on Twitter, Nov. 24, 2020.

197   **"I want to see his . . . face"**: *El Diario* Editorial Office, "Caro Quintero Is Involved in the LeBaron Massacre," Nov. 25, 2020.

197   **"taking bags of food"**: Grillo, "9 American Mormons."

198   **"to us in slow motion"**: Quotations in this paragraph from Hérika Martinez Prado, "He Directed Acquaintance of the LeBaron to Hitmen: Fidencio G. Took the Video and Was the One Who Yelled to Burn the Truck," *El Diario de Chihuahua*, Jan. 20, 2021.

198   **"This memorial will be a permanent"**: https://mexiconewsdaily.com/news/memorial-to-victims-of-lebaron-family-massacre-unveiled-in-sonora/.

198   **"the love of God"**: *The Book of Mormon,* 1 Nephi 11:22–23.

199   **"victims of cartel violence"**: https://mexiconewsdaily.com/news/memorial-to-victims-of-lebaron-family-massacre-unveiled-in-sonora/.

200   **"It was emblematic"**: Quotations in this paragraph from author's interview with a close relative of Ervil LeBaron.

201   **"wants to appropriate land"**: *Animal Politico*, "LeBaron Family Denounces Burning of Their Land and Attacks Due to Territorial Conflict in BC," Dec. 31, 2020.

201   **"Carlos Hafen is the son of us"**: Quotations in this paragraph from Vanessa Job and Kenia Hernandez, "Community Founded by the LeBaron Family Faces Former PRD Candidate by Land," *Milenio*, Jan. 19, 2021.

202   **"It is illegal, and we are not going to leave"**: Antonio Heras, "Invasion of Properties and Burning of Houses in San Quintín, Denounces LeBaron," *La Jornada Baja California*, Jan. 2, 2021.

202   **"This story has been written"**: Quotations in this paragraph from Cesar Martinez, "They File Complaints for Invasion in Baja California," *San Diego Union-Tribune*, Jan. 4, 2021.

Epilogue: Sisterhood

203 **"Until now I only have the monument":** Quotations in this paragraph from Adrian LeBaron post on Twitter, May 25, 2021.

203 **"They killed my lawyer":** *Saxon*, "They Kill the Lawyer of the Massacre of Mormons Who Was Running for Mayor in Mexico," May 14, 2021.

203 **"We are all crying here":** Quotations in this paragraph from Carmen Morán Breña, "Assassinated Abel Murrieta, Electoral Candidate and Lawyer of the Massacred LeBaron Family," *El País*, May 13, 2021.

204 **"I don't want hugs":** Adrian LeBaron post on Twitter.

204 **"enough evidence in that spider's web":** Prado, "He Directed Acquaintance of the LeBaron to Hitmen."

204 **"López Obrador doesn't want":** Quotations in this paragraph from author's interview with Michael S. Vigil.

205 **"held down the fort":** Author's interview with a granddaughter from Colonia LeBaron.

205 **"It is the strength of the women":** Author's interview with a widow from Colonia LeBaron.

205 **"The men have always been absent":** Author's interview with a granddaughter from Colonia LeBaron.

205 **"the standards and ways of being":** Author's interview with a widow from Colonia LeBaron.

205 **"We believe that God is the same today":** Ana Gabriela Rojas, "In the Line of Fire," BBC *World News*, March 23, 2020.

Works Cited

Books

Anderson, Jack, with Daryl Gibson. *Peace, War, and Politics: An Eyewitness Account.* New York: Forge Books, 1999.

Anderson, Scott. *The 4 O'Clock Murders: The True Story of a Mormon Family's Vengeance.* New York: Bantam Doubleday Dell, 1993.

Andrus, Hyrum Leslie, and Helen Mae Andrus. *They Knew the Prophet.* Salt Lake City: Bookcraft, 1974.

Bagley, Will. *Blood of the Prophets: Brigham Young and the Massacre at Mountain Meadows.* Norman: University of Oklahoma Press, 2002.

Beith, Malcolm. *The Last Narco: Inside the Hunt for El Chapo, the World's Most Wanted Drug Lord.* New York: Grove Press, 2010.

Bennion, Janet. *Desert Patriarchy: Mormon and Mennonite Communities in the Chihuahua Valley.* Tucson: University of Arizona Press, 2004.

Berman, Sarah. *Don't Call It a Cult: The Shocking Story of Keith Raniere and the Women of NXIVM.* Lebanon, NH: Steerforth Press, 2021.

Bigler, David L. *Forgotten Kingdom: The Mormon Theocracy in the American West, 1847–1896.* Logan: Utah State University Press, 1998.

Black, Robert Rey. *The New and Everlasting Covenant,* 2nd ed. Bloomington, IN: Author House, 2006.

Black, Susan Easton, and Larry C. Porter, eds. *Lion of the Lord: Essays on the Life and Service of Brigham Young.* Salt Lake City: Deseret Book Company, 1995.

Bosch, Lolita. *45 Voices Against Barbarity.* Ocean. http://www.oceano.mx/ficha -libro.aspx?id=12833.

Bradlee, Ben, Jr., and Dale Van Atta. *Prophet of Blood: The Untold Story of Ervil LeBaron and the Lambs of God.* New York: G. P. Putnam's Sons, 1981.

Brodie, Fawn M. *No Man Knows My History: The Life of Joseph Smith the Mormon Prophet.* New York: Alfred A. Knopf, 1990.

Brooks, Juanita. *The Mountain Meadows Massacre.* Norman: University of Oklahoma Press, 1962.

_____. *John Doyle Lee: Zealot, Pioneer Builder, Scapegoat*. Logan: Utah State
   University Press, 1992.

Chynoweth, Rena, with Dean Shapiro. *The Blood Covenant: The True Story of the
   Ervil LeBaron Family and Its Rampage of Terror and Murder*. Fort Worth: Eakin
   Press, 1990.

Coates, James. *In Mormon Circles: Gentiles, Jack Mormons, and Latter-Day Saints*.
   Reading, MA: Addison-Wesley Publishing, 1991.

Corchado, Alfredo. *Midnight in Mexico: A Reporter's Journey Through a Country's
   Descent into Darkness*. New York: Penguin Books, 2014.

del Bosque, Melissa. *Blood Lines: The True Story of a Drug Cartel, the FBI, and the
   Battle for a Horse-Racing Dynasty*. New York: Ecco, 2017.

Denton, Sally. *American Massacre: The Tragedy at Mountain Meadows, September 1857*.
   New York: Alfred A. Knopf, 2003.

_____. *Faith and Betrayal: A Pioneer Woman's Passage in the American West*. New York:
   Alfred A. Knopf, 2005.

_____ and Roger Morris. *The Money and the Power: The Making of Las Vegas and Its
   Hold on America*. New York: Alfred A. Knopf, 2001.

DeVoto, Bernard. *The Year of Decision, 1846*. New York: Truman Talley Books, 1942.

Ebershoff, David. *The 19th Wife*. New York: Random House, 2008.

Embry, Jessie. *Mormon Polygamous Families: Life in the Principle*. Salt Lake City:
   University of Utah Press, 1987.

Fielding, Robert Kent. *The Unsolicited Chronicler: An Account of the Gunnison
   Massacre, Its Causes and Consequences, Utah Territory, 1847–1859*. Brookline, MA:
   Paradigm Publications, 1993.

_____, ed. *The Tribune Reports of the Trials of John D. Lee for the Massacre at Mountain
   Meadows*. Higganum, CT: Kent's Books, 2000.

Freeman, Judith. *The Latter Days: A Memoir*. New York: Anchor, 2016.

Gibbs, Josiah F. *The Mountain Meadows Massacre*. Salt Lake City: Salt Lake City
   Tribune Publishing Company, 1910.

Gilmore, Mikal. *Shot in the Heart*. New York: Doubleday/Anchor, 1994.

Grant, Richard. *God's Middle Finger: Into the Lawless Heart of the Sierra Madre*. New
   York: Free Press, 2008.

Grillo, Ioan. *El Narco: Inside Mexico's Criminal Insurgency*. New York: Bloomsbury
   Press, 2011.

Gunnison, Lieut. J. W. *The Mormons, or Latter-Day Saints, in the Valley of The Great
   Salt Lake: A History of Their Rise and Progress, Peculiar Doctrines, Present Condition,
   and Prospects, derived from Personal Observation during a Residence Among Them*.
   Philadelphia: Lippincott, Grambo & Co., 1852.

Hafen, Lyman. *Far from Cactus Flat: The 20th Century Story of a Harsh Land, a Proud
   Family, and a Lost Son*. St. George, UT: Arizona Strip Interpretive Association,
   2006.

Harline, Paula Kelly. *The Polygamous Wives Writing Club*. Oxford: Oxford
   University Press, 2014.

Henrie, Samuel Nyal, ed. *Writings of John D. Lee*. Tucson: Hats Off Books, 2001.

Hernández, Anabel. *Narcoland: The Mexican Drug Lords and Their Godfathers*. London, New York: Verso, 2010.

Hirshson, Stanley P. *The Lion of the Lord*. New York: Alfred A. Knopf, 1969.

Janzen, Rebecca. *Liminal Sovereignty: Mennonites and Mormons in Mexican Culture*. Albany: SUNY Press, 2018.

Johnson, Benjamin Franklin. *My Life's Review: Autobiography of Benjamin Franklin Johnson*. Independence, MO: Zion's Printing & Publishing, 1947.

Kamstra, Jerry. *Weed: Adventures of a Dope Smuggler*. Santa Barbara, CA: Ross-Erikson Publishers, 1983.

Krakauer, Jon. *Under the Banner of Heaven: A Story of Violent Faith*. New York: Random House, 2004.

Lair, Jim. *The Mountain Meadows Massacre: An Outlander's View*. Marceline, MO: Walworth Publishing, 1986.

LeBaron, Anna, with Leslie Wilson. *The Polygamist's Daughter*. Carol Stream, IL: Tyndale House Publishers, 2017.

LeBaron, Charlotte K. *Maud's Story: With Entire Sections in Her Own Words*. Bloomington, IN: Author House, 2014.

LeBaron, E. Dale. *Benjamin Franklin Johnson: Friend to the Prophets*: Provo, UT: Grandin Book Company (Benjamin F. Johnson Family Organization), 1997.

LeBaron, Verlan M. *The LeBaron Story: The Saga of a Modern Cain and Abel*. Lubbock, TX: Keels & Co., 1981.

Lee, John D. *Writings of John D. Lee*. Edited by Samuel Nyal Henrie. Tucson: Hats Off Books, 2001.

_____. *Mormonism Unveiled, or The Life and Confession of John D. Lee*. Albuquerque: Fierra Blanca Publications, 2001.

McBride, Spencer W. *Joseph Smith for President: The Prophet, the Assassins, and the Fight for American Religious Freedom*. New York: Oxford University Press, 2021.

McLynn, Frank. *Villa and Zapata: A History of the Mexican Revolution*. New York: Carroll & Graf, 2001.

Mills, James. *The Underground Empire: Where Crime and Governments Embrace*. New York: Dell Publishing, 1986.

Molloy, Molly, and Charles Bowden, eds. *El Sicario: The Autobiography of a Mexican Assassin*. New York: Bold Type Books, 2011.

Moody, Michael D. *Mitt, Set Our People Free! A 7th Generation Mormon's Plea for Truth*. Bloomington, IN: iUniverse, Inc., 2008.

Moore-Emmett, Andrea. *God's Brothel*. San Francisco: Pince-Nez Press, 2014.

Oxenberg, Catherine. *Captive: A Mother's Crusade to Save Her Daughter from the Terrifying Cult NXIVM*. New York: Gallery Books, 2018.

Park, Benjamin E. *Kingdom of Nauvoo: The Rise and Fall of a Religious Empire on the American Frontier*. New York: Liveright, 2020.

Peterson, Levi. *Juanita Brooks: Mormon Woman Historian*. Salt Lake City: University of Utah Press, 1988.

Piercy, Frederick Hawkins. *Route from Liverpool to Great Salt Lake Valley*. Edited by
Fawn Brodie. Cambridge: Belknap Press/Harvard University Press, 1962.

Quinn, D. Michael. *The Mormon Hierarchy: Origins of Power*. Salt Lake City:
Signature Books, 1994.

Reisner, Marc. *Cadillac Desert: The American West and Its Disappearing Water*. New
York: Viking, 1986.

Rodriguez, Teresa. *The Daughters of Juárez: A True Story of Serial Murder South of the
Border*. New York: Atria Books, 2007.

Romney, Thomas Cottam. *The Mormon Colonies in Mexico*. Salt Lake City:
University of Utah Press, 1938.

Sánchez-Moreno, Maria McFarland. *There Are No Dead Here: A Story of Murder and
Denial in Colombia*. New York: Nation Books, 2018.

Schmidt, Susan Ray. *His Favorite Wife: Trapped in Polygamy, A True Story of Violent
Fanaticism*. Twin Falls, ID: Kassidy Lane Publishing, 2006.

Shipps, Jan. *Sojourner in the Promised Land: Forty Years Among the Mormons*.
Champaign: University of Illinois Press, 2000.

Smith, John L. *Saints, Sinners, and Sovereign Citizens: The Endless War Over the West's
Public Lands*. Reno: University of Nevada Press, 2021.

Smith, Joseph F., Jr., and Richard C. Evans. *Blood Atonement and the Origin of Plural
Marriage: A Discussion*. Salt Lake City: Deseret News Press, 1905.

Solomon, Dorothy Allred. *Predators, Prey, and Other Kinfolk: Growing Up in
Polygamy*. New York: W. W. Norton, 2003. Reprinted as *Daughter of the Saints:
Growing up in Polygamy*, 2004.

_____. *The Sisterhood: Inside the Lives of Mormon Women*. New York: Palgrave
Macmillan, 2007.

Spencer, Irene. *Shattered Dreams: My Life as a Polygamist's Wife*. N.p.: Gold-Donn
Opportunities Publishing, 2019.

_____. *Cult Insanity: A Memoir of Polygamy, Prophets, and Blood Atonement*. New
York: Center Street, 2009.

Stenhouse, T. B. H. *The Rocky Mountain Saints: A Full and Complete History of the
Mormons, From the First Vision of Joseph Smith to the Last Courtship of Brigham Young*.
London: Ward, Lock, and Tyler, 1871.

Taylor, Samuel W. *The Last Pioneer: John Taylor, a Mormon Prophet*. Salt Lake City:
Signature Books, 1976.

Traven, B. *The Treasure of the Sierra Madre*. New York: Farrar, Straus and Giroux
2010.

Turner, Wallace. *The Mormon Establishment: How Does This Uniquely American
Religion Rule the Lives of Two and a Half Million Americans Today?* Boston:
Houghton Mifflin, 1966.

Twain, Mark. *Roughing It*. New York: Penguin, 1987.

Urquidi, Javier Ortega. *Los Güeros del Norte*. Kindle (Spanish edition). June 1, 2016.

Van Wagoner, Richard S. *Mormon Polygamy: A History.* Salt Lake City: Signature Books, 1989.

Ward, Kenric F. *Saints in Babylon: Mormons and Las Vegas.* Bloomington, IN: 1stBooks Library. 2002.

Wariner, Ruth. *The Sound of Gravel.* New York: Flatiron Books, 2015.

Wasserman, Mark. *Persistent Oligarchs: Elites and Politics in Chihuahua, Mexico. 1910–1940.* Durham (NC) and London: Duke University Press, 1993.

Werner, M. R. *Brigham Young.* New York: Harcourt, Brace, 1929.

Wiley, Peter, and Robert Gottlieb. *Empires in the Sun: The Rise of the New American West.* Tucson: University of Arizona Press, 1982.

Wise, William. *Massacre at Mountain Meadows: An American Legend and a Monumental Crime.* New York: Thomas Y. Crowell, 1976.

Young, Ann Eliza. *Wife No. 19: The Story of a Life in Bondage, Being a Complete Exposé of Mormonism, and Revealing the Sorrow, Sacrifices and Sufferings of Women in Polygamy. By Ann Eliza Young, Brigham Young's Apostate Wife.* Hartford, CT: Dustin, Gilman and Co., 1875.

Periodicals

Abrams, Garry. "A Family's Legacy of Death: Ervil LeBaron Said God Told Him to Kill Anyone Who Strayed from His Polygamist Cult. A Tenacious Salt Lake Investigator Tracked the LeBarons for 15 Years. Now, an Anonymous Tip May Have Helped Him Close a Case That Claimed as Many as 30 Lives." *Los Angeles Times,* Sept. 20, 1992.

Adams, Brooke, and Maria Villasenor. "Two with Polygamous Roots Gunned Down in Mexico." *Salt Lake Tribune,* July 8, 2009.

Agren, David. "How an Isolated Group of Mormons Got Caught Up in Mexico's Cartel Wars." *The Guardian,* Nov. 8, 2019.

———. "The Mormons Standing Up to Mexico's Drug Cartels: 'We Have to Overcome Our Fears.'" *The Guardian,* Jan. 23, 2020.

———. "Mexican Cartel Boss Arrested Over Mormon Massacre in Which Nine Died." *The Guardian,* Nov. 24, 2020.

Ahmed, Azam. "After Mormon Family's Terror in Mexico, a Message Emerges: No One Is Safe." *New York Times,* Nov. 7, 2019. *Akronoticias.com.* "Chihuahua News," May 2020.

———. "Chihuahua Removes Mega Ranch from Former Governor to Hand It Over to the People," Feb. 3, 2021.

———. "LeBarons Request Intervention of the Federal Government in the Conflict Between Barzonistas and La Mojina Ranch," May 29, 2020.

Allyn, Bobby. "FBI Joins Investigation into Killing of 9 Members of Mormon Family in Mexico." NPR, Nov. 11, 2019.

Althaus, Dudley. "Defying Mexican Gangs Costs Mormons Their Lives." *Houston Chronicle,* July 10, 2009.

Andrade, Julían. "The Ghost of Kiki Camarena and the LeBarons." *Forbes Mexico*, Dec. 10, 2019.

Andrews, Suzanna. "The Heiresses and the Cult." *Vanity Fair*, Oct. 13, 2010.

Animal Politico. "LeBaron Family Denounces Burning of Their Land and Attacks Due to Territorial Conflict in BC [Baja California]." Dec. 31, 2020.

Armendáriz, Jaime. "They Detect 12 'Illegal' Wells in the Carmen Basin." *El Diario MX*, Nov. 29, 2017.

Arrington, Leonard. "Scholarly Studies of Mormonism in the Twentieth Century." *Dialogue: A Journal of Mormon Thought*, 1966. Vol. 1 (no. 1): 15–32.

Assmann, Parker. "How Mexico's 'Small Armies' Came to Commit a Massacre." *Mexico News Daily*, Nov. 28, 2019.

Associated Press. "Mexico Farm Town Prepares Funerals After 9 Americans Slain," Nov. 7, 2019.

Baptiste, Nathalie. "God Said to Make the Desert Bloom, and Mormons Are Using Biblical Amounts of Water to Do It." *Mother Jones*, May 9, 2018.

Barry, Tom. "The Coming Water Wars in Mexico." *New Mexico Mercury*, Part 1, April 14, 2013; Part 2, June 10, 2013.

_____. "Politics of Climate Change in Chihuahua." *New Mexico Mercury*, June 23, 2013.

Beith, Malcolm. "A Long Fall from Grace: The Trial of Genaro García Luna, Mexico's Former Security Chief." *Literary Hub: CrimeReads*, Nov. 20, 2020.

Beauregard, Luis Pablo. "The Mormon Clan of the LeBaron, a Family Broken by Kidnappings and Violence in Mexico." *El País*, Nov. 6, 2019.

Booth, William. "Ambushed by a Drug War." *Washington Post*, July 23, 2009.

Boots, Michelle Theriault. "LeBaron Family, with Nine Members Killed in Mexico Massacre, Has Anchorage Ties." *Anchorage Daily News*, Nov. 7, 2019.

Breña, Carmen Morán. "Assassinated Abel Murrieta, Electoral Candidate and Lawyer of the Massacred LeBaron Family." *El País*, May 13, 2021.

Briones, Pedro Sanchez. "Julian LeBaron Returns to Mexico After Quarrel." *Reforma*, April 21, 2020.

Browning, Dan. "Williston Family Members Slain in Mexico Were Preparing for Wedding." *Star Tribune* [Minneapolis], Nov. 6, 2019.

Cannon, Lou. "Violent Death Shadows Polygamist Sect." *Washington Post*, Aug. 8, 1977.

Carlisle, Nate. "I Do Not Feel Safe Here." *Salt Lake Tribune,* Nov. 7, 2019.

_____. "Families Plan to Move Out of Mormon Community in Mexico, But for Some It Won't Be Easy to Leave." *Salt Lake Tribune*, Nov. 9, 2019.

_____. "Video of Killings of US Citizens in Mexico Shows Gunmen Poised to Torch SUV, Says Relative." *Salt Lake Tribune*, Nov. 22, 2019.

_____. "Here Is What Polygamous Sect Member Ross LeBaron, Jr. Wrote in Support of the Bundy Family." *Salt Lake Tribune*, Feb. 20, 2016.

Carranza, Rafael. "Lawsuit Against Juárez Cartel Sheds New Details on Deadly Ambush South of Arizona Border. *Arizona Republic*, July 31, 2020.

Castillo, Ricardo. "Who Slaughtered the Innocent Mormon Family?" *Pulse News Mexico,* Nov. 11, 2019.

"The Chihuahua Diary: They Lament the Indolence of the Government in the Case of the Murder of Barzonistas." *El Diario MX*, Aug. 22, 2018.

Correa, Carla. "A Timeline of the Nxivm Sex Cult Case." *New York Times*, Nov. 27, 2020.

Daily, Angel. "Massacre to US Citizens Was Due to Water Disputes and Sex Cult with the LeBarons and Not Cartels." Medium.com, Nov. 7, 2019.

Delgado, René. "LeBaron Points Out Police Chief for Massacre." *Reforma*, June 5, 2020.

Del Pozo, Melissa. "Organized Crime Bloodied the Mormon Paradise." *Proceso*, Nov. 13, 2019.

Del Valle, Gaby. "Everyone Has a Different Theory About Why the Mormon Family Was Massacred in Mexico. VICE News, Nov. 7, 2019.

Denton, Sally. "Romney and the White Horse Prophecy." *Salon*, Jan. 29, 2012.

_____. "A Utah Massacre and Mormon Memory." *New York Times*, May 24, 2003.

_____. "What Happened at Mountain Meadows?" *American Heritage*, Oct. 2001.

Devereaux, Ryan. "Prosecution of Top Mexican Security Official Exposes the Façade of the Drug War." *The Intercept*, Jan. 26, 2020.

DeVries, Sarah. "In Water Disputes, What to Do if Authorities Can't Be Counted On to Fix It?" *Mexico News Daily*, Nov. 13, 2019.

Díaz, Gloria Leticia. "The LeBarons Are Concerned About the Impact of the Security Law on US Agencies." *Proceso*, Jan. 18, 2021.

Diaz, Lisbeth. "After Burying Last Victims, Some in Mexico's Breakaway Mormon Community Head North." Reuters, Nov. 9, 2019.

_____. "Killed American Family May Have Been 'Bait' in Mexican Cartel Fight: Relatives." Reuters, Nov. 6, 2019.

_____. "Mexico Mormon Family Has Tearful Christmas After Cartel Murders." Reuters, Jan. 5, 2020.

_____. "Nine Americans Killed in Mexican Ambush, Trump Urges Joint War on Drug Cartels." Reuters, Nov. 4, 2019.

Dickson, E. J. "How People Leave One Cult—And End Up in Another." *Rolling Stone*, May 23, 2019.

Dillon, Nancy. "Funerals Begin as Mormon Families Grapple with 'Unimaginable' Grief Following Mexico Cartel Massacre. *Daily News* [NY], Nov. 7, 2019.

_____, and Larry McShane. "Mormons Mourn Last of Nine Massacre Victims in Mexico, Head for Safer Pastures in US Under Renewed Spotlight." *Daily News* [NY], Nov. 9, 2019.

Duran, Thelma Gomez, and Patricia Mayorga. "The Desert Where Water Is Trafficked." *Los Explotadores del Agua,* Oct. 29, 2019.

Edmonds, Lauren. "Mormon Father Whose Daughter and Four Grandkids Were Massacred in Mexico Wants to Set Up 'Wild West-Style Militias' to Take On the Cartels Because He Doesn't Trust the Government." *Daily Mail*, Dec. 21, 2019.

El Diario Editorial Office. "Caro Quintero Is Involved in the LeBaron Massacre," Nov. 25, 2020.

Estrada, Jesús. "Authorities Overlap Illegal Depredation of Aquifers in Chihuahua." *La Jornada*, May 9, 2018.

Ferri, Pablo. "The LeBaron Family's Journey to Horror." *El País*, Nov. 7, 2019, https://elpais.com/internacional/2019/11/06/actualidad/1573063851_970260.html.

Feuer, Alan. "El Chapo Found Guilty on All Counts; Faces Life in Prison." *New York Times*, Feb. 12, 2019.

_____. "The Prosecution Rests Its Case, and El Chapo Decides Not to Testify." *New York Times*, Jan. 28, 2019.

Fierro, Juan Omar, and Sebastián Barragán. "Kindergarten NXIVM: The School That Raniere Gave to the Children of Salinas and Rosa Laura Junco." *Aristegui Noticias*, Dec. 8, 2020.

Fitzgerald, Sandy. "Mexican President Refuses Meeting with Peace March Organizers." Newsmax, Jan. 27, 2020.

Forbes Staff. "LeBaron Residents Fear Exodus Due to Violence." *Forbes Mexico*, Nov. 8, 2019.

Freedman, Michael. "The World's Strangest Executive Coach: Keith Raniere's Rich and Famous Clients Pay Thousands of Dollars, Bow and Call Him 'Vanguard.'" *Forbes*, Oct. 2003.

Fruen, Lauren. "Life in the LeBaron Mormon Stronghold." *Daily Mail*, Nov. 5, 2019.

Gándara, Sugeyry Romina. "Alex LeBaron, former PRI Deputy in the César Duarte Era, Raises Dust for Asking Trump for Help." Sinembargo.mx, Nov. 27, 2019.

García, Jacobo. "Mexico Attributes the Massacre of the LeBaron Family to a Confrontation Between Cartels." *El País*, Nov. 7, 2019.

Gavin, Robert. "Mexican Slaughter Victims Were from NXIVM Recruiting Ground." *Times Union* [Albany, NY], Nov. 8, 2019.

_____. "Raniere Lawyers Say NXIVM Lawyers Prevented Crime, Brought Peace to Mexico." *Times Union* [Albany], Sept. 20, 2020.

Gaytán, Berenice. "Oral Proceedings Against 'Hawk' Begin in Plagiarism of LeBaron." *El Diario*, Jan. 17, 2013.

González, Carlos. "4 Years After Not Knowing the Whereabouts of Seven Men: They Were Installing Radio Communication Equipment Antennas for the FGE." *El Diario de Chihuahua*, Aug. 30, 2019.

Gonzalez, Jose Luis. "Faith in Mexico Shaken for 'True Believer' Mormon Communities." Reuters, Nov. 6, 2019.

Gonzalez, Sydnee. "Church Releases Statement Following Shooting in Mexico." *Daily Universe*, Nov. 5, 2019.

Graham, Dave. "Mexican Leader Blasts Critics After Supporters Hector Grieving Family." Reuters, Jan. 27, 2020.

Grant, Will. "How a US Mormon Family Ended Up Dead." BBC News, Nov. 8, 2019.

Grigoriadis, Vanessa. "Inside NXIVM, the 'Sex Cult' That Preached Empowerment." *New York Times*, May 30, 2018.

Grillo, Ioan. "9 American Mormons Died in a Brutal Ambush in Mexico. This Is the Untold Story of the Hunt for Justice by Those Left Behind." Insider.com, May 7, 2020.

_____. "Dismantling Mexico's Narco State." *New York Times*, Feb. 5, 2020.

_____. "Trump's 'Narco-Terrorism' Label Could Backfire." *New York Times*, Dec. 3, 2019.

Groves, Stephen. "Family of 9 Slain Mexican-Americans Sues Juárez Drug Cartel." AP News, July 29, 2020.

Heras, Antonio. "Invasion of Properties and Burning of Houses in San Quintín, Denounces LeBaron." *La Jornada Baja California*, Jan. 2, 2021.

Hollenhorst, John. "Retired Prosecutor Speaks Candidly About High-Profile Cases." *Deseret News,* Feb. 3, 2014.

Hong, Nicole, and Sean Piccoli. "Keith Raniere, Leader of NXIVM Sex Cult, Is Sentenced to 120 Years in Prison." *New York Times*, Nov. 27, 2020.

Infobae. "They Knew, Before They Shot, That They Were Women: The Story Behind the LeBaron Massacre on the Border Between Sonora and Chihuahua," Nov. 6, 2019.

Ilizaliturri, Arturo. "Colonia LeBaron: 10 Years of Harassment." Newsbeezer. com, Nov. 6, 2019.

Janzen, Rebecca. "Mormons in Mexico: A Brief History of Polygamy, Cartel Violence, and Faith. *The Conversation*, Nov. 6, 2019.

Job, Vanessa. "Who is Julian LeBaron?" *Milenio,* Nov. 11, 2019.

_____, and Kenia Hernandez. "Community Founded by the LeBaron Family Faces Former PRD Candidate by Land." *Milenio,* Jan. 19, 2021.

Johnson, Scott, and Rebecca Sun. "Her Darkest Role: Actress Allison Mack's Descent from 'Smallville' to Sex Cult. *Hollywood Reporter*, May 16, 2018.

Kari, Doug. "How an American Mom Died at the Hands of a Mexican Cartel." *Las Vegas Review-Journal*, Dec. 20, 2019.

Kelly, Jamie. "Family, Friends Reeling After 9 Killed in Ambush in Northern Mexico." *Williston* [ND] *Herald*, Nov. 5, 2019.

Krauze, León. "The Brutal Murder of the Mormon Family in Mexico Was Almost Inevitable." *Slate,* Nov. 6, 2019.

_____. "What Did NXIVM Want in Mexico?" *Slate,* May 23, 2019.

_____. "What the Hell Did I Do? The Story of the ESP Movie in Mexico." *Letras Libres*, Oct. 23, 2017.

_____. "This Family Suffered a Brutal Attack in Mexico. Now It Has a Message for Washington." *Washington Post*, Dec. 12, 2019.

Kryt, Jeremy. "A New Twist in the Horrific Massacre of American Moms and Kids in Mexico." *Daily Beast*, Nov. 11, 2019.

_____. "Trump Labeling Mexico's Cartels 'Terrorists' Makes Things Worse." *Daily Beast*, Dec. 5, 2019.

LaFuente, Javier, and Pablo Ferri. "The Brutal Murder of a Family Opens a New Front in the Relationship Between Mexico and the United States." *El País*, Nov. 7, 2019.

La Verdad. "The LeBaron Slaughter Was Not a Mistake; They Were Threatened by the Huachicolero Group," Nov. 5, 2019.

LeBaron, Julian. "Julian LeBaron: A Petition to the Mexican People." *Dallas Morning News*, April 16, 2010.

Ledo, Rocio Muñoz, and Juan Omar Fierro. "Emiliano Salinas's Movement Raised 9.5 Million Pesos to Promote the NXIVM Leader." *Aristegui Noticias*, July 16, 2018.

Linthicum, Kate. "For Mexico Ambush Victims, There Was No Safety in Numbers." *Los Angeles Times,* Nov. 6, 2019.

_____. "There Is Only One Gun Store in All of Mexico. So Why Is Gun Violence Soaring?" *Los Angeles Times,* May 24, 2018.

_____. "This Was the Moment Mexican Forces Captured the Son of 'El Chapo.' Soon After, They Freed Him." *Los Angeles Times*, Oct. 30, 2019.

Lira, Ivette. "Father and Son Were Killed for Taking Care of the Water in Chihuahua." *Ocmal*, June 15, 2018.

López, Julio Hernández. "The Young Guru Salinas, Emiliano with Sicilia, LeBaron, ESO's Ally." *La Jornada,* April 23, 2012.

Loudis, Jessica. "Fall of the House of NXIVM." *London Review of Books*, June 25, 2019.

Madi, Mohamed, and Ana Gabriela Rojas. "Mexico Ambush: Mormon Families Waiting for Justice a Year on from Massacre." BBC News, Nov. 9, 2020.

Malkin, Elisabeth. "Side Effect of Mexico's Drug War: Fear and Death in a Mormon Town in Mexico." *New York Times*, July 26, 2009.

Martinez, Cesar. "They File Complaints for Invasion in Baja California." *San Diego Union-Tribune*, Jan. 4, 2021.

Martinez, Chris. "The Return of the Caro Quintero Brothers, Rafael Leading the Caborca Cartel and Miguel One Year 'Out' of Victorville Federal Prison. *Borderland Beat*, Aug. 7, 2020.

Martinez, Erendira. "The Mormon Family Killed in Mexico." *Nuestra Verdad Publicacion*, Dec. 5, 2019.

Martinez, Milton. "Familia LeBaron Rejects the 'Confusion' Hypothesis in the Attack: The Question Is Why Did They Do It?" *Proceso*, Nov. 7, 2019.

Mayorga, Patricia. "Activists Demand to Guarantee the Life of Members of El Barzón Threatened with Death." *Proceso,* May 23, 2018.

_____. "Barzonistas Denounce That LeBaron Family Put a Price on Their Heads." *Proceso,* May 21, 2018.

_____. "'Even if the Earth Shakes, I Will Continue Looking for My Son': Mother of Disappeared in Chihuahua." *Proceso*, Dec. 4, 2015.

_____. "They Block the Way to Demand a Substantive Solution to the Barzon-LeBaron Conflict." *Proceso*, April 21, 2020, https://www.proceso.com.mx/

nacional/estados/2020/4/21/bloquean-via-para-exigir-solucion-de-fondo-al
-conflicto-barzon-lebaron-241698.html.

———. "Water Fight Confronts Ejidatarios with the LeBaron Family in
Chihuahua." *Proceso*, April 30, 2018.

———. "Six Employees Who Placed an Antenna in Chihuahua Have Been Missing
for Two Months." *Proceso*, Oct. 28, 2015.

———. "Pifia: After Three Years in Prison, They Release Someone Involved in the
LeBaron Crime." *Proceso*, March 12, 2013.

McGahan, Jason. "The Cartels vs. a Mormon Sect: The Story Behind a Massacre."
Daily Beast, Nov. 6, 2019.

Meier, Barry. "Inside a Secretive Group Where Women Are Branded." *New York
Times*, Oct. 17, 2017.

Mendoza, Gardenia. "Peasant Organization, Suspected of the Massacre of the
LeBaron Family of Mormons in Mexico." *LaOpinion*, Nov. 7, 2019.

Mexico News Daily. "Attackers Not Confused: They Knew They Were Killing
Women, Children," Nov. 6, 2019.

"The Mormons in Mexico." *New York Times*, June 29, 1885.

"The Nation: A Deadly Messenger of God." *Time,* Aug. 29, 1977.

Odato, James M., and Jennifer Gish. "Secrets of NXIVM." *Times Union* [Albany,
NY], Feb. 11, 2012.

———. "In Raniere's Shadows." *Times Union* [Albany, NY], Feb. 28, 2012.

Orsi, Peter. "After Mourning, Mexico Town Realizes Fear Left by Attacks."
Associated Press, Nov. 9, 2019.

———. "Last Victim of Mexico Ambush Killings to Be Laid to Rest." Associated
Press, Nov. 9, 2019.

———. "Mexico Farm Town Buries 3 of 9 Americans Slain. Associated Press, Nov.
7, 2019.

Padgett, Tim. "Why I Protest: Javier Sicilia of Mexico." *Time,* Dec. 14, 2011.

Padilla, Liliana. "We Have No Other Place in the World Than Galeana and
Bavispe." *Milenio*, Nov. 16, 2019.

Palmer, Emily, and Alan Feuer. "El Chapo Trial: The 11 Biggest Revelations from
the Case." *New York Times*, Feb. 3, 2019.

Paterson, Kent. "Mexico's Disappeared Who Won't Disappear." *Counterpunch*, Sept.
1, 2016.

Piñon, David. "LeBaron-Barzon, 6 Decades of Conflict Over Aquifer Dispute." *El
Sol de Mexico*, Dec. 30, 2020.

Polemon. "Javier Sicilia and the LeBarons Were Financed by the NXIVM Sect,"
https://polemon.mx/javier-sicilia-y-los-lebaron-fueron-financiados-por-la
-secta-nxivm/.

Prado, Hérika Martinez. "The Journal of Juárez." *El Diario MX*, Jan. 20, 2021.

———. "The Demand for Justice, a Difficult Road." *El Diario MX*, Dec. 21, 2020.

———. "He Directed Acquaintance of the LeBaron to Hitmen: Fidencio G. Took the Video and Was the One Who Yelled to Burn the Truck." *El Diario de Chihuahua*, Jan. 20, 2021.

Proceso Staff. "Julian LeBaron Announces His Separation from the Movement for Peace," Feb. 24, 2012.

Reilly, Katie. "Here Are All the Times Donald Trump Insulted Mexico." *Time*, Aug. 31, 2016.

Reyes, Gerardo. "The Keith Raniere Saga." *Univision Noticias*, July 9, 2018.

Ríos, Lorena. "Mexican President Declines Trump's Help After Mormon Family Killed in Attack." Bloomberg, Nov. 5, 2019.

Roberts, Alyssa. "Mexico Arrests Mastermind Behind Killings of 9 Members of Family with Utah Ties." KUTV, Nov. 25, 2020.

Rodríguez, César. " 'I Tried to Take Photos That Meant Something': After the Cartel Ambush in Mexico." *Time*, Nov. 9, 2019.

Romero, Simon, Elizabeth Dias, Julie Turkewitz, and Mike Baker. " 'Innocence Is Shattered': A Storied Mormon Family Reels After Mexico Murders." *New York Times,* Nov. 7, 2019.

Rose, Jaimee. "Cousin Up a Storm." *Washington Post*, Aug. 7, 2005.

Rose, Joel. "This Grieving Family Wants the US to Designate Mexican Cartels as Terrorists." NPR *Morning Edition,* Dec. 13, 2019.

Schindler, Hal. "Brigham Young's Favorite Wife." *Salt Lake Tribune*, July 30, 1995.

Sieff, Kevin. "How Mexico's Cartel Wars Shattered American Mormons' Wary Peace." *Washington Post*, Nov. 7, 2019.

Smith, Lynn. "The Mormon Enclave in Mexico: Descendants of Pioneers Gather to Celebrate Centenary." *Los Angeles Times,* Aug. 18, 1985.

Stevenson, Mark. "At Least 9 U.S. Citizens Killed in Cartel Attack in North Mexico." Associated Press, Nov. 5, 2019.

Stilwell, Blake. "Mormon Colonies Are Fighting Drug Cartels in Mexico." VICE News, April 29, 2020.

Tahir, Tariq. "Cartel Kingpin El Mencho Who Is Even More Savage than El Chapo May NEVER Be Captured, Says Legendary Narco Cop." *Irish Sun*, Feb. 19, 2021.

Tames, Alfonso. "Vanguard Region 4." *Animal Politico*, Feb. 9, 2011.

Taylor, Scott. "Mexicans to Rally for Tougher Laws in the Wake of Kidnappings." *Deseret News*, July 1, 2009.

teleSurHD. "Water Wars: Ranchers Clash Over Scarce Resources in Mexico." May 2, 2018.

Tolson, Mike. "Cult Leader's Daughter Faces Trial in 4 Deaths Father Ordered." *Houston Chronicle,* May 14, 2010.

Torres, Adry. "Mormon Father Relives the Morning His Daughter and Four of His Grandchildren Were Brutally Executed Along with Four Others in Mexico—and Says the Family Is Still Awaiting Justice." DailyMail.com, Nov. 4, 2020.

Turati, Marcela. "The Courage of the LeBaron." *Proceso*, Aug. 17, 2011.

Turley, Jeremy. "Williston Vigil Remembers Family Killed in Mexico." Forum News Service, Nov. 8, 2019.

Villapando, Rubén. "Corral Protects Aquifer Looters, Say Barzonistas." *La Jornada*, May 22, 2018.

Vincent, Isabel. "Defiant Patriarch Wants to Start Militias to Fight Mexican Cartels After Mormon Family Massacre." *New York Post*, Dec. 21, 2019.

Walch, Tadd. "She Planned for Marriage on Monday. Instead She Buried Her Family in Mexico." *Deseret News*, Nov. 7, 2019.

Whelan, Robbie. "Family That Lost Nine Members in Attack Has a Long History in Mexico." *Wall Street Journal*, Nov. 5, 2019.

Whittle, Andrea. "*W* Club TV: Can't Get Enough of the NXIVM Story? Time to Watch 'Seduced.'" *W*, November 21, 2020.

Willmore, Alison. "Before NXIVM and *The Vow*, Mark Vicente Directed a Truly Bizarre Hit Documentary." *Vulture*, Oct. 22, 2020.

Yakowicz, Will. "When We Exposed Keith Raniere, the Leader of the NXIVM 'Sex Cult.'" *Forbes*, May 15, 2019.

———. "Dark Capital. From Heiress to Felon: How Clare Bronfman Wound Up in 'Cult-Like' Group NXIVM." *Forbes*, May 31, 2019.

Yucatan Times Staff. "The LeBaron Family in Mexico . . . a History of Conflict," Nov. 5, 2019.

Zavala, Susana. "Bryan LeBarón After Murder Video: They Are 'Highly Trained Terrorists.'" *El Universal*, July 9, 2020.

Zhao, Christina. "Republican Senator Says U.S. 'May Have to Take Matters into Our Own Hands' Regarding Mexico Drug Cartel Violence." *Newsweek*, Nov. 6, 2019.

Zimmerman, Amy. "Inside the NXIVM Sex Cult's Secret Plot to Take Over Mexico." *Daily Beast*, Aug. 9, 2018.

Television Interviews, Documentaries, Audiotapes, YouTube Videos, Social Media, Oral Histories, Blogs

ABC *World News Tonight with David Muir*. "American Father Speaks Out for the 1st Time Since Deadly Mexican Ambush." Nov. 10 and 11, 2019. Two parts.

ABC *Good Morning America*. Nov. 11, 2019.

BBC News *Mundo*. "In the Line of Fire." Ana Gabriela Rojas, March 23, 2020, https://www.facebook.com/amber.compton.589/videos/4138812756132719/ UzpfSTU0MTI4ODYzMzoxMDE1NzEzMjc5NzgzMzYzNA/?fref=sear ch&__tn__=,d,P-R&eid=ARA3kmVLcJfU9C2IIWp-e1S6pcLvtyfo67AcEuXo 5PVc0bRabE1CctU2lq3PFpKmPM7kj1Bb10fXiysl.

Blust, Kendal, and Murphy Woodhouse. "After La Mora Bids Loved Ones Farewell, Grieving Community's Future Unclear." KJZZ Radio, Nov. 14, 2019, https://kjzz.org/content/1303486/after-la-mora-bids-loved-ones-farewell -grieving-communitys-future-unclear.

CNN *New Day*. Nov. 6, 2019, https://www.youtube.com/watch?v=r3naF3fJUwM.

Cooper, Anderson. *Full Circle*. "Sister-in-law of Mexico Victim Describes Scene of Massacre." CNN, Nov. 6, 2019, https://www.cnn.com/videos/us/2019/11/05/acfc-full-kendra-lee-miller-mexico-ambush-vpx.cnn.

Facebook: La Mora Family Massacre.

Forbes Video. "Dark Capital: From Heiress to Felon: How Clare Bronfman Wound Up in NXIVM." Dec. 7, 2020, https://www.forbesafrica.com/video/2020/12/07/from-heiress-to-felon-how-clare-bronfman-wound-up-in-nxivm-dark-capital-forbes/.

Fox News. Nov. 6, 2019, https://video.foxnews.com/v/6101003917001—sp=show-clips.

Hafen, DeWayne, interview with Dale Van Atta, https://holyorder.org/2018/08/14/dewayne-hafen-interview-to-dale-von-atta-1978/.

Jack's Newswatch. "It's All About the Water." Nov. 11, 2019, https://xxy.zaa.mybluehost.me/its-all-about-the-water/.

KVIA ABC-7. "Mexican Soldiers Arrest Suspect in Deadly LeBaron Kidnappings," April 25, 2010.

La Opcion de Chihuahua. Interview with Joel LeBaron Soto, Nov. 7, 2019, http://laopcion.com.mx/noticia/252904.

Lara Logan Investigates. Fox News. Jan. 31, 2021, https://nation.foxnews.com/lara-logan-investigates-mexican-mormon-massacre-nation/.

LeBaron, Heber. *My Name Is William Heber LeBaron. Federal Prisoner Number 22254-077,* http://www.people.vcu.edu/~dbromley/undergraduate/spiritualCommunity/ChurchOfTheLambOfGodReadingsLink.html.

NBC News. "Family Member of Mexico Ambush Victims Reacts: 'How Is This Even Real?'" Nov. 7, 2019, https://www.msn.com/en-us/news/us/family-member-of-mexico-ambush-victims-reacts-how-is-this-even-real/vi-AAJZuqj.

NPR. "Law-Abiding Mexicans Taking Up Illegal Guns." John Burnett, Jan. 28, 2012, https://www.npr.org/2012/01/28/145996427/mexican-community-takes-taboo-stance-on-guns.

Payne, Daniel. "Relative of Mormons Massacred in Mexico Goes on CNN, Tells Americans 'Fight for Those Guns.'" CNN, Nov. 11, 2019.

Rivers, Matt. "Mexico Family Ambush: Le Baron Family Interview. ABC4Utah, Nov. 7, 2019, https://www.youtube.com/watch?v=mZrNlenzD4M.

Salinas, Emiliano. "Emiliano Salinas' Mission for a Non-Violent Mexico," April 25, 2018, https://medium.com/@esalinas1819/emiliano-salinas-mission-for-a-non-violent-mexico-e95a5760aac4.

Saxon. "They Kill the Lawyer of the Massacre of Mormons Who Was Running for Mayor in Mexico," May 14, 2021.

Smith, Shane. "The Mexican Mormon War." VICE News, Sept. 26, 2012.

Winslow, Ben. "FBI Arrests Fugitive Mormon Fundamentalist Wanted for

Murders Ordered by Her Violent Cult Leader Father." Fox News, May 13, 2010.

YouTube: "LeBaron Family in the U.S. Says Mexico Massacre Was 'Total Shock.'" Bryan LeBaron interview, https://www.youtube.com/watch?v=i5 -G0IvTPRs&feature=youtu.be&fbclid=IwAR0o7Km1Y1dY5F9aQrvoCOI49i fMIF85fSa6a4LW-3HgvqP2E2X3HhV-Uyw, Nov. 7, 2019.

YouTube: "Langford Family Member Talks About What People Got Wrong About Her Family." Emily Langford interview, https://www.youtube.com/ watch?v=cYNJBTQOIZ4&feature=share&fbclid=IwAR0GmVDFYyiuuag -YRdQXTjgEWz4GUdzGdp8rBtfOi_yBiMDlXzgLlNNQYk, Nov. 10, 2019.

Papers

Benjamin F. Johnson (1818–1905), Letter to George S. Gibbs, 1903. Church Archives. Available at https://archive.org/stream/BenjaminFJohnsonLetterto GeorgeFGibbs.

Dale Van Atta Collection, 1969–92. L. Tom Perry Special Collections, Harold B. Lee Library, Brigham Young University, Provo, UT.

Theses and Miscellaneous Documents

Henson, Elizabeth. "Madera 1965: Obsessive Simplicity, the Agrarian Dream, and Che." Department of History, University of Arizona. Electronic dissertation, 2015.

Higbee History and Stories. Special Collections, Gerald R. Sherratt Library, Southern Utah University, Cedar City (includes synopsis of interview with eighty-five-year-old massacre survivor Sallie Baker Mitchell in September 1940).

LeBaron, Charlotte K. "Events Incident to the Martyrdom and Burial of Joel Franklin LeBaron," http://mormonpolygamydocuments.org/wp-content/ uploads/2015/01/MF0223.pdf.

LeBaron, E. Dale. "Benjamin Franklin Johnson in Nauvoo: Friend, Confidant, and Defender." BYU Studies, 1992, file://localhost/Users/sallydenton/ Downloads/32.1-2lebaronbenjamin-778b5df3-2796-475a-8cdb-884ee486353b (1).pdf.

_____. Benjamin Franklin Johnson: Colonizer, Public Servant, and Church Leader, https://scholarsarchive.byu.edu/etd/4869/.

Schwartzlose, Richard. "Mormon Settlements in Mexico," 1952, http:// thecardonfamilies.org/Documents/MormonSettlementsInMexico.

Tanner, Sandra. "Joseph Smith's 'White Horse' Prophecy." Salt Lake City: Utah Lighthouse Ministry. Undated post on utlm.org.

Teixeira, Antonio Trevisan. "Was Ross LeBaron a Mormon Fundamentalist?" *Ross LeBaron, the Holy Order and the Church of the Firstborn,* Holyorder.org, https:// holyorder.org/2020/01/27/was-ross-lebaron-a-mormon-fundamentalist/.

Wills, John A. "The Twin Relics of Barbarism." *Historical Society of Southern*

California, Los Angeles (1890), vol. 1, no. 5, 1890, pp. 40–44, JSTOR, www.jstor
.org/stable/41167826. Accessed March 13, 2021.

Government Documents and Court Cases

US House of Representatives. *Mountain Meadow Massacre. Special Report of the
Mountain Meadow Massacre by J. H. Carleton, Brevet Major, United States Army,
Captain, First Dragoons.* Doc. 605. 57th Cong., 1st sess., 1859.

Howard Miller et al. vs. Juárez Cartel, La Línea, Vicente Carrillo Fuentes
Organization and CFO. US District Court for the District of North Dakota.
Case: 1:20:cv-00132-DMT- CRH. Filed July 23, 2020.

The Government's Sentencing Memorandum as to Defendant Keith Raniere.
United States of America against Keith Raniere, Defendant. US District Court,
Eastern District of New York. Docket No. 18-cr-204 (S-2) (NGG), https://
wnyt.com/wnytimages/Keith-Raniere-sentencing-memorandum.pdf.

Index

Page numbers in *italics* refer to photos and illustrations. Page numbers after 211 refer to notes.

ON THE MORNING OF NOVEMBER 4, 2019, an unassuming caravan of women and children was ambushed by masked gunmen on a desolate stretch of road in northern Mexico controlled by the Sinaloa drug cartel. Firing semiautomatic weapons, the attackers killed nine people and gravely injured five more. The victims were members of the LeBaron and La Mora communities—fundamentalist Mormons whose forebears broke from the LDS Church when their religion outlawed polygamy.

In *The Colony*, best-selling investigative journalist Sally Denton picks up where the initial reporting on the attacks ended and delves into the story of the LeBaron clan. Her tale spans from the first polygamist emigrations to Mexico in the late nineteenth century through the LeBarons' internal blood feud in the 1970s—started by Ervil LeBaron, known as the "Mormon Manson"—and up to the family's recent alliance with the NXIVM sex cult. In seeking answers to what happened on that fateful day, Denton ultimately presents an unforgettable account of the sisterhood that can flourish in polygamist communities, against the odds.

"An excellent history of a polygamist subculture. . . . [A] testament to what happens when male power, under the guise of religious conviction, goes unchecked."—J U L I A S C H E E R E S, *New York Times Book Review*

"A mesmerizing deep dive into Mormon fanaticism, violence, deceit, mental illness, and misogyny."—L E W I S B E A L E, *Daily Beast*

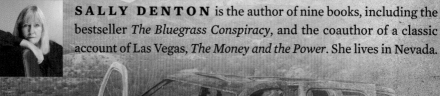

S A L L Y D E N T O N is the author of nine books, including the bestseller *The Bluegrass Conspiracy*, and the coauthor of a classic account of Las Vegas, *The Money and the Power*. She lives in Nevada.

Cover design: Richard Ljoenes Design LLC
Front cover photograph: Adriana Zehbrauskas / *New York Times* / Redux Pictures
Back cover photograph: © César Rodriguez
Author Photograph: Arron Mayes

Liveright
An Imprint of W. W. Norton & Company
WWNORTON.COM

TRUE CRIME

ISBN 978-1-324-09408-1

51795

9 781324 094081

$17.95 USA $23.95 CA